SWISS TRAVEL WONDERLAND

By the same Author

Swiss Travel Wonderland

CECIL J. ALLEN

FRSA, FCIT

LONDON

IAN ALLAN

Originally published in 1967 with the title of
Switzerland—Its Railways and Cableways,
Mountain Roads and Lake Steamers

This enlarged and revised edition first published 1972

SBN 7110 0296 7

© Cecil J. Allen 1972

Published by Ian Allan Ltd., Shepperton, Surrey and printed in the United
Kingdom by The Press at Coombelands Ltd., Addlestone, Surrey.

Contents

Author's Preface

IN THE MINDS of Swiss engineers the word "impossible" hardly seems to exist. This is why travel in their entrancing country is such a fascinating experience. Whether in running their railways through the heart of the Alps, or in devising means to carry sightseers and winter sports enthusiasts up to the heights, the most difficult *terrain* has been a challenge rather than an obstacle, and the feats that they have accomplished may possibly have equals but certainly no superiors in any other part of the world.

So it is that to one like myself, both an engineer and a lover of the mountains (whose distinctive forms eventually take on the character almost of personal friends), Switzerland exercises an annual attraction which is irresistible. Moreover the unceasing completion of new mountain lines of the cable suspension type, to higher and higher altitudes and over ever-lengthening cable spans, means that even to so constant a visitor as myself there is every year something new and exciting in mountain travel to stir the pulses.

Switzerland is a country in which no more than half the railway mileage has been nationalised, the remainder being owned by a very large number of independent companies. So in this book I have attempted to bring under review, not merely all the main lines of the Swiss Federal system, but also almost all the minor lines, with the great majority of which I have personal acquaintance, and some of which are of sufficient importance to justify chapters of their own. The same familiarity applies to the astonishing collection of mountain lines, whether rack-and-pinion, funicular, or of the cable suspension type, an increasing number of which are now carrying passengers right up to the eternal snows.

Also in compiling this book I have realised that some of the road engineering in Switzerland, over the mountain passes or now beginning to tunnel under them, is but little less spectacular than that of the railways, and this prompted a tour during 1966 by the most efficient motorcoaches of the Swiss postal service of almost all these routes, in the interest of the chapter in this book which describes and illustrates them. And to complete this survey of Swiss travel, it has been impossible to omit the beautiful lakes and their steamer and motorship services which delight so many holidaymakers in that country.

So this book aims to be a comprehensive travel guide to Switzerland, and especially for those with an interest in railways. For the guidance of tourists a chapter is included setting out the Swiss fare system, the special types of holiday ticket available, and the various regional season tickets—such a worth-while investment to those who want to make the very most of their time in the country—with the precise cost and coverage of each.

7

Then, by way of illustration, there are very nearly 200 photographs, which I can claim with some justification to be one of the finest collections of views ever assembled in a single Swiss book of travel. The railways and cableways, the mountain roads and the lake craft, can never be divorced from their scenic setting, and this is apparent in full measure in the pages that follow. These I hope may both help readers in deciding to which parts of Switzerland to plan their future trips, and also may serve as nostalgic reminders on their return of what they have seen and so greatly admired.

Finally I have to acknowledge the help that I have received from many friends in compiling the text and collecting the illustrations that follow. They include Mr. A. Kunz, General Manager of the Swiss National Tourist Office in London, and his Publicity Manager, Mr. Jürg W. Schmid, who most kindly read through the whole of the text and made a number of valuable suggestions; Mr. W. Wenger, former Chief of the Press Service of the Swiss Federal Railways in Berne and his successor, Mr. Alex Amstein; Messrs. R. Widmer and S. Zehnder, Directors of the Montreux–Oberland Bernois and Furka–Oberalp Railways respectively; Mr. E. Cadalbert, Publicity Manager of the Rhaetian Railway; Mr. Hugo Wirz, Publicity Manager of the Lötschberg Railway; and Messrs. Martin Mengelt, Armin Moser and Raoul Sommer, the respective Directors of the Tourist Offices of Central Switzerland, North-East Switzerland and the Grisons.

If this book helps to arouse in the hearts of any of its readers the affection for this charming country that I have gradually developed after more than half-a-century of intimate acquaintance with it, the writing will have been well worth while.

CECIL J. ALLEN

ONE

Railway Beginnings in Switzerland

NOT UNTIL the year 1898 did Switzerland decide to possess a national railway system, as the result of a referendum. In this a substantial majority of the nation voted for the passing of a "Redemption Law", which laid it down that "The Swiss Confederation is legally empowered and commissioned to purchase any railway which, in its opinion, serves from a military defence or economic point of view the interests of the Confederation or a major part of it, and to operate it under the name of Swiss Federal Railways". So it was that nationalisation of the principal Swiss railways took place on January 1st, 1902. The Swiss Confederation itself had not come into existence until 1848, and until 1852 concessions for railway building were in the hands of the individual cantons; but after that date, although railways were still a matter of private enterprise, for reasons of strategy the Federal Government exercised the right to approve all new proposals for railway construction.

Railways in Switzerland had a comparatively late start. It was in June, 1844, that the first railway came into operation on Swiss territory, and this was not Swiss, but the termination at St. Louis, a suburb of Basle, of a French line. Switzerland's own first railway was opened in August, 1847, and it was over the 14½ miles between Zürich and Baden. It soon received the nickname of "Spanisch-Brötli-Bahn" because the traffic in the Spanish buns baked in Baden, which were a delicacy highly esteemed by the citizens of Zürich and until then had travelled by road, was promptly transferred to the new railway and expedited in consequence. Soon after the Confederation had come into being, the British engineer, Robert Stephenson, was commissioned to prepare a scheme for a Swiss railway system which would not merely link the largest towns, but would also have strategic importance to a country surrounded by nations whose reputations, on the whole, were not as peaceful as they might be.

The principal Swiss cities were, and still are, Geneva, Lausanne, Berne, Basle, Biel, Lucerne, St. Gallen and Zürich. Stephenson's plan was for a trunk route from south-west to north-east, starting at Geneva, skirting the Lake of Geneva to Lausanne, and from there turning inland along the south-eastern shores of the Lakes of Neuchâtel and Biel through Morat and Lyss to Solothurn, after which the line would run along the southern slopes of the Jura through Olten to Brugg and Baden; from here the metals of the "Spanisch-Brötli-Bahn" would be used into Zürich. There would be branches from Olten to both Basle and Lucerne; the main line would continue from Zürich to Romanshorn on the Lake of Constance, along the south of that lake through Rorschach to the Austrian frontier at St. Margrethen, and from there up the Rhine valley to Chur, capital of the Canton of the Grisons. All these lines were built eventually, and presented no great engineering difficulties; but as yet no line through the great main chain of the Alps had been seriously considered. The only change from Stephenson's plan, in the early stages, was that his route was altered from the south-east to the north-west sides of the Lakes of Neuchâtel and Biel between Lausanne and Solothurn, thereby giving direct railway communication to the growing towns of Neuchâtel and Biel. From Biel a branch was thrown out to the capital of the country, Berne.

The various sections of these lines, as well as a number of others, were built by numerous privately-owned companies, which by 1872 had amalgamated into four fair-sized groups—the North-Eastern, Central and United Swiss Railways eastwards from Berne, and the largest, the straggling Jura–Simplon Railway, which covered all the west and south-west, from Geneva, Pontarlier and Delle on the French frontier to Lausanne, Neuchâtel, Biel and Berne, and up the Rhône valley to Brigue. It was this company that built the direct line from Lausanne to Berne through Fribourg, which now forms part of the main Geneva–Zürich trunk route, and it is not without interest that the present main office building of the Swiss Federal Railways in Berne, adjacent to the Hauptbahnhof, was formerly that of the Jura–Simplon Railway. Eventually a line was built along Stephenson's planned route from Lausanne to Solothurn through Morat and Lyss, but this has never played more than a secondary role.

Meantime another company of the greatest importance had been formed. Even as early as 1848 there had been dreams of a direct north-south railway through the Alps, and a conference at Berne in 1869, with German and Italian representation, had decided that the Reuss and Ticino valleys would provide the most suitable course, with a lengthy tunnel between them. France was opposed to any such scheme, as she considered that traffic through her new Mont–Cenis tunnel would suffer by such competition, but this was a matter in which France could have but little say. Eventually German and Italian support was sufficient to encourage the formation at Lucerne in 1871 of the Gotthard Railway Company, and a start in 1872 on the work of construction. The Swiss, German and Italian Governments all contributed handsomely to the capital required, and after engineering difficulties on an unprecedented scale had been overcome, including the spiral planning at Wassen and the four helicoidal tunnels between Rodi–Fiesso and Giornico, not to mention the $9\frac{1}{4}$-mile Gotthard tunnel itself, the line was ready for opening by 1882. It was destined to become, and still remains, the principal rail traffic artery between South Germany and North Italy.

The original Gotthard Railway started from Rotkreuz, on the Lucerne–Zug–Zürich line; it was not until later years that a slightly more direct line was laid out from Lucerne along the lakeside round the Meggen promontory to Küssnacht and across the narrow neck of land between the Lakes of Lucerne and Zug to join the line from Rotkreuz at Immensee. As the station at Lucerne was terminal, all through trains required to reverse there, and the majority of the passenger trains still do, but certain important sleeping car trains, as well as practically all the through Gotthard freight traffic, use a different route entirely from Olten southwards, which, as we shall see later, takes them over the original Gotthard line between Rotkreuz and Immensee.

The formation of the Swiss Federal system was a gradual process. The beginning of 1902 saw the acquisition of the North-Eastern Railway, 433 route miles in all, and later in the same year the 204 miles of the Swiss Central and 85 miles of minor lines were added, followed by the 183 miles of the United Swiss and Toggenburg Railways. In May, 1903, Switzerland's biggest railway, the Jura–Simplon, with 552 route miles of line, became part of the national system, with the 46 miles of the Brünig Railway, the only narrow-gauge section of the Swiss Federal. The Gotthard Railway remained independent until May, 1909, when its 140 miles of line also were acquired; in succeeding years various other minor lines came in, so that today the Swiss Federal Railways own a total of 1,818 route miles. During recent years there has been much discussion as to the possibility of adding the Lötschberg group of lines, and the Rhaetian Railway in the east, to the national system, especially the former, which forms part of an international route in the heart of Swiss Federal territory, but for the time being at least these proposals are in abeyance.

Even this, however, is little more than one-half the total railway mileage of the country; the remainder, excluding the mountain railways and cable suspension lines, is divided between more than 80 privately-owned companies, with a route mileage of 1,265 miles in all. As will be described later, a number of the minor lines now operate in groups, with centralised management, and in the interests of economy the Swiss Government is taking active steps to encourage the extension of this grouping. Of all descriptions of railway in Switzerland there is a total of 3,178 miles, contained in a country which in extreme length from southwest to north-east measures no more than 226 miles, and in extreme breadth from north to south only a maximum of 137 miles. Indeed, Switzerland owns a mile of railway for every 1,150 of its population. As already mentioned, the only portion of the national system which is not of standard gauge is the 46 miles of the Brünig line, but the major part of the privately-owned railways is laid to the metre gauge.

Because of the three languages—German, French and Italian—spoken in the different areas of Switzerland, the Swiss Federal system is known by three names, "Schweizerische Bundesbahnen", "Chemins de Fer Fédéraux" and "Ferrovie Federali Svizzere" respectively. The corresponding initials are "SBB", "CFF" and "FFS". At one time all three sets of letters used to appear on the sides of locomotives and coaches, but for reasons of economy the present practice is to show "SBB" and "CFF", with the Swiss national flag between, on one side of each rolling stock unit, and "SBB" and "FFS" on the other. It is curious, by the way, that although the German and Italian titles specify Swiss ownership, "Chemins de Fer Fédéraux" might indicate any country with a Federal Government!

Large-scale electrification of the Swiss railways began at a relatively late date, but the First World War brought home to the Swiss nation the serious handicap of being dependent on other countries for its supplies of fuel, which during the latter part of that war nearly dried up altogether; by 1916 imported coal had risen to six times its prewar price. The first experimental electrification in the country had been in 1888, of the tramway between Vevey and the Castle of Chillon, on the Lake of Geneva, and the first electrified railway had been a small metre-gauge line between Sissach and Gelterkinden, operated electrically for the first time in 1891; this ceased to exist in 1916 after the opening of the Lower Hauenstein tunnel between Basle and Olten. Next, in 1899, the Emmental–Burgdorf–Thun Railway started to run the first standard-gauge electrically-hauled trains in the country, with a 30-ton 0-4-0 locomotive of 300 h.p., which is still preserved in the Transport Museum at Lucerne; this used alternating current at 750 volts, 40 cycles.

The first single-phase electrification, with current at 15,000 volts a.c. and a frequency of 15 cycles, was carried out on another small line, that from Wettingen to Seebach, near Zürich, in 1904, using for the first time a rotary converter on the locomotive. Its success was such that in 1910 the Lötschberg Railway, in preparation for the opening throughout in 1913 of its main line to Brigue, equipped in similar fashion the portion of the latter from Spiez to Frutigen. The Swiss Federal Railways followed in 1919 with their first electrified line, that between Berne and Thun, connecting at Thun with the Lötschberg, also at 15,000 volts a.c., but at 16 2/3 cycles, which was to be established as standard for both the Swiss Federal and the Lötschberg systems.

Meantime, by 1913, just before the outbreak of World War One, the Swiss Federal management had decided to electrify the Gotthard main line, traffic over which was increasing to such an extent that steam power was finding great difficulty in coping with it. The war delayed the work and not until 1921 was traffic at last being worked over the mountain sections between Erstfeld and Biasca by electric power; electrification of the entire route was completed in the following year. By 1960 the electrification, in six stages, of practically the entire Swiss Federal system had been completed, a remarkable achievement in so comparatively short a period. The minor railways have all followed suit, with the sole exception of the diesel-operated mountain line up Monte Generoso, on the Lake of Lugano, and the steam-worked line up the Brienzer Rothorn, in the Bernese Oberland, both with rack-and-pinion traction. So far as railways are concerned, Switzerland is now the most completely electrified country in the world, with electricity generated entirely by its abundant resources of water power.

One of the best ways in which to study all these developments is by a visit to the Swiss Transport Museum, or, as it is generally known, the "Verkehrshaus", at Lucerne. This most admirable collection, beautifully housed beside the lake about a mile outside the town, contains some of the oldest Swiss steam and electric locomotives, some sectioned to show their working, as well as a similar full-size model showing in illuminated fashion all the way in which the electric equipment of a large Ae 6/6 functions. There is also a range of one-tenth scale models of steam and electric locomotives and rolling stock: a striking model of the spiral construction of the Gotthard main line between Erstfeld and Göschenen, fully signalled and with a number of passenger and freight trains in operation simultaneously; and much else of railway interest. There are similar collections to illustrate the development of transport by road and air, and of communications generally. This is an exhibition not to be missed by any visitors who stay at or are within reach of Lucerne.

TWO

The Swiss Federal Railways

THE PRINCIPAL Swiss Federal main lines may be regarded as four in number. First there is the great traffic artery, much as originally planned by Robert Stephenson, from Geneva through Lausanne and Berne to Zürich. This is crossed at Olten by the second most important route, from Basle to Lucerne, the Gotthard line, Bellinzona and Chiasso, on the Italian frontier. The third is from Basle through Zürich to Sargans and Chur, using the same metals as the Berne–Zürich trains between Brugg and Zürich. The fourth is from Vallorbe on the French frontier through Lausanne and up the Rhone valley to Brigue, continuing through the Simplon Tunnel to Domodossola in Italy.

Then there are several secondary main lines of importance. One is the original route from Lausanne to Yverdon, Neuchâtel, Biel, Solothurn and Olten, with the line, branching from it just beyond Biel, that passes through the Grenchenberg Tunnel to Delémont and Basle, used by the principal express trains between Geneva and Basle. Another is the continuation from Zürich of the line from Berne to St. Gallen and Rorschach, and on through St. Margrethen and Buchs to join the Zürich–Chur line at Sargans. A third is the line from Berne direct to Lucerne, of which the line from Lucerne to Zug and Zürich also may be regarded as a continuation, and the fourth and fifth are the lines from Zürich to Schaffhausen (used by the through expresses to Stuttgart in Germany), and from Zürich to Romanshorn.

Among minor lines that may be mentioned are those from Rupperswil, east of Aarau on the Berne–Zürich main line, through Lenzburg, Wohlen and Rotkreuz to Immensee, between Lucerne and Arth-Goldau, over which, as described later on in this chapter, the heavy Gotthard freight traffic is worked. There is the line in the north of the country from Stein-Säckingen, between Basle and Zürich, to Eglisau, on the Zürich–Schaffhausen main line; and in the same area that south of the Lake of Constance from Schaffhausen to Kreuzlingen (Konstanz), Romanshorn and Rorschach. And, finally, there is the line from Palézieux through Morat (or Murten) and Lyss to Solothurn. We have now to consider these routes in detail.

Geneva–Lausanne–Berne–Zürich

This main line may be regarded with justification as the most important in Switzerland. It starts from the Cornavin station at Geneva, used also by trains of the French National Railways from the Lyons direction.

The 37.4 miles from Geneva to Lausanne provide one of the few racing tracks in this mountainous country, with gentle curvature and inconsiderable gradients, over which speeds up to 80 m.p.h. are common. In the middle 1950s the fastest time over it came down to 32 minutes, demanding a start-to-stop average of 70.1 m.p.h., but the task then began of replacing a number of level crossings by underpasses or overbridges, and to allow for speed restrictions while this work was in progress times were increased to 39 minutes, but the former times were restored in 1967. Approaching Lausanne, between Denges and Renens, we pass the immense marshalling yard that has been laid out recently, with a spur connection to the Neuchâtel and Biel main line, which is joined at Renens. About 60 express trains use the Geneva–Lausanne section daily; some run to and from Zürich and beyond; others, which have to reverse at Lausanne, are for Neuchâtel, Biel and Basle; and there are those for the Simplon line and Italy.

Leaving Lausanne the Berne trains face a hard task—the 10-mile climb to Corbéron, on a gradient of 1 in $53\frac{1}{2}$–55, that lifts each train some 775 ft.; but even a locomotive no more weighty than a 79-ton Re 4/4 II Bo-Bo type will mount this gradiant at a steady 60 m.p.h. with a train of up to sixteen coaches. When travelling in the opposite direction, on emergence from a tunnel between Puidoux-Chexbres and Corbéron one comes suddenly on one of those sensational views that are a feature of a mountainous country such as this—a vast expanse of the Lake of Geneva far below the train. The highest point between Lausanne and Berne, 2,493 ft., is reached at Vauderens; we then pass the picturesque walled town of Romont, and the important city of Fribourg, before reaching the capital.

In the city of Berne the immense task at long last has been completed of rebuilding and extending the Hauptbahnhof, or main station. The first railway to reach Berne did so from the north, and ran into a terminal station facing the Holy Ghost Church in what became known as the Bahnhof-Platz. The later extension of the line to Fribourg and Lausanne branched off by a sharp curve in a south-westerly direction just short of this terminal. On this curve the new station was built, and to provide the necessary space much blasting had to take place into the rock of the high ground on the west side. The old terminal then became a parcels depot, and so continued until 1970, but has disappeared in the reconstruction. This has required considerably more room on the west side, with blasting on an extensive scale, in order to increase the former five platforms, with their nine platform faces, to six island platforms, from 985 to 1,180 ft. long, with twelve platform faces.

Above the station has been built a garage for 500 cars and a bus terminal; below are a spacious subway 52 ft. 6 in. wide and four other subways for luggage and mails, all reached by both stairs and ramps. Two new railway tunnels have been needed, one to bring the Bern-Neuenburg, Belp and Schwarzenburg trains of the Lötschberg group into the westernmost platform, and the other to enable the trains of the Berne–Zollikofen-

Solothurn line to be transferred from the street outside the station—the Bahnhof-Platz—to a new four-platform underground terminal. The scheme includes an immense new Post Office block, now in full use, and has been completed by the erection of a fine range of station offices.

It was in 1956 that the plans were first agreed between the Swiss Federal Railways and the canton and city of Berne, and in the following year were approved by a popular vote. In May, 1957, the formidable task began. The first new platform, No. 6, came into use in 1961, and the last, No. 1, in September, 1966, by which time all the alterations to track and the electric signalling had been completed. The Swiss Federal Railways and the Postal Authorities between them have invested over £23,000,000 in this immense enterprise, to which the city and canton have made a handsome contribution. The result of some fourteen years of hard work has been to provide the capital of Switzerland with a station of which it may well be proud.

Immediately after the exit from the Hauptbahnhof at Berne the four-track railway has to cross the River Aar, in its deep gorge, which it does by the magnificent Lorraine Bridge. This remarkable reinforced concrete structure, with a clear span of 150 metres, or 492 ft., for some time after its construction was the largest of its kind in the world. It is used also by the trains for Thun and the Lötschberg line, which shortly afterwards diverge to the east.

The Zürich main line continues through hilly country with constant changes of gradient and a number of moderate speed restrictions for curves, through Burgdorf and Langenthal, where traffic is exchanged with some of the minor railways mentioned in Chapter 10, to Aarburg, where the line from Lucerne, carrying the Gotthard traffic, is joined. A short distance further on, the line from Biel *via* Solothurn comes in from the west, just before reaching Olten, which is one of the busiest junctions in Switzerland. Within a short distance from the station, the Basle main line takes off to the north, so that through Olten, and entirely over flat junctions, three great streams of traffic—the Berne–Zürich, Biel–Zürich and Basle–Lucerne—cross one another's paths. But a costly scheme has now been prepared to ease the pressure; it will include a new station, and a flyover to carry non-stopping Berne–Zürich trains, chiefly freight, over the Basle–Olten line. Already, however, the important international freight traffic between Basle, the Gotthard line and Italy avoids both Olten station and Lucerne by taking a route described in the second section of this chapter.

Travelling eastwards from Olten, the Zürich main line first passes Dulliken, where a large new marshalling yard is to be laid out in connection with the Olten improvement scheme, and passing through Aarau reaches Brugg, where it is joined by the main line carrying the heavy Basle–Zürich traffic. Here another flyover has been completed recently for the Basle–Gotthard freight trains, as also described a little later. Between Brugg, Baden and Zürich is the most densely occupied main line in Switzerland, and here also elaborate plans have been worked out

Top: The reinforced concrete approach viaduct to the main station at Berne, with the Lorraine bridge at the extreme right.

Above: The magnificent Lorraine bridge across the River Aar, carrying four tracks over a clear span of 495ft.

Below: The locomotive *Limmat* of the former Swiss Northern Railway, with a train of the period. Weighing 35 tons, it was capable of a maximum speed of 25mph.

[All, Swiss Federal Railways

The main station at Berne, as rebuilt and greatly extended.
The Post Office building is at the right, and has an extension
across the station.

The well-lit and cheerful platform area, now completely
covered in and a transformation from the past.

Zürich, Switzerland's principal traffic centre. In the distance, the main passenger station; curving from it to the right, the main lines to Basle and Chur; curving by the flyover to the left, the main line to Winterthur and St. Gallen; below, the line to Schaffhausen and siding tracks.

The new all-electric signalbox, with the radio tower which is in communication by walkie-talkie equipment with all those engaged in train marshalling and operation in and around the station.
[Both, Swiss Federal Railways

Lucerne station, with its former handsome façade, on the right; to the left the Kunsthaus in which concerts and other large gatherings are held, with the well-known fountain. Unfortunately a disastrous fire in February 1971 destroyed the main station building, and complete reconstruction is now in progress.

Between Lucerne and Arth-Goldau—the Gotthard line rounding the promontory at Meggen. The pointed peak in the background is the Stanserhorn.

[Both, Swiss Federal Railways

The Gotthard line as it borders the most scenic stretch of the Lake of Lucerne, at Sisikon.

Entry to Lucerne from the Gotthard line—a push-and-pull train crosses the River Reuss, with the old town wall in the background.   *[Both, Swiss Federal Railways*

Left: The northbound Gotthard line alongside the southern extremity of the Lake of Lucerne, between Brunnen and Flüelen. The southbound line, added at a later date, is in tunnel. *[Swiss Federal Railways*

Above: Intschi bridge, between Amsteg and Gurtnellen, carrying the Gotthard line 256ft above the River Reuss. The inverted truss below the main girders was added in later years to adapt the bridge to carry the heavier modern stock. *[I Keller*

Above left: The lowest level of the Gotthard line opposite the village of Wassen, with the TEE "Ticino" Zürich-Milan express about to enter the semi-spiral Wattinger tunnel, which will temporarily reverse its direction of running from south to north.

Above right: Pfaffensprung spiral tunnel, lifting the Gotthard line 115ft; the entry is seen below on the right.

Below: The middle Meinreuss bridge, on the centre section of the double loop at Wassen, recently rebuilt in reinforced concrete.
[All, *Swiss Federal Railways*

Göschenen station, looking north. On the right is the car-loading platform, with a motorcar train about to enter the Gotthard tunnel.   [G M Kichenside

The north portal (to the right) of the 9¼-mile Gotthard tunnel. The left-hand tunnel, penetrating about ½-mile, was added in recent years to facilitate shunting from the enlarged marshalling yard; at its inner end it is possible to pass on to the main line.   [Swiss Federal Railways

Left: The three levels of the Gotthard line near Giornico. In the foreground is the entrance to Piano Tondo tunnel; below to the left is the line between Piano Tondo and Travi tunnels; to the right is the exit from Travi tunnel, 300ft below. The train is carrying about 150 Italian motor-cars. *[Franz Marti*

Above: Two levels of the Giornico spirals as seen from the opposite mountainside, with the improved main road construction in progress. *[Swiss Federal Railways*

Below: Piano Tondo viaduct as seen from the middle level of the line. The locomotive at the head of the freight train is the unique twin-unit No 11852, of 11,100hp. *[Franz Marti*

The TEE "Gottardo", en route from Zürich to Milan, passing the historic Romanesque church of San Nicolao, at Giornico.
[Swiss Federal Railways

Lugano and its lake, as seen from Monte Bré. The Gotthard line passes round the base of the conical peak (Monte San Salvatore) to the Melide causeway across the lake (extreme left).
[Lugano Tourist Office

The Melide causeway, carrying the Gotthard line across
the Lake of Lugano, as seen from Maroggia. During 1966
the doubling of the line between Melide and Maroggia—
the last remaining single-track section of the Gotthard line,
was completed.

Southbound Gotthard express leaving Bellinzona, capital
of the Canton Ticino.   *[Both, Swiss Federal Railways*

Western end of the Simplon main line—the Orbe viaduct, near Vallorbe.

The Milan-Paris TEE "Cisalpin", passing the Castle of Chillon, on the Simplon line just east of Montreux.
[Both, Swiss Federal Railways

Top: The western entrance to the $12\frac{1}{4}$-mile Simplon Tunnel. The original tunnel was opened in 1906; from the second tunnel, brought into use in 1921, a Milan-Paris express emerges. *[All, Swiss Federal Railways*

Above: Grandfey viaduct, carrying the Lausanne-Berne main line across the gorge of the Sarine near Fribourg. Originally consisting of steel spans on masonry piers, it has been rebuilt in more recent years in reinforced concrete.

Below: Passing the 11th century castle of Grandson—an express from Lausanne to Neuchâtel, Biel and Basle. *[Both, Swiss Federal Railways*

A lovely winter impression of the Swiss Federal main line from Lausanne to Berne, near Romont. In the centre background is the precipitous Moléson.

The great Barberine dam, 935ft long and 250ft high, impounding a lake which feeds the Swiss Federal Châtelard power-station on the Franco-Swiss frontier.

[Both, Swiss Federal Railways

for its relief. They include diverting the Berne–Zürich traffic from Rupperswil, beyond Aarau, to Lenzburg, and from there over an existing single track, which is being doubled, to Othmarsingen and Mägenwil. Thence a new double-line spur is being built, including a lengthy tunnel under the Heitersberg ridge, to rejoin the existing Olten–Zürich main line at Killwangen, and four tracks will be available from there into Zürich.

Between Killwangen and the next station, Dietikon, an immense new marshalling yard is being laid out in which all the marshalling operations for the Zürich region will be carried out with the latest mechanised equipment. From Altstetten, at the immediate approach to Zürich, another new spur already is complete, beginning with a lengthy concrete viaduct and finishing through the new Käferberg tunnel, to enable freight trains to run between this main line and that to Winterthur and beyond, which is joined at Oerlikon, without reversal. Then the approaches to the 16-platform main station at Zürich are to be completely remodelled, with underpasses which will eliminate conflicting train movements. Work has begun already on this vast scheme, and has been carefully planned in a sequence of operations which is expected to need a total of 18 years for completion.

Although reversal is necessary in Zürich-Hauptbahnhof of the through passenger trains, the main Zürich–St. Gallen line in effect is a continuation of that from Berne to Zürich. It leaves the main station by a lengthy curved viaduct over many of the approach tracks, and makes its way through Oerlikon to the important manufacturing town of Winterthur. It then continues, through rolling country and with no outstanding engineering features, through Wil to the five-platform station in the city of St. Gallen, used also by the Bodensee–Toggenburg Railway (Chapter 8). After the St. Fiden station in that city the line becomes single track as it descends to the port of Rorschach, on Lake Constance. The continuation up the Rhine valley also is mainly single track; it passes the important junctions of St. Margrethen and Buchs, where traffic is exchanged with the Austrian Federal Railways, at the former for Bregenz and Munich, and at the latter for the Arlberg line, Innsbruck and Vienna. But the principal trains from Zürich for the latter take the shorter course *via* Ziegelbrücke and Sargans, where they reverse to travel the 10 miles to Buchs.

In the early days of the trains composed of lightweight stock, the fastest time over the 178 miles between Geneva and Zürich, with intermediate stops at Lausanne and Berne only, came down to 3 hours 13 minutes. In recent years these times were slightly eased, but now six "Inter-City" expresses each way daily complete the journey in 3 hours 12 to 16 minutes. Non-stop, the fastest time over the 60.4 miles between Lausanne and Berne is made by a distinguished newcomer to this route, the German T.E.E. "Rheingold", the four-coach Geneva section of which is hauled in each direction by a Swiss Re 4/4 type Bo-Bo locomotive; the time allowance is 63 minutes southbound. Between Berne and Basle this

B

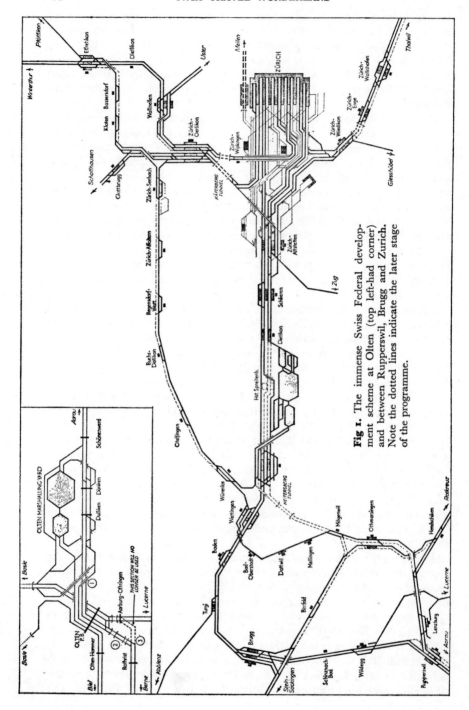

Fig 1. The immense Swiss Federal development-scheme at Olten (top left-had corner) and between Rupperswil, Brugg and Zurich. Note the dotted lines indicate the later stage of the programme.

is the only non-stop train of the day, taking 70 minutes only for the 66 miles in the southbound direction.

Between Geneva and Zürich one of the quickest services is provided by the "Rhône-Isar" express. This is one of the several through services to and from Munich, in German Bavaria; reversing in Zürich they travel through St. Gallen and Rorschach to be handed over to the Austrian Federal Railways at St. Margrethen, having to cross two frontiers in rapid succession, here and at Lindau. Another is the recently introduced "Bavaria"; taking the name of a former Geneva–Munich express, this is now a first class only T.E.E. service between Zürich and Munich. Express trains run at roughly 80-minute intervals throughout the day between Geneva, Berne and Zürich; some take the alternative route from Lausanne *via* Neuchâtel, Biel and Solothurn to Olten; most continue from Zürich, either to St. Gallen and Rorschach or to Romanshorn, also on the Lake of Constance. Many of these trains have grown to a considerable weight, and formations of 12 to 15 coaches are common; these for the most part are now handled by the new 6,320 h.p. Re 4/4 II type Bo-Bo locomotives but a few by the numerous RBe 4/4 motorcoaches of 2,720 h.p. The majority of the trains are made up into set formations, and despite their length some work on the push-and-pull principle, a driving compartment being provided in the brake-coach at the opposite end of the train when the motive power is in rear. It is a somewhat startling experience to be propelled in a train of such length at speeds up to 80 m.p.h.

The Gotthard Line

Strictly speaking, the Gotthard main line runs between Lucerne and Chiasso, but in effect it forms the continuation of the earlier line from Basle through Olten to Lucerne, so that Basle–Chiasso may be regarded as a continuous route. On leaving the Swiss (SBB) station at Basle, the trains first pass the great marshalling yards at Muttenz, much extended in recent years and handling three-fifths of all the freight traffic passing through Switzerland. All wagons running through from France and Germany by the Basle gateway are sorted here according to their destinations in Switzerland and Italy; the Italian traffic is moved southwards over the Gotthard line. Freight from Germany can run direct from the Badischer Bahnhof in Basle to Muttenz by a spur line which avoids the SBB station; all the passenger trains, however, run into the SBB station and reverse there, except the night "Italia" and "Riviera" sleeping car trains, which also take the direct spur; of these more later.

Five miles out of Basle, at Pratteln, the Zürich and Olten lines separate, and the latter then begins a steady ascent past Liestal. Beyond Sissach, 13 miles out, the original line climbed to 1,844 ft. altitude at Läufelfingen before passing through the 1½ miles of the Upper Hauenstein Tunnel, the earliest tunnel of any length in Switzerland, which took from 1853 to 1858 to complete. But in order to bypass the toilsome approach gradient, as steep in parts as 1 in 38, in 1916 a new line was opened from Sissach to Olten, climbing no higher than to 1,444 ft. at Tecknau, but at the cost of boring the 5 miles 95 yards of the double-line Lower Hauenstein tunnel. Immediately after the exit from this we cross the swiftly flowing River Aar and enter Olten. Just short of Olten a spur diverges to the east to join the Olten–Zürich main line; this is used by the Gotthard line freight trains and the night sleeping car trains already mentioned, following a route of which more in a moment.

Between Olten and Lucerne the only town of importance is Zofingen, at which many of the expresses stop. Beyond here in clear weather a distant view is obtained to the south-west of the snowclad Bernese Alps; then, on the opposite side of the line, over almost level track, we skirt the Lake of Sempach. Presently there appear ahead the mountainous forms of the Rigi and Pilatus before, with curvature on a considerable scale, we join, at Emmenbrücke and Sentimatt, the lines from Zürich and Berne respectively. Then, after the Gotthard line has crossed the Reuss to join us, there comes the complete semi-circle, partly through tunnel and the remainder between high retaining walls, that leads into the capacious terminal at Lucerne. The station is on the lake front, and its handsome frontage was a considerable ornament to the town until a disastrous fire early in 1971 destroyed the building. Lucerne, incidentally, is an extremely difficult station to work. Apart from the metre-gauge Brünig line, from Sentimatt it has no more than two approach lines over which to work all its busy traffic in and out, and over which all Gotthard line trains must pass twice. Widening this section would be an extremely costly business, and the best has been made of an onerous task by signalling both lines for either-way working.

On leaving Lucerne, the nose of a Gotthard locomotive is pointing due south. In the first half-mile we negotiate the same semi-circle as on entry, and then, branching eastwards at Sentimatt, cross the Reuss and plunge into Wesemlin tunnel, which in just over 1¼ miles carries us right under the town to emerge at Halde; already the train has travelled not far short of 3 miles, though the station from which it started is only just across a narrow stretch of water. The course is now south-east along the Luzernersee—the north-western arm of the lake—until the line is compelled by the lake's cruciform shape to turn round the Meggenhorn to the north-east until it reaches the head of the north-eastern arm of the lake at Küssnacht. Opposite is the massive bulk of the Rigi, which we are circling. A short run from Küssnacht takes the line across the narrow neck of land separating the Lakes of Lucerne and Zug; the latter we reach, turning a right-angle a second time (in addition to having boxed the compass out of Lucerne) at Immensee.

Here the line from Lucerne is joined by the original Gotthard line, which started from Rotkreuz, on the line between Lucerne, Zug and Zürich, and it is over the line from Rotkreuz that the Gotthard freight traffic moves today. As mentioned already, the freight trains from Basle have been using the Olten line until just short of that station, then proceeding by the eastern spur to join the Olten–Zürich line; this they have followed for 11 miles through Aarau to Rupperswil. Here they have turned south through Lenzburg and Wohlen to reach Rotkreuz. Much of this route until now has been single track, but such is the increase in the Gotthard freight traffic that it is being doubled; the work is now nearly complete, including a new flyover at Rotkreuz to carry the Wohlen–Immensee trains over those from Lucerne to Zürich.

But this is not all. To avoid undue congestion on the Berne–Zürich main line between Olten and Rupperswil, the revised route of the freight trains from Basle to the Gotthard line is by the Basle–Zürich line as far as the approach to Brugg, where the new flyover already mentioned has been built over the Berne–Zürich line to connect with the branch from Brugg which passes through Othmarsingen to join the Aarau–Wohlen line at Hendschiken. Also, as previously mentioned, there are important future plans for keeping the Berne–Zürich and Basle–Zürich streams of traffic separate by connecting Othmarsingen direct with Killwangen in the Limmat Valley, from which there will be four tracks into Zürich. The route of many Zürich trains from Olten will then be *via* Aarau, Rupperswil, Lenzburg, and Othmarsingen to Killwangen. This plan involves a stretch of new line, including a lengthy new tunnel under the Heitersberg, which is now nearly complete.

A short run from Immensee brings the Gotthard trains to the important junction of Arth-Goldau, where the line comes in over which the Gotthard trains from Zürich travel by way of Thalwil and Zug. The station is also used by the trains of the Südostbahn or South Eastern Railway, described in Chapter 8, and by those of the Arth-Rigi rack-and-pinion railway, which start from a viaduct above the station. Beyond Arth-Goldau the line passes through the debris produced by a disastrous landslide that broke away in 1806 from the Rossberg mountain and devastated four villages; there is a reminder of this grim happening in the great boulders strewn on both sides of the line. We are now skirting the east side of the Rigi, and turn at last due south, in our proper direction, as we pass the historic town of Schwyz and reach the lake once again at Brunnen. Though at this point the direct distance from Lucerne is no more than 15 miles, already the train, by the circuits described, has travelled 24½ miles.

From Brunnen the railway, much tunnelled, skirts the almost precipitous eastern wall of the Urnersee, the southernmost stretch of the Lake of Lucerne. Above is the famous Axenstrasse road, also with a number of tunnels; as to the railway, the longer tunnels are all on the southbound track, which was added to the original line, now carrying the northbound trains, in comparatively recent years. The extreme end of the lake is reached at Flüelen, and the railway now enters the valley of the River Reuss. For 5½ miles, past Altdorf, it is level, but at Erstfeld, a small manufacturing town ensconced between high mountain walls, and an important railway centre at which are maintained the 5,940 h.p. Ae 6/6 type locomotives that work the line, climbing begins in earnest.

The ruling gradient decided on at the time of construction was between 1 in 38½ and 1 in 40, and this continues with only minor interruptions for

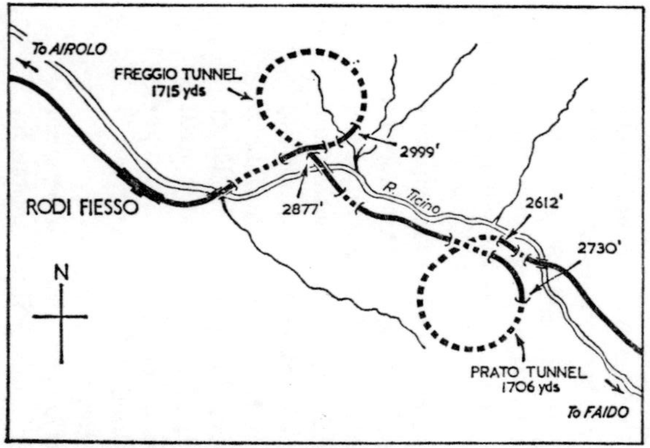

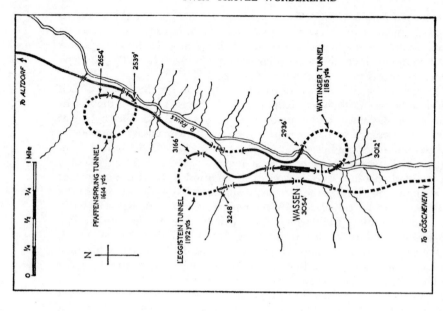

Fig 4. Spiral location of Gotthard main line at Wassen.

Fig 2. Spiral location of Gotthard main line in Piottino Ravine.

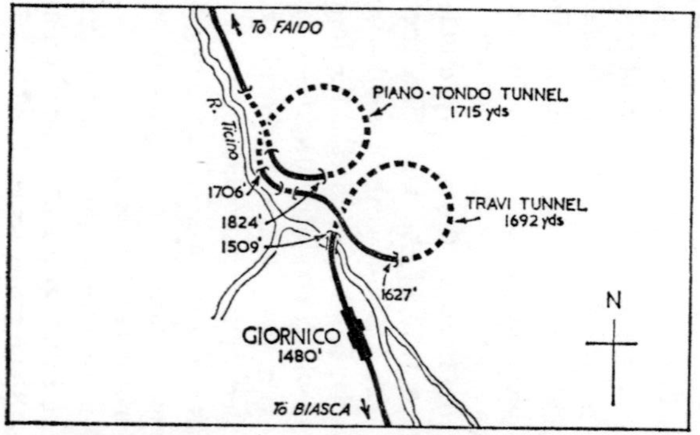

Fig 3. Spiral location of Gotthard main line near Giornico.

18 miles to Göschenen, during which the trains are lifted through a difference in level of 2,080 ft. The line first mounts the east wall of the valley to a level some 200 ft. above the valley floor, through the station at Amsteg and across the great Kärstelenbach viaduct, 178 ft. high at its maximum and 440 ft. long, spanning the deep gorge at the entrance to the Maderanertal. The Reuss valley itself now narrows to a gorge down which the river forces its way by a series of falls, and which the railway crosses by a single span 255 ft. above the river. By the end of the gorge the valley floor has risen almost to the railway level, despite the latter's continued climbing, and more drastic measures now had to be taken by the engineers. Beyond the village of Gurtnellen these begin with the completely spiral Pfaffensprung tunnel, which in a length of 1,685 yds. lifts the line some 115 ft.

A little further on we come to the famous stretch past the village of Wassen, with its white church perched on a rocky eminence, and the gorge of the tributary Meienreuss stream immediately to the north of it. This the railway crosses by the lower Meienreuss bridge, beyond which it tunnels under the church, and after a short distance crosses the Reuss to enter the semi-spiral Leggistein tunnel. Emerging and recrossing the Reuss the railway now travels northwards instead of southwards past the village, and beyond the imposing middle Meienreuss bridge, 260 ft. above the stream, enters yet another semi-spiral tunnel which reverses the direction of the line for a second time, and carries it over the upper Meienreuss bridge to the uppermost level, looking down on the village and both lower stretches of the line. By this bold development, which of course adds to the distance covered, the railway is lifted roughly 400 ft., but without any steepening of the ruling gradient.

At Göschenen, 55½ miles from Lucerne, the climbing is virtually at an end. The next stretch of the valley is the deep, narrow and steeply rising Schöllenen gorge, up which in later years, with the help of considerable tunnelling and avalanche protection, the Schöllenen Railway has been built from Göschenen to Andermatt, but this has only been possible with a maximum gradient of 1 in 5½, operated with rack-and-pinion. The Gotthard Railway, however, here enters the Gotthard tunnel, 9¼ miles long, and in it attains its maximum altitude of 3,786 ft., having ascended some 2,350 ft. since leaving the Lake of Lucerne. From Göschenen station two tunnel entrances are seen; the right one is the main tunnel, but the left goes in for about half-a-mile only; it was bored at a time when the freight marshalling yard at Göschenen was being extended, and in the very restricted space of the valley had to be laid out on both sides of the stream; an extension therefore was needed at the south end to facilitate shunting movements. There is a through track from the inward end of this second tunnel to the southbound main line.

One very considerable activity in the Gotthard tunnel is the movement through it of motorcars, whose drivers wish to avoid the further climb of 3,145 ft. over the Gotthard Pass, and in winter in any event cannot pass over the latter, because of blockage by snow. Loading the cars on to the motorcar trains at both ends of the tunnel, Göschenen and Airolo, has been brought to a fine art. The trains themselves are composed of flat wagons joined by flaps which in effect turn each train into a road, and are worked push-and-pull fashion with a locomotive permanently at one end and a driving cabin at the other.

Needless to say, the movement of these trains has complicated the operation over this densely-occupied line, but this is greatly facilitated by the automatic signalling now installed through the length of the tunnel. It comprises a total of 13 block sections, so that several trains can be running on each track through the tunnel simultaneously, adequately protected by this signalling. In the centre of the tunnel, also, there is a double crossover line between the two tracks which can be brought into use in case of emergency. On the signalling panel in Göschenen station, under the control of the stationmaster, the position of every train in the tunnel can be clearly seen. Now, however, a road tunnel is being bored under the Gotthard pass, and on completion this will ease the pressure on the railway considerably.

On emergence from the tunnel at Airolo the trains enter the valley of the Ticino, which at this point changes its easterly flow to a southerly direction, roughly in line with that of the Reuss valley. In the 28½ miles from Airolo to Biasca a descent of 2,785 ft. has to be negotiated, and over some stretches engineering similar to that at Wassen has been necessary in order to keep pace with the rapid fall in the valley floor. The most interesting section is the 15 miles between Rodi-Fiesso and Giornico, through the Piottino and Biaschina ravines. Here four completely spiral tunnels are passed through, Freggio and Prato, between Rodi-Fiesso and Faido, and Piano-Tondo and Travi, between Faido and Giornico. The two last-mentioned are side by side, and from the train, as it enters Piano-Tondo Tunnel, it is possible to look straight down the mountainside to the exit from Travi Tunnel, some 300 ft. below. By Biasca the valley floor is flattening out, and a fairly straight track permits some fast travel before the capital town of the Canton Ticino, Bellinzona, is reached. The lowest point on the whole line, Giubiasco, 767 ft. above the sea, is 1½ miles further on.

The original Gotthard line continued from Giubiasco along the Ticino Valley and the eastern shore of Lake Maggiore to the Italian frontier at Luino, whence the Italians worked the through trains to Milan. A branch was thrown off at Giubiasco, climbing all but 800 ft. up the steep slope on the east side of the valley at 1 in 38½–40 to a tunnel under Monte Ceneri, which led to the station at Rivera-Bironico, at 1,558 ft. altitude. From here the branch, now the main line proper, descended the neighbouring valley to reach the popular resort of Lugano, on the lake of that name, and to continue to Chiasso and Como.

From Lugano station, high above the lake, the railway descends through the suburb of Paradiso, skirting the lower slopes of the precipitous Monte San Salvatore until it reaches Melide. Here a promontory extending well out into the lake prompted the discovery of an under-water ridge coming nearly to the surface of a lake which opposite the town of Lugano is some 900 ft. deep. On to this ridge material was dumped to form a substantial causeway right across the lake, carrying both the railway and the public road. The task was completed in 1966 of widening this causeway to enable the single railway track—the last single line section on the entire Gotthard line—to be doubled, and for the road also to be converted to a dual carriageway.

Curving sharply round at Maroggia, the railway then continues along the eastern shore of the lake past Capolago—lower terminus of the rack-and-pinion railway up Monte Generoso—to Chiasso, on the Italian frontier. Here, as at Basle on the French and German frontier, a vast amount of money has been spent recently in the extension on a very considerable scale and mechanisation of the freight yards, in order to handle the constantly growing international freight traffic more expeditiously. Part of the work was the boring of a tunnel at Balerna to carry southbound freight trains into the yard without fouling the northbound main line.

In all, in coping with natural obstacles, Gotthard line trains travel 140 miles between Lucerne and Chiasso as compared with the direct distance of 92 miles between these two towns. Including the 9¼-mile Gotthard Tunnel, a total of 80 tunnels aggregating in length 28½ miles had to be bored, and 324 bridges of more than 32 ft. span had to be built, in carrying out this great enterprise. Today one of the busiest main lines in the whole of Europe, it has more than justified the heavy expenditure involved.

Working over the Gotthard main line hitherto has been almost entirely by the Co-Co 5,940 h.p. locomotives of Class Ae 6/6, with loads up to 600 tons on the long climbs. Freight trains may be made up to 1,200 tons, with a second Ae 6/6 locomotive cut into the centre of the train to avoid undue strain on drawbars. Speed on the mountain section is limited by curvature to 75 km.p.h. (46 m.p.h.). For this reason the two T.E.E. trains which work daily between Zürich and Milan, the "Ticino" and "Gottardo", are little faster in actual running than the ordinary expresses, though they gain their quicker overall times by making no stops en route other than Lugano and Como, and having no lengthy stops at Chiasso for frontier formalities. They are the only trains booked to pass Chiasso without stopping; this they are able to do, despite the change from the Swiss 15,000 volts a.c. to the Italian 3,000 volts d.c., by the multi-current equipment which the inventive Swiss have been the first to think out. The T.E.E. trains take 3 hours 47 minutes to 4 hours for the 183-mile journey between Zürich and Milan.

Through coaches belonging to many different countries are seen every day on the Gotthard main line, travelling between Scandinavia, Holland, Belgium, France and Germany and Italian destinations ranging from Milan to the Riviera, Rome and the Adriatic coast. Among the most interesting are the night "Riviera" and "Italia" expresses, which use the freight route already described between Basle and Arth-Goldau via

Aarau, Lenzburg and Rotkreuz, and have no publicly booked stop between Basle and Bellinzona, though in point of fact they halt at Erstfeld to change crews.

But seven other international trains, including the T.E.E. "Roland", do make the longest actual non-stop runs in Switzerland, over the 105.6 miles between Lucerne and Bellinzona, in a best time of 2 hours 9 minutes; considering the gradients, speed restrictions and the considerable weight of the trains concerned, this is at a most creditable average speed of 49.1 m.p.h. As to weight, on one evening in September 1966 I saw the northbound "Italy–Holland Express" at Lucerne made up to 15 coaches, including sleeping cars and some of the heavier Continental stock, with a total weight of 698 *tonnes* (688 tons), and yet hauled by a single Ae 6/6 type locomotive. Loads up to 15 and 16 coaches, largely of the lighter Swiss vehicles of 26 to 28 *tonnes*, are common over this route at peak periods. But the ubiquitous new Re 4/4 II and III type Bo-Bo electrics have now taken over the Gotthard passenger workings.

Basle–Zürich–Chur

This is a main line on the improvement of which the Swiss Federal Railways have spent a considerable amount of money in recent years; its passenger traffic includes three T.E.E. (Trans-Europe Express) trains making their way to Zurich—the "Arbalète" from Paris, the "Edelweiss" from Amsterdam and the "Helvetia" from Hamburg—as well as the handsome Austrian "Transalpin", running between Basle and Vienna. Other trains running from Basle to the Austrian frontier at Buchs and thence over the Arlberg route are the "Arlberg Express" from Paris and Calais to Innsbruck and Vienna, and the pleasantly named "Wiener Walzer" sleeping car train between Basle and Vienna. Then this main line provides the chief access to the famous resorts in the Canton of the Grisons—Arosa, Davos, St. Moritz and Pontresina—carrying the coaches of many countries between Basle and Landquart and Chur, where passengers change into the metre-gauge trains of the Rhaetian Railway.

The line is on rising gradients from Basle for the first 29 miles, to Effingen, mounting just over 600 ft. to an altitude of 1,522 ft., and after passing through the 1½-mile Bötzberg Tunnel enters the valley of the Aar, which is crossed just before the entry to Brugg. Here we join the main line from Berne and Olten. Just short of the crossing is the divergence of the new flyover line which, as described earlier in this chapter, now carries the heavy freight traffic from Basle to the Gotthard line. Shortly after Brugg the River Reuss is crossed, and beyond Baden the River Limmat, so completing the crossing of the three principal Swiss streams that feed the Rhine. At the approach to Baden we pass the famous Brown Boveri engineering works, and beyond the station is the tunnel recently bored in order to eliminate level crossings in the centre of this important town. There is no further engineering work of note until, at the approach to Zürich, we see on the left the massive reinforced concrete viaduct, which, with a tunnel, provides the new direct connection from this main line to that from Zürich to Winterthur and beyond, so eliminating the reversal of through freight trains.

The great terminal station at Zürich, with its 16 platforms, is the busiest in Switzerland. With the present layout, it is impossible to avoid many conflicting train movements, especially with the through trains between Berne and the Romanshorn and St. Gallen lines, but as mentioned in the first section of this chapter, a complete transformation of the station approaches is now in prospect. Some of the through passenger trains between Basle and both the Arlberg line and Chur—the "Arlberg Express", for example—avoided reversal in the Hauptbahnhof at Zürich by taking a direct spur line, and stopping instead at the Enge station; certain night trains still take this route.

From Basle to Zürich is a distance of 55 miles; another $72\frac{1}{2}$ miles bring us to Chur. At Thalwil, $7\frac{1}{2}$ miles from Zürich, we come to a further recently completed improvement—the flyover line that carries trains from Zürich to Lucerne and to the Gotthard line over the northbound main line. Then, after having skirted the Lake of Zürich for a considerable distance, we come to Ziegelbrücke, $35\frac{1}{2}$ miles from Zürich (the junction for Glarus and Linthal), and to the most costly of all the improvements along the route, which was completed in 1970. Until comparatively recent years this main line was single-tracked beyond Ziegelbrücke; the change includes double-tracking over most of its length. The worst difficulty in so doing has been that over much of the 12 miles between Weesen and Walenstadt the railway is carried at the foot of the mountains bordering the Walensee lake, in part so precipitous as to leave no room for an additional track. It was also decided to straighten out the extremely sinuous stretch of line between Ziegelbrücke and the lake.

The first task, therefore, was to bore the double-line Kerenzerberg tunnel, $2\frac{1}{2}$ miles long. Next, a comparatively straight line has been laid between the western end of this tunnel and Ziegelbrücke, including a new station for Weesen and the short Biberlikopf tunnel between there and Ziegelbrücke. A short length of single track still remains from the eastern end of Kerenzerberg tunnel between Mühlehorn and Murg, but from there onwards there is now double track as far as Sargans and Bad Ragaz. Some fine scenery lends attraction to this stretch; the snowclad summit of Glärnisch is in view after leaving Ziegelbrücke, and the pale green Walensee, bordered on the opposite side by the Churfirsten, in appearance like a row of giant's teeth, is quite spectacular.

At Sargans this main line meets that which has come up the Rhine valley from Rorschach by way of Buchs. It is unfortunate that for through trains to and from the Austrian Arlberg line the junctions at Sargans and Buchs are both trailing; all these trains, therefore, have to reverse direction twice in a distance of 10 miles, and with the time required for passport and customs examination at Buchs this part of the journey is the reverse of speedy. Trains to and from Chur, however, have no such handicap. Passing Bad Ragaz they come on to single track; Landquart, where the Rhaetian trains for Klosters and Davos are waiting, is the next important stop; and up the wide Rhine Valley, here bordered by high mountains, the trains proceed until they reach the commodious exchange station at Chur. From Landquart to Chur the Swiss Federal and Rhaetian lines run parallel, as also the main motorway up the valley; at Zizers the Rhaetian line crosses over the Swiss Federal from the east to the west side, and so continues into Chur. Doubling the Swiss Federal line from Bad Ragaz to Chur, with a new station at Landquart, is now in progress.

As to the train service, the faster trains take 1¾ hours or slightly less between Zürich and Chur, at roughly two-hour intervals; in some cases the Chur and Arlberg portions are combined between Chur and Sargans, but the more important Arlberg trains run independently. From Chur the most interesting of all the trains starts at 8.19 in the evening, including in a single formation Swiss, Dutch, Belgian and French coaches and German and International Sleeping Car Company sleeping cars for Basle, Frankfurt, Amsterdam, Oberhausen, Ostend, Calais and Paris— an international collection indeed!

The Simplon Line

In effect, the Simplon main line begins on the French frontier at Vallorbe; it forms the principal route from Paris to Milan and North Italy. Originally the through trains travelled from Dijon by way of Pontarlier; in 1915 a new line was opened from Frasne direct to Vallorbe, which cut off a considerable corner, though it required the boring of the Mont d'Or tunnel, 3¾ miles in length. The Pontarlier route, however, is still used twice daily by through trains between Paris and Berne, which provide Neuchâtel also with through facilities.

Vallorbe is 2,655 ft. above the sea, and in descending the very winding stretch of line to the junction with the Neuchâtel–Lausanne line at Daillens, near Cossonay, fine views are obtained of this distant chain of the Alps, from the Jungfrau to Mont-Blanc. A little short of Renens, first a spur line leaves on the right to the great new mechanised marshalling yard at Denges, and then the main line from Geneva is joined. After a brief run of 29 miles from Vallorbe, we are in the busy main station at Lausanne. From here the railway skirts the Lake of Geneva—a most pleasant stretch of line—past Vevey, turning a little inland through Montreux but back to the lake by Territet, and then past the historic Castle of Chillon to the eastern end of the lake at Villeneuve.

Up the length of the Rhône valley the gradients are inconsiderable, and high speeds can be run; indeed, over certain sections the T.E.E. "Cisalpin" is allowed to speed up to 140 km.p.h. (87 m.p.h.), which is the record for Switzerland. Many start-to-stop runs of other expresses also are timed at well over 60 m.p.h., including one scheduled in 37 minutes over the 42.3 miles from Sion to Montreux, at 68.6 m.p.h. start to stop. The "Cisalpin" makes the best time over the 90.4 miles between Lausanne and Brigue non-stop—85 minutes eastbound and 83 minutes westbound—but the "Simplon Express", a heavy sleeping car train, makes the run in no more than 90 minutes eastbound and 88 minutes westbound. These times include a number of speed restrictions at different points, and single line working over certain sections east of Sion, which in part are now being doubled.

After leaving the Lake of Geneva the line passes a number of stations— Aigle, Bex and Martigny—where connection is made with the minor railways described in Chapter 11, and at St. Maurice there comes in the Swiss Federal line from St. Gingolph, the French frontier town on the south side of the lake. At Martigny non-stopping trains swing round the long curve by which the railway adjusts itself to the great right-angled bend made by the Rhône valley at this point. The important town of Sion, with its new station, is passed, a prominent object in the view here being the two castles of Tourbillon and Valère, perched on their. two conical rocky hills.

The station at Sierre precedes the longer single line section previously referred to, recently widened as far as the next station, Salgesch. Speed must be reduced through the narrow curving gorge of the river at Leuk, but then follows a fast running stretch past Visp, junction for the Zermatt line, to Brigue. From Gampel onwards we have an intriguing view, at an immense height up the north wall of the valley, of the Lötschberg main line; from its coming into view at Hohtenn we can follow a train gradually descending, crossing viaducts and disappearing from view through tunnels, until eventually the two lines meet in Brigue station.

With a number of the trains Swiss local stock is detached at Brigue and the through portions from both Lötschberg and Simplon lines for Italian destinations are amalgamated. They still remain in custody of Swiss locomotive power, for the Swiss locomotives, mainly Swiss Federal but in one or two cases Lötschberg, work through the Simplon tunnel and finish their journeys on Italian territory at Domodossola.

The entrance to the Simplon tunnel is $1\frac{1}{2}$ miles beyond Brigue station. "Tunnels" is the more correct description, for there are two parallel bores, with their centre-lines 56 ft. apart, the original tunnel on the left, opened for traffic in 1906, and the second tunnel, on the right, completed in 1921. A book might be written about the almost incredible difficulties experienced before both first and second tunnels were carried through to completion. Like the Gotthard, these tunnels handle a thriving motorcar traffic, with efficient loading facilities at the two ends—Brigue and Iselle— and are also equipped with automatic signalling and a central cross-over. For some years they possessed a central signalbox, which signalmen had the somewhat unenviable task of manning in shifts, deep in the bowels of the mountain, but with automatic signalling this human element is no longer required.

Of the principal trains using the Simplon line the Swiss T.E.E. six-coach "Cisalpin" has been mentioned already. The westbound train takes 7 hours 44 minutes to cover the 508 miles from Milan to Paris, and the eastbound 9 minutes more. Another T.E.E. train, which runs between Geneva and Milan, is the Italian "Lemano"; the original two lengthy cars have now become a locomotive-hauled train. At night, as also mentioned already, there is the "Simplon Express"; in former years this was the "Simplon-Orient", but its through portions now run no further than Belgrade, Zagreb and Rijeka in Yugoslavia, as well as to Trieste, Milan traffic is carried by the following "Lombardie Express", which also serves Venice and Trieste.

The only through train over this route which still serves the Middle East is but a pale shadow of its former self. It is the "Direct Orient", which on various days includes in its formation through sleeping cars for Belgrade, Sofia, Athens and Istanbul, but it is far slower than formerly, and between Lausanne and Brigue stops at all the principal stations. There are other fast services each day between both Paris and Geneva and Italian destinations, including Florence, Rome, Pescara and Bari on the Adriatic, and as far distant in one case as Brindisi, almost to the toe of Italy.

Basle–Delemont–Biel–Neuchâtel–Lausanne

While the original route from Basle to Lausanne was by way of Olten and Berne, and is still followed by some of the expresses, in particular the TEE "Rheingold", most of the services between Basle and Geneva take the more westerly route which enables them to serve the important towns of Biel and Neuchâtel. From Basle this line diverges almost immediately from that to Olten, and makes its way up the picturesque valley of the Birs past Laufen to Delémont. Here it is joined by the line which once carried the principal traffic from Calais and Paris to Berne and the Bernese Oberland, until French electrification diverted most of these trains *via* Thionville, Metz, Strasbourg and Basle. This was a pity, for the Delle route makes a most attractive entry into Switzerland, in particular the stretch of line from Porrentruy past St. Ursanne, high above the Doubs valley. There are still two services each way between Paris and Berne by way of Delle, but one involves a change of train at Belfort.

At Delémont the Basle–Geneva trains must reverse direction. They then enter the lower reach of the Birs valley, which here becomes a spectacular gorge known as the Val Moutier, through the heart of one of the ridges of the Jura, flanked with huge limestone rocks of fantastic shapes, and thread a whole succession of tunnels. But the longest of these is after Moutier; it is the $5\frac{1}{4}$-mile Grenchenberg tunnel, which as described in Chapter 3 forms part of a cut-off built by the Lötschberg Railway and opened in 1916 to shorten the circuitous route *via* Sonceboz used previously. So the Basle–Geneva expresses use this straight bore through the last ridge of the Jura to the station at Grenchen-Nord, from which they swing down over the line from Olten to Biel to join the latter at Lengnau. The line from Olten through the historic town of Solothurn is part of the original route between Lausanne and Zürich, and is of sufficient importance to have had its remaining single-track sections doubled in recent years. A few of the Geneva–Zürich trains still use it, for the benefit chiefly of Neuchâtel and Biel, though the faster main line through Berne is the usual route.

Biel is an important city, in the Canton of Berne second only to the capital, and a centre of the watch-making industry. For many miles beyond Biel the railway is carried between the wooded slopes of the Jura and the Lakes of Biel and Neuchâtel, with distant views eastwards of the Alpine chain; the Lake of Neuchâtel has that city at its north-eastern end and the town of Yverdon at its south-western extremity. At Neuchâtel we are joined, coming from the east, by the Bern–Neuenburg section of the Lötschberg system, and beyond the town there branch in succession two lines to the west. One climbs very steeply to Les Hauts-Geneveys and Convers—a station deeply hemmed in a narrow rock-girt valley between two long tunnels, and at 3,444 ft. altitude the highest station on the line—to reach the busy towns of La Chaux-de-Fonds and Le Locle, two further watch-making centres. The other is the line which makes its way up the Val de Travers to Les Verrières, the last Swiss station, and Pontarlier in France, providing the route mentioned in Chapter 3 which is followed by two Paris–Berne trains daily. Though some widening has been carried out, three single-track sections still remain between Biel and Yverdon, but from there onwards there is double-track, first through rolling hill country to Daillens, where the Vallorbe line comes in, and to Renens, where the main line from Geneva is joined just short of Lausanne.

With the double reversals of the Basle–Geneva expresses, at Delémont and Lausanne, the use of push-and-pull train sets saves valuable minutes, and most of the point-to-point times between Biel and Lausanne are at start-to-stop speeds up to 60 m.p.h. By far the most interesting express over this route, however, is one which requires to be re-engined at both the stations mentioned. This is the "Hispania", which daily connects Hamburg in Germany with the Spanish frontier. Formerly this train started from Copenhagen in Denmark, and included in its formation a through sleeping car from Sweden's capital, Stockholm. Now, however, connections only from Scandinavia bring passengers to the "Hispania", which begins its journey at Hamburg at 9.0 a.m. Travelling by way of Hanover, Frankfurt and Heidelberg, the "Hispania" is into the Swiss station at Basle by 5.25 p.m.; it has been preceded by another express bringing through coaches from Emmerich, on the Dutch frontier, by way of Cologne, Bonn and Mannheim. At 5.50 p.m. the combined express is away from Basle, and after reversal at Delémont and Lausanne is into Geneva by 8.56 p.m. Here sleeping cars are added, and finally, after travelling through France by way of Lyons, Avignon and Narbonne, the "Hispania" makes its way into Port Bou, on the Spanish frontier, at 6.24 a.m., after a journey of just under 21½ hours from Hamburg.

Other Main Lines

There are one or two other Swiss lines in the main line category that merit description. One of these, which, until the boring of the Simplon tunnel provided the route from Berne to North Italy, connects the capital with Lucerne. For a happy impression of pastoral Switzerland one cannot do better than to travel over this 59-mile route. Seven fast trains, formed of push-and-pull sets, run over it in each direction daily, taking an average of 80 minutes for the journey, with three intermediate stops.

Lucerne trains leave Berne by the Thun line, which is followed for 4½ miles to Gümligen; from here onwards the line is single track throughout, and with some considerable gradients, much curvature, and intermediate stops at Konolfingen, Langnau and Wolhusen, the times demand some smart locomotive work. After the Gümligen divergence we begin rapidly to climb, for a short distance with a magnificent view of the glittering peaks of the Bernese Alps from the Wetterhorn to the Blümlisalp. At Konolfingen we intersect the principal line of the E.B.T. or Emmental–Burgdorf–Thun group (Chapter 10), that from Thun to Burgdorf and Solothurn. Climbing continues through the pleasant Emmental, noted for its agriculture and cattle-breeding, and in particular for its cheese. Before the junction of Langnau another branch of the E.B.T. group comes in, from Burgdorf by way of Ramsei.

The valley of the Grosse Emme now narrows considerably, and the line winds incessantly beside the stream between high and thickly-wooded slopes. After Langnau higher mountains come into view, particularly at Wiggen, where we see up a lateral valley to the south the rocky crest of the 6,864 ft. Schrattenfluh. For a time the valley broadens again, as the summit level of the line, 2,805 ft., is reached at Escholzmatt. We now cross into the valley of the Kleine Emme, which begins as a narrow defile, with more incessant windings and a number of short tunnels, until the train runs into Wolhusen; this is the third of the junctions with the EBT group lines, one which has come from Langenthal by way of Huttwil and Willisau.

Soon after Wolhusen the gorge of the Kleine Emme ends, quite picturesquely, with the church and monastery of Wertenstein perched on a rocky promontory, round the base of which the railway, road and stream wind sharply. We then emerge into a broad valley, over which the line is fairly straight and level and the fast trains travel at a steady 75 m.p.h. To the south towers Pilatus, here seen as the termination of a long mountain ridge, and not as the bold shape that fronts the Lake of Lucerne. Finally, passing through a ¾-mile tunnel, we join at the Sentimatt junctions the main Basle–Lucerne line, and negotiate its semi-circle to reach the terminus at Lucerne.

As mentioned in Chapter 1, the Lucerne–Zürich line may in effect be regarded as a continuation of that just described, though the latter is much the busier of the two. Eight-coach push-and-pull trains with RBe 4/4 motor coaches run at about 80-minute intervals throughout the day between Lucerne and Zürich, in times ranging from 47 to about 60 minutes, according to stops, for the 36 miles. Many of the trains require extra vehicles, and one amusing service is the 5.36 p.m. from Zürich, very popular with commuters, on which the motorcoach pushes eight and pulls six 73 ft. coaches at speeds up to 75 m.p.h. on the straighter sections between Zug and Lucerne.

The viaduct carrying the Zürich - Schaffhausen line across the Rhine at Eglisau, with a main span of 295ft.

A winter scene on the Swiss Federal metre - gauge Brünig line. A snowplough has been in use to keep the track clear.
[*Both, Swiss Federal Railways*

The vast new mechanised marshalling yard at Denges, west of Lausanne. The main line from Lausanne to Geneva is seen on the right, between the yard and the motorway.

Containers have now invaded Switzerland. A container train passing Immensee, where the Gotthard line borders the Lake of Zug.　　　*[Both, Swiss Federal Railways*

Above: A second class open coach of the Swiss Federal standard lightweight type for internal service, with ten bays of 80 seats in all and two lavatories. Its tare weight is 27 tons.

Right: Swiss first class comfort — interior of a standard centre-corridor first.

Right: One of the latest Swiss restaurant cars. Current for cooking is drawn from the overhead conductors by the car's own pantograph.
[*All, Swiss Federal Railways*

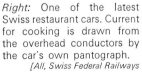

Top: One of the early freight locomotives built for the Gotthard line after electrification, nicknamed "Crocodiles". It is of the 1C-C1 type, weighing 129 tons and of 2,460hp.

Above: No. 11852, one of three experimental locomotives built some years ago for heavy service on the Gotthard line. It has the 1BoIBoI+1BoIBoI wheel arrangement, weighs 233 tons and is rated at 11,100hp.

[*Both, Swiss Federal Railways*

Below: A standard Ae 6/6 locomotive, No. 11401, of 5,940hp and 118 tons weight. 120 of these fine machines are now in service. [*Cecil J Allen*

Above: The first Swiss Federal Bo-Bo locomotives, now classified as Re 4/4 I, are of 2,520hp and 58 tons weight. They have all now been fitted for push-and-pull operation.

Left: One of the Swiss Federal multi-current TEE train sets, used on the "Cisalpin", "Gottardo" and "Ticino" workings. To accommodate more passengers, a sixth coach has now been built into each set.

[*Both, Swiss Federal Railways*

Below: The German TEE "Roland", from Milan to Basle and Bremen, headed by a Swiss Re 4/4 II type locomotive. Though no more than 79 tons in weight, these Bo-Bos are rated at 6,320hp. Of the type 163 are being built.

[*Railphot*

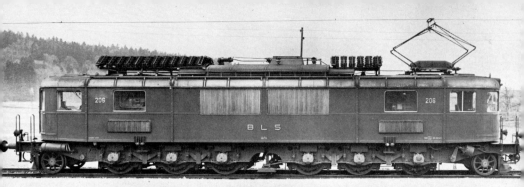

Above: The Lötschberg Railway has always taken a lead in Swiss locomotive design. No. 206 is one of the 1Co-Co1 locomotives introduced in 1926, recently rebuilt and uprated to 6,000hp.

Left: One of the later Lötschberg 6,200hp Bo-Bo units climbing the 1 in 37 gradient from Frutigen to Kandersteg with a heavy freight train.
[Both, Bern-Lötschberg-Simplon

Below: Entering Kandersteg station, after climbing to 4,067ft altitude is the Lötschberg tunnel with a heavy freight train, is one of the most powerful BLS locomotives, a 158 - ton twin Bo-Bo unit of 8,800hp.
[Edward G Hodgkins

The twin motorcoaches of the Lötschberg line are used both for local service and also in summer for the "Blue Arrow" excursion trips over longer distances. This twin is running between Thun and Spiez, with the Lake of Thun and the Bernese Oberland peaks in the background.

A Lötschberg "Blue Arrow" train-set at speed in the Kander Valley, with the snowmantled Balmhorn and Altels as an impressive background.

[Both, Bern-Lötschberg-Simplon

The handsome station building at Spiez, focal point of the Lötschberg system, where the Brigue, Interlaken and Zweisimmen lines separate.

A number of Western Europe's car-sleeper trains now serve or pass through Switzerland. This example is seen near Thun on the Lötschberg line en route from Ostend to Milan via Brigue; others terminate at Lyss (near Berne) and Biasca. *[Both, Bern-Lötschberg-Simplon*

Switzerland has its steam enthusiasts, like those of Great Britain. Approaching Klosters is a special metre-gauge train of the Rhaetian Railway, hauled by steam 2-8-0 No. 107, which has just descended a 1 in 20 gradient from the Davos direction.   [Brian Stephenson]

Swiss railfans now have their own railway, having taken over the disused metre-gauge line from Chamby to Blonay, above Montreux. It is described as "Switzerland's First Tourist Railway".   [Swiss National Tourist Office]

An historic picture, showing the one-time "Oberland Express" *train-de-luxe*, composed entirely of sleeping cars and headed by two of the original Lötschberg 1E1 locomotives, crossing the Kander viaduct.

The striking steel arch across the Bietschtal gorge, with its span of 312ft and maximum height of 255ft above the valley floor. The bridge is prepared for eventual double-tracking of the Lötschberg main line.

[Bern-Lötschberg-Simplon

Looking down on Mitholz station and the middle section of the double loop at this point, over which the direction of travel is reversed. At the upper right is seen the top level of the line.

Goppenstein, where the main line emerges from the 9-mile Lötschberg tunnel into the Lonza valley.

[Both, Bern-Lötschberg-Simplon

High above the Lonza gorge—the Lötschberg line descending the southern ramp from the main tunnel through a succession of avalanche shelters.

The startling emergence at Hohtenn from the Lonza gorge into the Rhône valley, with the Lötschberg line 1,450ft above the valley floor. *[Both, Bern-Lötschberg-Simplon*

Top: Lügelkinn viaduct, perched on a precipitous mountain-side above the Rhône valley.

Above: Typical of the many gorges crossed by the Lötsch-berg main line on the descent from Hohtenn to Brigue-Baltschieder viaduct.

Below: The Viktoria tunnel, so named because of the alleged resemblance of the rock face to the profile of the late Queen Victoria. *[All, Bern-Lötschberg-Simplon*

Bietschtal bridge, seen far below from the path made by the Lötschberg management from Hohtenn to Ausserberg and Lalden, high above the Rhône valley. The path is seen passing under the railway at the opposite side of the gorge.   [Bern-Lötschberg-Simplon

Railway engineering extraordinary—how the Lötschberg
line is carried along the precipitous mountainside above
the River Rhône.

Another view of the Baltschieder viaduct, with the short
Viktoria tunnel in the right background.
                    [Both, Bern-Lötschberg-Simplon

A Lötschberg byway — a twin motorcoach from Spiez to Zweisimmen passes the picturesque castle of Wimmis, near Spiez.

Approaching Zweisimmen, with the Rinderberg mountain in the background. The connecting Montreux - Oberland Bernois line crosses the mountain shoulder high above the village.

[Both, Bern-Lötschberg-Simplon

On leaving Lucerne the Zürich trains take the Basle line to a junction at Sentimatt just beyond that with the Berne line, and then skirt the Rotsee, a lengthy narrow sheet of water renowned for its annual rowing contests. Passing at Ebikon the great Schindler factory, noted for lifts and elevators, we reach Rotkreuz, here intersecting the Gotthard freight route already described. The Lake of Zug is reached at Cham, a pleasant lakeside resort, and we then run into Zug, a town of considerable size, and an important junction at which all the Lucerne trains stop. But not so all those between the Gotthard line and Zürich, which skirt the east side of the Lake of Zug from Arth-Goldau and join the Lucerne line here; these include the T.E.E. trains "Gottardo" and "Ticino".

The section between Zug and Thalwil, carrying both the Gotthard and the Lucerne trains, is a very busy one, but operation is hampered by two single-track tunnels, Albis and Horgenberg, 2 miles and 1½ miles long respectively, the cost of double-tracking which has not as yet been regarded as justifiable. Between them is the station of Sihlbrugg, junction for the Sihltal line into Zürich, and here a loop has been laid in long enough to permit trains in the two directions to pass one another without stopping. From Horgen, at the exit from the Horgenberg tunnel, the line has been doubled in recent years down to Thalwil, including a flyover to permit trains from Zürich to the Zug direction to cross the Chur–Zürich main line without fouling the latter. From Thalwil over the 7½ miles into Zürich is a busier section still; it is, of course, double track, and eventually, as part of the great Zürich reorganisation, a third track is to be laid in, but that may not be for a good many years yet.

From Zürich there is another main line of sufficient importance to be double-tracked throughout to Romanshorn on the Lake of Constance, part of its importance being due to the fact that it carries freight wagons for the train-ferries across the lake to and from the German port of Friedrichshafen. The Romanshorn trains use the St. Gallen main line as far as Winterthur, and branch from there through Frauenfeld for their 52-mile journey. At one time this line was noted for the extremely sharp timings of its trains, such as 10 minutes start-to-stop for the 10.8 miles between Frauenfeld and Weinfelden, and though these have since been slightly eased, 35 minutes by the fastest train from Amriswil, near Romanshorn, over the 31 miles to Winterthur, with two intermediate stops, does not leave much to spare. There are eight express trains each way daily, most taking 64 to 67 minutes with four stops *en route*; two in each direction are through to and from Geneva.

In the same vicinity there is the main line from Zürich to Schaffhausen, on the German frontier, 35½ miles distant, which carries a substantial traffic for Stuttgart and beyond, including three trains with through coaches to and from Italy by the Gotthard line; between Oerlikon, point of divergence from the St. Gallen line, and Schaffhausen this is single track. Beyond Eglisau the line has to cross the deep valley of the Rhine, and does so by one of Switzerland's biggest and most imposing viaducts. With the arched masonry approaches the viaduct is some 500 yards in

C

length, and the central girder span, 200 ft. above the river level, is 295 ft. across. The Rhine comes into prominence again as we pass Neuhausen, a suburb of Schaffhausen; here the famous Rhine Falls are in full view to the right of the train. Between Zürich and Schaffhausen there are seven expresses every day in times of 37 to 43 minutes, and a number of other trains with intermediate stops.

The curious will find in the timetable two intriguing trains each way daily between Zürich and Eglisau which bear the designation "Badezug". These branch at Eglisau to reach Zurzach, where there are some warm springs of great renown which feed open-air baths. Their curative properties can be sampled by the citizens of Zürich in either a morning or an afternoon by these "Badezug" specials, which normally are "Red Arrow" railcars, suitably timed for a start out of Zürich after an early breakfast or after lunch.

Zurzach, incidentally, is on a secondary line of some importance which leaves the Basle–Zürich main line at Stein-Säckingen, and parallels the left or south bank of the Rhine through Koblenz to Eglisau; several semi-fast trains use this route between Basle and Winterthur. Also from Schaffhausen there is, in effect, a continuation of the line last mentioned through Kreuzlingen (just south of Konstanz) and along the southern shore of the Lake of Constance to Romanshorn and Rorschach—a route of considerable interest to those who wish to follow the course of the Rhine at close quarters. From Rorschach, of course, the journey can be continued up the Rhine valley to Sargans and Chur, and then by the Rhaetian and Furka–Oberalp Railways through Disentis practically to the source of the Vorder-Rhein near Tschamut.

The Brünig Line

The Swiss Federal Railway system incorporates one metre-gauge line which is of no small importance, especially to tourist traffic, for it provides the direct communication between Lucerne and the heart of the Bernese Oberland. This is also the only Swiss Federal line on which the steeper gradients require rack-and-pinion traction. It became a part of the Swiss Federal system in the same year, 1903, as the Jura-Simplon Railway; it was worked by steam power until 1941–42, when electric operation took over.

In the terminal station at Lucerne, the two tracks on the eastern side of the station (the exit from which points due south) are used by the Brünig trains, and, since the completion of the Hergiswil connection, by those of the Lucerne–Stans–Engelberg Company also. Thus there is quite a substantial passenger service between Lucerne and Hergiswil of some 30 trains daily in each direction, some through to or from Engelberg and others making Engelberg connections at Hergiswil; in certain cases the trains for both the Engelberg and Brünig lines run coupled together over this section. From Hergiswil, like the Engelberg line the Brünig line tunnels under the Lopperberg, and shortly after emergence reaches Alpnachstad, lower terminus of the Pilatus Railway

Up to this point there have been attractive views on the left of the Lake of Lucerne, and we have not travelled far before another lake comes into view, on the opposite side of the train. This is the Lake of Sarnen, the eastern shore of which is skirted after the train has stopped at Sarnen, capital of the Canton of Obwalden. At the further end of this lake is Giswil, where all trains stop before beginning the climb of the first rack-and-pinion section. Many trains detach coaches here, and it is customary also to change locomotives, all the heavier trains being hauled by a couple of locomotives over the rack section. As far as Giswil it is possible to bring standard gauge wagons with their loads on transporters, and considerable use is made of this facility, by Sarnen in particular.

Climbing now begins, at 1 in 10, high above the valley of the Sarner Aa, until, like passing over a gigantic step in the valley floor, we come rather dramatically to a higher basin of the valley embosoming another beautiful lake, that of Lungern; the rack ceases before Kaiserstuhl, and climbing then continues on an easier gradient to Lungern station. It should have been remarked that from Sarnen it is possible to take a motorcoach to Melchtal and from there the lengthy *Luftseilbahn* up to Melchsee-Frutt; equally from Lungern we have at our disposal the very attractive cable line in two sections—*Luftseilbahn* and *Gondelbahn*—up to Schönbüel, from which there is a grand view of the Bernese Alps. But in this case a walk of over a mile is needed round the head of the lake from Lungern station to the lower, or Obsee, terminal of the Schönbüel line.

At Lungern the rack reappears, and two rack sections, with an adhesion section between, are needed to get the train up to the crest of the Brünig pass at Brünig–Hasliberg station. Since leaving Lucerne we have climbed 1,857 ft. to an altitude of 3,287 ft. above the sea. The ensuing descent is considerably more abrupt. The line now bends eastwards, and on a ruling gradient of 1 in 8 rapidly descends the north wall of the Aar valley. We might here have expected to see the Wetterhorn, the ice-mantled summit of which was briefly in view before Lungern, but at the beginning of the descent it is hidden by intervening heights, and further down the mountainside is so thickly wooded that no extensive view is possible. In no more than 3 miles we descend some 1,325 ft. and reach the station at Meiringen. This is terminal, so that the train has to reverse.

From Meiringen it is a level and fairly straight run to Brienz, on which the metre-gauge train attains a speed but little short of 50 m.p.h. Here we reach the fourth lake of our journey, that of Brienz, and stop at a station which has the lake pier on the left, and the lower terminus of the steam-operated Brienzer Rothorn Railway on the right. The remainder of the Brünig journey is along the steep southern slope of the Brienzer Grat, well above the northern shore of the Lake of Brienz, and commanding beautiful views; the end of the 45¾-mile run, which by the faster trains take just under two hours, is in Interlaken Ost station, where traffic is interchanged with the Lötschberg and Berner Oberland Railways. In the summer two Brünig trains in each direction include through coaches to the B.O.B., one to and from Lauterbrunnen and the other to and from Grindelwald.

For its Brünig services the Swiss Federal Railways have developed powerful locomotives which are in part brakevans, and which can operate at up to 75 km.p.h. by adhesion, and at 30 km.p.h. (18½ m.p.h.) by rack-and-pinion up gradients as steep as 1 in 8. Some fine rolling stock also has been built for this scenic route, in particular first class saloon cars furnished with armchairs; most of the stock, both first and second class, is fitted with wide picture windows giving the maximum possible extent of view.

Locomotives and Motorcoaches

Locomotive building for Swiss railways is carried out by several private firms, and for this purpose there is close collaboration in design between the Swiss Federal locomotive authorities and the Swiss Loco-motive Company of Winterthur, which is responsible for the mechanical parts, and Brown Boveri & Company of Baden and the Oerlikon Company of Zürich, with assistance in some cases from the firm of Sécheron at Geneva, for the electrical equipment. This admirable team work has been of benefit equally to the railways and to the manufacturers.

For the first electrification, which was of the Gotthard line, two classes of locomotive were produced in 1920—a massive 110-ton 1B–B1, known as type Be 4/6, of 1,760 h.p., for passenger service, and the familiar 1C–C1 or Ce 6/8 type, weighing 128 tons, nicknamed "Crocodiles" because of their distinctive central cabs and sloping bonnets, for freight. A second version of the latter, type Be 6/8, built from 1926 onwards, was more powerful, with an hourly rating of 2,460 h.p., and a rebuilt form of these engines, from 1942 onwards, increased the rating to a much higher 3,640 h.p. These veterans are now disappearing, but a passenger type introduced in 1927, and built over seven succeeding years to a total of 127 units, is still doing excellent service. This is the ubiquitous Ae 4/7 class, having the 2–Do–1 wheel arrangement, with a weight of 118 tons and a h.p. of 2,800 as first turned out, increased in later examples to 3,120 h.p. and 123¼ tons. It should be added that meantime, between 1922 and 1926, over 200 locomotives of the 1C1 and 2C1 types had been built for the less exacting duties, of from 1,800 to 2,000 h.p., and weights ranging from 81-85 tons with the 1C1s to 98 tons with the bigger 2C1s. It is of interest to recall that some of the latter were modified to run the first lightweight express trains between Geneva and Zürich, before the appearance of the first Re 4/4 Bo–Bos. Many of these locomotives are still going strong.

From 1931 onwards some interesting experiments were made with a view to hauling heavier loads over the Gotthard line without double-heading. Three immense twin locomotives of the 1Bo1Bo1+1Bo1Bo1 type were built in succession, No. 11801 of 7,500 h.p. in 1931, No. 11851 of 8,800 h.p. in 1932, and No. 11852 of 11,400 h.p.—the most powerful locomotive in the world—in 1939. With an overall length of 111 ft. 6 in., this last monster weighed 232 tons. It is still in service, but has proved too cumbersome to justify the building of any further examples. The next experiment, from 1941 to 1945, was the production of an Ae 4/6 type, with the 1Do1 wheel arrangement, weighing 105 tons and with the unusually high output, for a single unit, of 5,540 h.p., but this class was not multiplied to a further extent than 12 units.

In 1946, however, there appeared the first of a most successful series of locomotives, the Re 4/4 class, of which the Bo–Bo wheel arrangement followed shortly on the Lötschberg *première* with this type, though of less power than the latter—2,480 as compared with 4,000 h.p. But for hauling the Swiss Federal express trains of lightweight stock the Re 4/4s have proved ideal. They are compact machines, measuring only 48 ft. 11 in. in length overall, and the later examples, with power slightly boosted to 2,520 h.p., weigh no more than 58 tons. In all, 50 of these locomotives were built between 1946 and 1951, and they have all been adapted for push-and-pull working. This is one of the four classes of locomotive that have now been standardised by the Swiss Federal Railways for main line service.

Even greater success has attended the next design, the Ae 6/6 type, with the Co–Co wheel arrangement, which took the rails for the first time in 1952; from then on building continued with but little intermission, and the total number of these machines is now 120. With an overall length of 60 ft. 4 in., and a weight of 120 tons, the Ae 6/6 locomotives have an hourly rating of 5,940 h.p. The vast advance that has been made since the introduction of the Ae 4/7 class in 1927 is seen in the fact that whereas the latter were rated as capable of working 1,000-*tonne* passenger trains (986 tons) on the level at 62 m.p.h. and 700-ton loads up 1 in 100 gradients at 40 m.p.h., the corresponding figures for the Ae 6/6 type are 1,200 *tonnes* (1,183 tons) at 68 m.p.h. and 1,000 *tonnes* (986 tons) at 56 m.p.h.

With freight trains the Ae 6/6 locomotives can move 2,000 *tonnes* (1,972 tons) at 46 m.p.h. on level track, and 1,400 *tonnes* (1,380 tons) at 43 m.p.h. up 1 in 100, thus more than doubling the capacity of their Ae 4/7 predecessors. They monopolise the Gotthard line freight service, sometimes in pairs, and work 592-ton loads up the continuous 1 in 38-40 gradients at the full permissible speed of 46 m.p.h., or, in pairs, 1,183-ton freight trains. All the locomotives of the Ae 6/6 type have been named after cantons, cities and towns in the country, the crests of which in colour they also proudly bear. One's only regret is that the beautiful polished steel bands which the earlier examples bore round the front and rear cabs have been abandoned with the later locomotives—a gain in economy, no doubt, but at the expense of public attraction.

The third standard type is not strictly a locomotive but a motorcoach. Various types of motorcoach had been built in the past, such as the familiar "Red Arrow" cars for excursion trips, and other more powerful types capable of hauling trailers at time of pressure. In 1959, however, a new RBe 4/4 type motorcoach was introduced, of considerably greater power, intended for use as locomotives pure and simple. This has developed into the now standard 2,800 h.p. type, hitherto used interchangeably with the Re 4/4 locomotives on the fast cross-country trains such as those between Geneva and Zürich. Each of these motorcoaches has 67 second class seats, which can be used as supplementary accommodation when trains are full. The majority of the 82 units of this type now in service were built in time for the great Swiss National Exhibition at Lausanne in 1964, when they rendered invaluable service.

In 1960 there appeared the first examples of a far more powerful version of the Re 4/4 Bo-Bo type, with the power-weight ratio increased from 43.5 to no less than 80 h.p. per ton. The pioneer units, classified as Re 4/4 II, were rated at 5,450 h.p., but after six of these had been built, the output was raised to 6,320 h.p. Later examples, with gearing slightly modified to increase the starting tractive effort, have the Re 4/4 III classification. So successful is this design that it has been built in numbers which are expected to produce a total of 163 units by the end of 1972. These are taking over all the principal passenger services in Switzerland, including those over the Gotthard line, on the 1 in 38-40 gradients of which the Re 4/4 III type is able to handle trains up to 570 tons in weight at speeds up to 50 m.p.h. This is not all, however, as a new and considerably more powerful Bo-Bo-Bo articulated type is in course of construction, with a potential output of no less than 10,600 h.p. This will be able to handle loads to a maximum of 800 tons up the Gotthard line gradients at a speed of 50 m.p.h., and should help considerably to ease the freight problem over this route. So the Swiss Federal Railways are continuing to keep abreast of the latest in electric locomotive technology.

Apart from these four standard types, many other locomotives, including the smaller types used in shunting and marshalling, are in service, too numerous to describe. But special mention is needed of the five self-contained T.E.E. or Trans-Europe-Express trains which have won considerable *kudos* for Switzerland. This is because the Swiss have been the first in the world to devise means whereby the same electric power plant can use any description of current, whether a.c. or d.c. and of whatever voltage. There is no parallel elsewhere in Europe to the journey made every day by one of these trains. It leaves Basle in the early morning as the "Ticino" for Zürich and the Gotthard line, climbing to the Gotthard tunnel and then descending to cross the Italian frontier at Chiasso; there it switches from the Swiss 15,000-volt a.c. to the Italian 3,000-volts d.c. Milan is reached shortly after midday.

After a lay-over of just over two hours there the train proceeds, now as the "Cisalpin", on its westward journey to Paris. At Domodossola comes the change back from 3,000 volts d.c. to 15,000 volts a.c., which is used as far as the French frontier at Vallorbe, whence the conductors carry 25,000 volts a.c. But only as far as Dôle; from there the French 1,500-volt d.c. system is used throughout to Paris. And, incidentally, between Dijon and Paris the train which has climbed to 3,786 ft. altitude in the Gotthard tunnel in the course of its 749-mile journey has to finish with a sprint over the 195¼ miles from Dijon to Paris in 147 minutes, at an average of 79.6 m.p.h. In the reverse direction the "Cisalpin", leaving Paris at 1.15 p.m. and heading the French "Mistral" at an interval of five minutes, has an even faster timing of 140 minutes, for an average of 83.7 m.p.h.—the fastest demanded of any Swiss train. These Swiss T.E.E. trains thus provide a daily 7¾-hour service between Milan and Paris, and two each way—the "Gottardo" and "Ticino"—between Milan and Zürich in 3½–4 hours, one of the latter, as just mentioned, extended to and from Basle. So popular have these trains become that a sixth coach has now been added to each original five-coach set.

A few words may now be appropriate concerning the training of Swiss locomotive drivers. This is a well-paid occupation, but is subject to strict conditions of entry. The driver-to-be must be a Swiss citizen, between 20 and 30 years of age and not less than 5 ft. 3 in. tall. Before joining the service he must have had an apprenticeship of at least four years as a fitter, mechanic, tool or instrument-maker, or some similar trade, followed by a year's practical experience in that trade. The first 300 days in the service are spent in the maintenance of motive power units at one of the principal depots, during which the entrant has to pass through nine courses on the design of motive power units. Then, after 12 days as assistant driver on a locomotive, followed by a fairly elementary examination, come 300 more days, now as an assistant driver, during which he is subjected to eight more courses on the rules of operation, marshalling and signalling, a detailed two-day examination following.

The third 300-day period is now entered, with the entrant still acting as an assistant driver, and four instruction courses on a driver's duties leading to a first driver's examination; in this two days are spent in a theoretical examination, followed by 30 days in which the driver-to-be, under the watchful eye of an experienced man, takes charge himself of locomotives for the first time. This period concludes with two days' practical examination in driving, after which the entrant is authorised to drive on his own, but at the assistant driver's rate of pay until, after yet another 300 days, there comes the second driver's examination, which is of a very thoroughgoing description. If this is passed successfully, appointment as a fully qualified driver follows, at the full rate of pay.

Thus, in addition to the five years of experience before entering the service, the Swiss driver spends another four years in the ways that have been described before final appointment, and it would be difficult to imagine a more comprehensive training. Moreover, on appointment he has sufficient experience to correct any minor fault that may occur on his locomotive during the course of a run; the result is that in Switzerland serious delays due to locomotive breakdowns are very rare. Since 1959 single-manning of locomotives has become the usual rule, except with certain night trains and when entrant drivers are under instruction. It may be added that there is a second grade of driver, on locomotives used only for shunting and marshalling; for these men the training is shorter and simpler, but they work at a lower rate of pay.

Coaches and Wagons

In the passenger rolling stock realm, as with the locomotives, there has been collaboration between the Swiss Federal Railways design staff and two coach-building companies—the Schlieren Company of Zürich and the Schweizerische Industriegesellschaft of Neuhausen. Between them there has been developed the characteristically Swiss lightweight type of coach, 74 ft. 6 in. in length and low-built, of which many hundreds are now in service, mainly inside Switzerland but some crossing into other countries. The whole of this stock is of the centre-corridor type, seating four abreast in the second class and three in the first. In the earlier stages of development these coaches were divided into three sections, separated by cross-lobbies giving access to the doors, and with end vestibules and lavatories at both ends; but all the latest cars are divided by a central glass partition into two sections, smoking and non-smoking, with the outer doors giving access to the end vestibules. The first class cars have eight bays of seats, and accommodate 48 passengers; the second have ten bays, and seat 80 apiece. As all over Western Europe, the comfort of the second class is a long way behind that of modern British main line second class stock, but the Swiss coaches have comfortably shaped seating, even if it is not elaborately cushioned, and clean and attractive interiors. The first class accommodation, however, matches the best anywhere else in Europe. It is now standard Swiss practice to upholster non-smoking compartments in green, and smoking compartments in red.

As already mentioned, nothing but centre corridor stock is built for internal Swiss use, but there are compartment coaches for many of the international runs. Recently the Swiss Federal Railways have been building *couchette* coaches which, conforming to what is now becoming the Western European standard, differ totally in appearance from the low-built Swiss stock. As in Germany, which first developed the standard, the length of each coach is 86 ft. 7 in., and the maximum roof height of 13 ft. 3 in. above rail makes the normal Swiss coaches look quite diminutive by comparison. The *couchette* coaches have ten compartments, providing 60 berths, with an attendant's compartment and two lavatories apiece. In addition, the Swiss are now building both sleeping and restaurant cars for the European pool of the International Sleeping Car Company, of the same dimensions; the restaurant cars seat 52 persons, and have ample kitchen and pantry accommodation. Like the restaurant cars which the Swiss build for their own internal use, pantographs are provided to collect current from the overhead conductors for cooking and other uses on the cars.

Freight traffic in Switzerland has been increasing on an intensive scale during recent years, particularly of iron and steel, oil, cement, wheat and coal and coke, which make up 53 per cent. of the internal freight traffic of the country. In addition to all this internal freight traffic there is the great volume of international traffic, especially that between Germany and Italy over the Gotthard route. This now includes the freight counterpart of the TEE high speed passenger trains—the TEEM

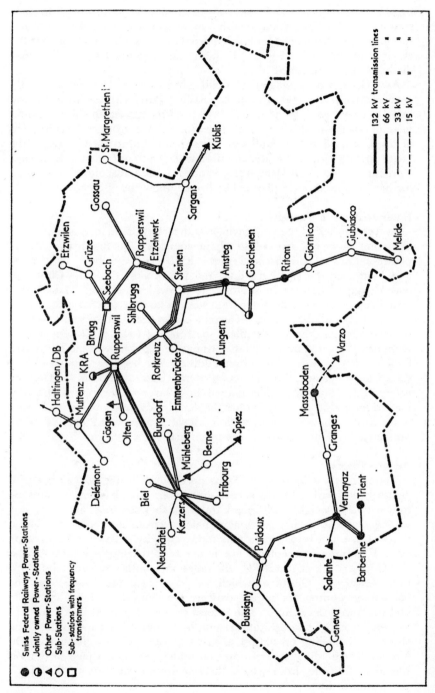

Fig 5. Plan of electric current supply to Swiss Railways.

freight trains, which with sealed wagons are able to pass through frontier stations like Basle and Chiasso with a minimum of customs delay. Many special wagons have been built for internal traffic, such as the types for the carriage of cement and grain, in both cases equipped for loading and discharge by compressed air.

As in Great Britain, wagon marshalling in Switzerland is being gradually concentrated in the great hump marshalling yards with the latest electric and electronic equipment which have been mentioned in the preceding sections—Muttenz (Basle) and Chiasso, at the frontier terminations of the Gotthard route; Dulliken (Olten) and Limmattal (Zürich), the latter now under construction and the former yet to be built, on the Berne–Zürich main line; and Denges (Lausanne) on the Lausanne–Geneva line; further installations are planned at Brigue and either Berne or Biel.

Hydro-Electric Power

In the matter of power, Switzerland is fortunate in possessing the abundant water resources of an Alpine country. The first hydro-electric power-stations of the Swiss Federal Railways were built at Amsteg and Piotta, on the Gotthard line, and were followed by the Châtelard and Vernayaz stations in south-western Switzerland and Massaboden near Brigue, all fed with water from storage lakes created at a high level by very substantial barrages. Current is also drawn from jointly-owned power-stations in the Etzel valley (south of the Lake of Zürich) and at Rupperswil, near Aarau, the latter using the rapid flow of the River Aar for its water power. The latest addition has been the jointly-owned station at Göschenen, drawing its water from a storage lake in the Damma valley; this power-station is housed in a large underground chamber blasted from solid rock, which has the double advantage of being cheaper to construct than a power-station above ground, and also of being protected from any possible enemy attack from the air.

Future Plans

Today the vast increase in Swiss north-south traffic is posing an increasing problem. The Gotthard line, even with passenger trains up to 600 tons in weight and freight trains up to 1,200 tons, and signalling arrangements to divide the longer block sections into shorter units, at times of pressure is loaded to maximum capacity. To ease the pressure several ambitious expedients are under serious consideration. One is the Gotthard "base tunnel", 28 miles in length through solid rock, from Amsteg to Giornico, which would replace the long, steep and curvaceous approaches to the existing Gotthard tunnel by a straight and practically level line. The second scheme, favoured by the eastern cantons, would be to use the existing line from Zürich to Linthal, and then, by tunnelling on almost as great a scale, to bore through to the Vorder Rhein valley at Trun and on under the Greina pass to the Val Blenio at Olivone, from which the line would continue to Biasca, on the Gotthard line.

A third plan would be to continue the Chur main line along the existing Rhaetian Railway route as far as Thusis, and from there continuing up the Hinter Rhein valley and under the Splügen Pass to reach Chiavenna, which would require a 21½-mile tunnel and also the willingness of the Italian State Railways to bring their line from Chiavenna through Sondrio and Lecco to Milan up to main line standards, a very costly business. Yet a fourth plan is a Kander base tunnel, some 17½ miles long, from Kandergrund on the Lötschberg line through to Raron in the Rhône valley, where the Simplon main line would be joined. This last would be the least costly of the four projects; the Gotthard base tunnel, estimated to cost about £150,000,000, would be the most valuable from the operating point of view and is the most likely of the four to be carried out. The Greina and Splügen schemes are almost certainly ruled out for reasons of cost and of more limited value. More immediately in prospect is the doubling of the remaining single-track sections of the Lötschberg line, which would give some relief at but a fraction of the cost of the other schemes mentioned, and work on which has already begun.

The new work at present in progress or recently completed, such as the rebuilding and extension of the main station at Berne, the extended or new mechanised marshalling yards just mentioned, the new flyover lines at Brugg and Thalwil, and relocation of the Zürich–Chur main line west of Ziegelbrücke, all form part of an immense programme authorised in the years 1956 and 1965, and estimated to cost a total of about £150,000,000, of which £100,000,000 will have been spent by the end of 1972. As described in the first section of this chapter, work has begun on a complete transformation of the Berne–Zürich main line between Olten and Zürich, including the great new Limmattal and other marshalling yards. The total expenditure on all the marshalling yards will be £64,000,000. Doubling of the few remaining single-line sections of the main lines, including those already dealt with, and new flyovers such as those now completed at Brugg and Thalwil, will have cost a total of some £37,000,000. Further plans include new or reconstructed freight depots, new or enlarged passenger stations, signalling modernisation, and other improvements.

One lesson which may be drawn from the contents of this chapter is that the Swiss have complete faith in the future of their railways, over which traffic continues steadily to expand, so that the closure of railways or stations in the country is practically unknown. Indeed, the railways are regarded as so essential part of the nation's life and wellbeing that the necessary finance is never withheld from any economically justifiable plans for their improvement.

THREE

The Berne-Lötschberg-Simplon Railway

THIS COMPANY, relatively small, but with an importance out of all proportion to the modest 155 route miles of itself and its associated lines, has been like an enclave in the heart of Swiss Federal Railways' territory, and in two directions has provided an essential link in the movement of international traffic. Up to the close of the last century rail traffic between the Canton of Berne and North Italy had to travel by way of Lucerne and the Gotthard line. In 1891 the then Jura-Simplon Railway, which had penetrated eastwards up the Rhône valley as far as Brigue, sought authorisation from the Swiss Federal Council for a bold scheme of extension—nothing less than a 12¼-mile tunnel under the Alps to provide a direct route to Milan. On completion this would provide a possible alternative route from Berne to North Italy, though by its having to follow the three sides of a square, with its corners at Lausanne and Martigny, the distance of 255 miles from Berne to Milan would still be 41 miles longer than the 214 miles via Lucerne. If the fourth side of the square could be closed by rail, it would be a different matter.

So it was that in 1899, by which time the Simplon tunnel was being bored, the proposal came to a head for a direct line from Berne to Brigue. French interests supported the scheme, as a new direct route to North Italy would be of considerable value to Belfort and other towns in Eastern France. The Swiss Federal Railways had a 19-mile line from Berne to Thun, which made an end-on junction there with the Thunerseebahn—a line which had come into existence in 1893 by extension from Därligen of the Bödelibahn; the latter, one of the earliest railways in Switzerland, had been opened in 1874 from Bönigen through Interlaken to Därligen in order to link the steamer services on the lakes of Brienz and Thun. In 1901 the Thunerseebahn had completed a branch from Spiez for 8½ miles up the Kander valley to Frutigen, so that just over 34 miles of the proposed route already were in existence. This left 37½ miles of new line to be driven through the heart of the Bernese Alps, an engineering task of very considerable magnitude, but offering the reward of a curtailment from 151 to 72 miles of the distance from Berne to Brigue, as compared with the existing route via Lausanne. The distance from Berne to Milan also would come down to 163 miles, 51 miles less than by way of Lucerne.

Some time was spent in getting the necessary concession, and not until 1906, the year of opening of the first of the two bores of the Simplon tunnel, did work commence. The line of route selected was up the Kander valley as far as Kandersteg, and then a 9-mile tunnel under the crest of the Bernese Alps through to the Rhône watershed, in the narrow valley of the Lonza. The Rhône valley would be reached at Hohtenn, and from there, roughly 1,450 ft. above the valley floor, the line would be brought gradually down the north wall of the valley to join the Simplon main line at Brigue. So a company was formed, with the imposing title of Berner Alpenbahn Bern–Lötschberg–Simplon, to carry the scheme through. The name Lötschberg, by which the line is usually known, was derived from the upper end of the Lonza valley, which is called the Lötschental.

Construction was delayed by the disaster which befell the boring of the Lötschberg tunnel in the summer of 1908, when the explosion of a charge caused a break-in to a deep waterlogged fissure under the Gasterntal, the existence of which was completely unsuspected. No fewer than 25 workers lost their lives, and the work was brought to a standstill. Finally the decision was reached to abandon and plug securely the affected part of the tunnel, and to introduce into it three curves, in order to be able to pass under the Kander at a point considerably higher up its course, so increasing the length of the tunnel from $8\frac{5}{8}$ to $9\frac{1}{8}$ miles. This was done successfully, and the main line of the Lötschberg Railway was brought into use in 1913, at which date the Thunerseebahn with its Frutigen branch was absorbed.

There were in existence a number of minor railways in the area, known as the "Berne Decree Railways", which had been built and were being worked under special guarantees from the Canton of Berne, and these were brought into the Lötschberg group for operational purposes though still retaining their financial identity and with their own rolling stock. This explains the varied lettering seen on the rolling stock used in the Lötschberg group, which is pooled between the parent and the minor companies. There were the Spiez-Erlenbach (opened in 1897) and Erlenbach-Zweisimmen (1901) Railways, effecting a junction with the Montreux-Oberland Bernois Railway at Zweisimmen and forming a part of the direct route between the Bernese Oberland and the Lake of Geneva; in 1942 these two amalgamated and formed the Simmentalbahn or Spiez-Erlenbach-Zweisimmen Railway (S.E.Z.).

An alternative route between Thun and Berne, known as the Gürbetalbahn, completed in 1901–02 and used only for local traffic, had branching from it at the Berne suburban station of Fischermätteli the Schwarzenburg line (1907); these also amalgamated in 1944 to become the Gürbetal-Berne-Schwarzenburg Railway, or G.B.S. Finally, the direct line from Berne to Neuchâtel, the Bern-Neuenburg or B.N., came into the Lötschberg group in 1901. The rolling stock of all four constituents is used indiscriminately over the whole system, but a strict account of this use is kept, so that each of the four companies may be duly credited with its share of the revenue.

One other development of importance came to fruition in 1915.

The through traffic from Eastern France crossed the Swiss frontier between Delle and Porrentruy, but between Delémont and Bienne had to follow a circuitous and steeply-graded course by way of Sonceboz. The Lötschberg Railway therefore completed and opened in that year a new 8¼-mile line, completely detached from the parent system, from Moutier to Lengnau, on the Swiss Federal main line from Olten to Biel, which shortened the journey by nine miles, and permitted a substantial acceleration of the trains. This was a costly proposition, for it involved the boring of the 5¼-mile Grenchenberg tunnel through the last ridge of the Jura.

The Grenchenberg cut-off still remains Lötschberg property, and it is still staffed by the B.L.S., including the one intermediate station, Grenchen-Nord, though its importance to the owning company has diminished considerably since the French National Railways diverted almost all the through trains for Switzerland by way of Basle. Conversely, it is now the Swiss Federal Railways that find the cut-off of the major use, for it is followed, as described in a section of Chapter 2, by most of the principal express trains between Basle, Lausanne and Geneva by way of Delémont and Biel, including the "Hispania". Moreover, the Lötschberg Railway has had its compensation in that the day and night trains between Paris and Berne now run over the electrified South-Eastern Region of the S.N.C.F. *via* Dijon and Pontarlier, so that the B.L.S. is responsible for their haulage over its subsidiary Bern–Neuenburg line between Neuchâtel and Berne.

Out of Thun the Lötschberg main line is double for the 6¾ miles to Spiez, a handsome five-platform station which is the hub of B.L.S. activity. In recent years some two million Swiss francs have been spent in a complete re-signalling of the station and its approaches, for between 1,500 and 1,800 shunting and marshalling movements are carried out here every day. From Thun the line has climbed some 200 ft., and the original Thunerseebahn now diverges to descend once again to the lakeside at Leissigen, and to keep at that level to Interlaken. The main line, however, continues to climb, curving southwards through the mile-long tunnel under the Hondrich-Hügel ridge into the Kander valley. From the tunnel exit at Hondrich-Süd the line quite recently has been doubled as far as Frutigen, passing on its way the station at Mülenen, adjacent to the lower terminus of the funicular up the Niesen. From Frutigen there begins the single track which extends to Kandersteg, with three intermediate passing loops.

The village of Kandersteg lies in a glacial basin 1,275 ft. above the level of Frutigen, though the two towns are only a little over five miles apart. Even to keep the ruling gradient down to 2.7 per cent., or 1 in 37, therefore, a lengthening of the line was necessary. So at Mitholz, where, despite the 1 in 37 ascent, the valley floor has come up to the railway level, the line doubles back on itself, climbing up the eastern wall of the valley until by a spiral tunnel—one of a number of tunnels along this length—it reverses direction once again from north to south. On the middle stretch is the station and passing loop of Blausee-Mitholz, the Blausee being a lake of vivid blue colour embosomed in the wood below the line. By Kandersteg the line has mounted 1,842 ft. above the level of Spiez, and has had to cover a distance of 19½ miles, 6¼ miles more than the direct distance between these towns.

At Kandersteg double track is resumed for the passage through the Lötschberg tunnel. The north portal of the tunnel is about 1½ miles beyond the village, with the imposing snowclad peaks of Balmhorn and Altels, which have been in view all the way up the valley, towering above. Close to the tunnel entrance is the lower station of the daring *Luftseilbahn* to Stock, described in Chapter 13. The exit from the tunnel, at Goppenstein, is into the gorge of the Lonza; here postal motorcoaches wait to carry passengers up into the wider stretches of the Lötschental, well known as a remote and unspoilt part of native Switzlerand. The Lonza gorge is subject to a great deal of avalanche risk, and for protection during the short run down the valley the railway, now single track once again, runs for most of its length through avalanche galleries. Then comes a longer tunnel, which curves to the eastward at its exit to introduce the passenger to one of the railway sensations of Switzerland. It is the wide Rhône valley, mountain-locked, but with its floor at a level lower by over 1,450 ft.

From Hohtenn, where the Rhône valley is reached, the Lötschberg has some 12 miles in which to descend, on its ruling gradient of 1 in 37, to join the Simplon line at Brigue. All the streams coming from the north to join the Rhône do so down deep gorges, which the railway crosses with some notable bridges or viaducts, and many tunnels through the mountain ridges that separate these valleys. Outstanding among the former is the Bietschtal bridge, a steel arch of 312 ft. span, straddling the gorge between two tunnels, and at its maximum with the rails 255 ft. above the stream.

Very little can be seen from the train of this notable structure, but with considerable enterprise the Lötschberg authorities have made a first-class view of it readily accessible to walkers. This is by means of a footpath that they have engineered, more or less parallel to the railway, from Hohtenn past Ausserberg and Lalden and finally down to the main road not far short of Brigue. I might add that it is a path requiring very considerable energy on the part of those using it; where the railway tunnels, the walkers must go over the top, and where a gorge is crossed the path goes a long way inwards so that not too much in the way of descending and getting out again may be called for. Another similar path has been laid out high above the Kander valley, from Kandersteg to the head of the Kiental chair-lift. The railway has been rewarded for its enterprise by very considerable public patronage.

Finally, after a fine view over the town of Visp up the Visp valley, crowned by the great peaks of the Mischabel group, the Lötschberg line runs into the busy station at Brigue, and the portions of its trains that are continuing through to Italy are joined to those of the Swiss Federal Railways which have come up the Rhône valley from Lausanne.

Passenger trains take just over the hour between Spiez and Brigue if non-stop, and a little more if stops at Frutigen, Kandersteg and Goppenstein are included. The scale of the traffic may be measured by the fact that over 40 passenger trains leave Thun for the Lötschberg line daily, some for both Interlaken and Brigue, dividing at Spiez, others for those destinations running independently, and the remainder local stopping trains, in addition to a heavy freight service. A number of the Interlaken trains are worked from Berne to their destination by Swiss Federal locomotives, and equally Lötschberg locomotives work the Brigue trains through from Berne, and in or two cases continue over Swiss Federal and Italian State tracks to Domodossola.

Many of the Lötschberg trains include through portions from France. Germany and beyond to Milan and other points in Italy; one of the most important in summer is the night "Riviera Express", from Copenhagen and Amsterdam to Genoa and Ventimiglia, which to relieve the Gotthard line travels by this route, and avoids Milan by running direct from Arona to Genoa *via* Alessandria. This train has no publicly booked stop between the Badischer Bahnhof at Basle and Brigue, but until now has had to halt at Berne for reversal. A short spur recently completed between the Olten-Berne and Berne-Thun lines near Ostermundigen, however, now makes this reversal unnecessary, and thus expedites the working of special through passenger trains and of freight trains from the north for the Lötschberg line and *vice versa*.

This brings us to Lötschberg locomotive power. From the very start this small company, like the Swiss Federal in conjunction with the Swiss Locomotive Company, Brown Boveri of Baden, the Oerlikon Company of Zürich and the Sécheron Company of Geneva, has been in the forefront of Swiss locomotive development, and in some technical respects, indeed, has led the world. Its first experiments in electric traction began in 1910, between Spiez and Frutigen, at 15,000 volts a.c., 15 cycles, later changed to the 16 2/3 cycles which became standard for the Swiss Federal Railways. For the opening in 1913 of the main line through to Brigue, 13 unique 2,500 h.p. locomotives were built with the 1–E–1 wheel arrangement, that is, five axles coupled with leading and trailing carrying wheels. Then the year 1926 saw the introduction of two magnificent 1Co–Co1 locomotives of 4,500 h.p., Type Ae 6/8, at that time the most powerful single-unit electric locomotives in the world; later their number was increased to eight, and their hourly output raised to 5,280 h.p. These were capable of handling loads up to 600 tons up the 1 in 37 gradients. Their output has now been increased further to 6,000 h.p.

A new record was established in 1944, with the introduction of the first electric locomotives in the world of the double bogie type with 1,000 h.p. motors mounted on their axles; these Bo–Bo units were of 4,000 h.p. each. They were designed to work 400-*tonne* loads (394 tons) up 1 in 37 at the maximum permissible speed (because of the curvature) of 75 km.p.h. (46 m.p.h.), though permitted to travel at up to 77½ m.p.h. on level track—a liberty which they have only been able to exercise on

Where the traveller to Jungfraujoch first comes into view at close quarters of the giants of the Bernese Alps— Wengernalp station, with the Eiger (left) and Mönch.

Kleine Scheidegg, with the Wengernalp Railway (left) and the Jungfrau Railway (right). On the extreme left is the triangular tunnel in which Wengernalp coaches can be turned end-for-end.   *[Both, Wengernalp & Jungfrau Railways*

The open-air stretch of the Jungfrau line, between Kleine Scheidegg and Eigergletscher, with the stately Jungfrau in the background.

The entry at Eigergletscher to the $4\frac{1}{2}$-mile tunnel leading to the Jungfraujoch terminus.

The highest railway station in Europe — Jungfraujoch, 11,333ft above the sea. In front of the train are seen some of the "huskies" from Greenland that pull sleighs across the glacier.

The icebound situation of Jungfraujoch station and hotel, with the observatory building to the right, and the observatory tower, reached by lift, high above on the Sphynx.
[Both,
Wengernalp & Jungfrau Railways

The formidable north face of the Eiger, with three white dots indicating the approximate position of Eigerwand station on the Jungfrau line.

Between Zweilütschinen and Grindelwald—a train of the Bernese Oberland Railway, with the Wetterhorn in the background. *[Both, Berner Oberland Railway group*

The spectacular climb of the rack - and - pinion railway from Wilderswil to the Schynige Platte, with the Eiger, Mönch and Jungfrau in the background.

Schynige Platte terminus, with part of its celebrated view. Above the train may be seen· the Lauterbrunnen valley, backed by the cone of the Breithorn, with the Jungfrau on the left.

[Both, Bernese Oberland Railway

The terminus of the tramway from Grütschalp is in the handsome new station opened recently at Mürren.

Another famous view—that of the Eiger, Mönch and Jungfrau as seen from the tramway that runs high above the Lauterbrunnen valley from Grütschalp to Mürren.
[Both, Bernese Oberland Railway

A Montreux-Oberland Bernois train, headed by two motorcoaches, descending the 1 in 13¾ gradient from Les Avants towards Montreux.

On the viaduct above Gstaad—a Montreux-Oberland Bernois train mounting towards Saanenmöser, on its way to Zweisimmen. The peak in the background is the Wildhorn. *[Both, Montreux-Oberland Bernois Railway*

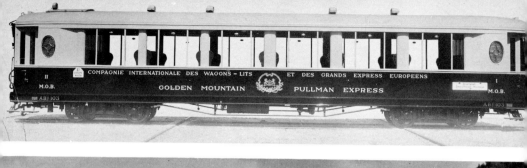

The two historic pictures (*above*) are of the only Pullman cars ever built for metre-gauge operation in Europe, by the International Sleeping Car Company. The train was the "Golden Mountain" Pullman of the Montreux-Oberland Bernois Railway, running between Montreux and Zweisimmen. The middle picture shows the train headed by one of the Bo-Bo-Bo locomotives specially built for its haulage during its short life. The picture (*below*) is of a train climbing the 1 in 13¾ gradient up from Montreux and the Lake of Geneva.   *[All, Montreux-Oberland Bernois Railway*

Solis bridge, carrying the Rhaetian Railway main line from Chur to St. Moritz 300ft above the Albula stream. The nearer bridge carries the Thusis-Tiefencastel road.

Tiefencastel, where the Rhaetian main line intersects the road from Chur through Lenzerheide and over the Julier pass to St. Moritz.   *[Both, Grisons Tourist Office*

Wiesen bridge, with its 180ft span masonry arch carrying the Davos-Filisur line 300ft above the Landwasser stream—a view giving a striking impression of the difficulty of the *terrain* through which the railways of the Grisons have been engineered.   [Grisons Tourist Office

The celebrated Landwasser viaduct on the Rhaetian main line, built to a radius of 330ft, 230ft above the valley floor, and with the last right-hand arch sprung directly from the precipice wall.

Climbing the 1 in 20 gradient from Klosters to Wolfgang, on the Davos line—a winter scene in the Grisons.
[Both, Grisons Tourist Office

Bergün, beginning of the amazing spiral location that lifts the Rhaetian main line 1,365ft in a direct distance of 4 miles. To the left of the village can be seen the first stage of the ascent, with two more stages on the extreme left.

More railway engineering extraordinary. Entering the picture at the extreme left, we follow the Rhaetian line into Toua spiral tunnel, emerge to cross the viaduct in the centre, circle across the valley and back into Zuondra spiral tunnel on the right, finally reaching the uppermost level, the whole on a gradient of 1 in 29.

[Both, Grisons Tourist Office

A modern Rhaetian Railway corridor train, with 2,400hp Bo-Bo-Bo locomotive, and rolling stock equal in comfort to the finest in Switzerland.   [*Rhaetian Railway*

Langwies bridge on the Chur-Arosa line, with its clear span of 315ft—a fine example of reinforced concrete construction.   [*Grisons Tourist Office*

Climbing a 1 in 14 gradient out of Morteratsch station on the Bernina line. In the background is the Morteratsch glacier, and the highest peak on the right is the Piz Bernina.

The highest through railway route in Europe—a train on the Bernina line near the Bernina Hospice station, at which the level is 7,410ft above the sea. *[Both, Grisons Tourist Office*

From ice and snow down to valley verdure — a Bernina line train alongside the public road passing the Lake of Le Prese, in the Poschiavo valley.

Spiral location without tunnelling — the final stage in the descent southwards of the Bernina line, in the Brusio defile.

[Both, Grisons Tourist Office

Looking down from Alp Grüm, with the first two stages of the 1 in 14 descent of the Bernina line in the centre, and in the distance the Lake of Le Prese and the Brusio defile.

Facing the ascent of 6,000ft in the 24 miles to the Bernina Hospice, a Bernina train passes the pilgrimage church of Madonna di Tirano.

[Both, Grisons Tourist Office

Swiss Federal metals between Berne and Thun. Eventually eight of these Bo–Bos were built. Next, in 1959, came the introduction of the most powerful locomotive type (with one single exception) in Switzerland, in effect two of the Type Ae 4/4 units permanently coupled together to make a locomotive of 8,800 h.p. These remarkable machines work loads of up to 900 *tonnes* (885 tons) up the 1 in 37 ruling gradient at the full permitted maximum of 46 m.p.h.; eight are now in service, and in normal working make three double trips daily between Thun and Brigue with loads up to the limit named, climbing a total of no less than 12,300 ft. in the process. Six of the older Ae 4/4 units were rebuilt to form three of the eight Ae 8/8 locomotives.

The final development, in 1964, has been the appearance of a new Bo–Bo type, the Ae 4/4 II, which then created yet another record by concentrating no less than 6,200 h.p. on four axles, that is, 1,550 h.p. per axle. These outstanding locomotives incorporate a number of unusual features, including ingenious arrangements for varying the proportion of the locomotives' weight coming down on each axle (to assist in starting), anti-slipping devices, and much else. On test, an Ae 4/4 II, though nominally limited to a load of 600 *tonnes* (592 tons), has started a train of 693 *tonnes* (683 tons), on a 1 in 37 gradient, and despite rails made slippery by a light fall of snow has accelerated this load to 46 m.p.h.

Various smaller types of locomotive undertake the minor duties, and the passenger stock includes a number of handsome electric motorcoaches, some of them twin-units of 1,600 and 2,000 h.p., capable if necessary of handling quite substantial trains of passenger coaches. Painted blue and white, these twins are used in summer for the regular "Blue Arrow" excursions, from Interlaken to Stresa in Italy, for the circuit *via* Brigue, Montreux and Berne back to Interlaken, and other attractive trips. As to other passenger rolling stock, the Lötschberg has built some of the finest coaches in Switzerland, which find their way into other European countries on the through international workings. There are times when such through coaches get put to unauthorised use; it is said that not long ago a missing Lötschberg coach was finally located in Sicily!

The expedition with which the Lötschberg Railway handles its busy traffic over the single-track sections between Spiez and Hondrich-Süd, Frutigen and Kandersteg, and Goppenstein and Brigue, is deserving of high praise. The six passing loops have all been lengthened to accommodate the lengthy freight trains which the high-powered locomotives have made it possible to operate. The Integra system of signalling, with colour-light signals, is in use throughout, and one of the loops, the remotely-situated Felsenburg crossing-place between Mitholz and Kandersteg, high above the Kander valley, does not require to be manned, for its points and signals are automatically operated, though under the supervision of the Kandersteg stationmaster. The recently-doubled section from Hondrich-Süd to Frutigen also is automatically signalled, with over-riding control from the station signal panel at Spiez.

The present-day growth of traffic is such, however, that work has

D

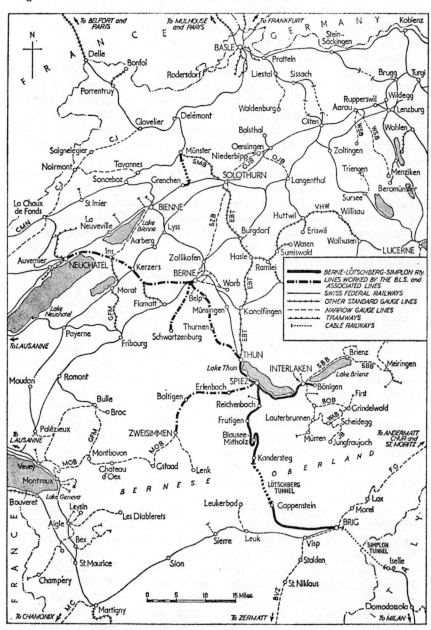

Fig 6. The Lötschberg railway system and other railways in the Bernese region.

begun on lengthening all the passing loops as part of doubling the remaining single track between Spiez and Brigue. These are from Spiez to the southern exit from the Hondrich–Hügel tunnel, from Frutigen to Kandersteg, and from Goppenstein to Brigue. The task will be simplified by the fact that most of the structures, both tunnels and bridges, have been prepared to receive a second track, and also that the passing loops at Felsenberg, Hohtenn, Ausserberg and Lalden have already been extended to considerable lengths, but even so the doubling will be an expensive business.

Such have been the technological advances made by this most efficiently managed and progressive railway. For some time past, as mentioned already in Chapter 1, there have been discussions as to the possibility of absorbing the line into the Swiss Federal system, which might be regarded as logical in view of the integral part which the Lötschberg plays in the movement of international traffic through the heart of Swiss Federal territory. But the movement towards national-isation seems now to be losing its impetus, and many, myself included, will feel no regret if, after just over half-a-century of distinguished history, the name "Bern–Lötschberg–Simplon" continues to play an intimate part in Swiss railway travel.

FOUR

The Bernese Oberland Railway Group

It was in the year 1890 that the first of a number of formerly independent railways, now under one common management at Interlaken, was opened to give access to one of the most scenic and popular regions in the whole of Switzerland. This was the Berner Oberland Bahn, from Interlaken to Zweilütschinen, there branching into two, one arm to Grindelwald and the other to Lauterbrunnen. It was laid to the metre gauge, and beyond Zweilütschinen each of the two branches required two sections of rack-and-pinion operation to climb sufficiently rapidly. Three years later Lauterbrunnen and Grindelwald became linked together by the Wengernalp Bahn, climbing from the former town through Wengen over the mountain pass known as the Kleine Scheidegg, and from there descending, at the foot of the famous north face of the Eiger, to Grindelwald. For reasons of economy, the gauge chosen for this line was the narrower one of 0.80 m. (2 ft. $7\frac{1}{2}$ in.)—an unfortunate decision, as in later years this was to preclude any through running between Interlaken, Kleine Scheidegg and Jungfraujoch. The Wengern-alp line has always been rack-operated throughout.

In 1893 there was also opened the rack-and-pinion line from Wilderswil, a suburb of Interlaken, to the Schynige Platte, a famous viewpoint; this was absorbed by the B.O.B. in 1895. Meantime the well-known winter sports resort of Mürren had been made accessible in 1891 by a cable-operated funicular railway from Lauterbrunnen up to Grütschalp, and an electric tramway high above the cliffs that form the western side of the Lauterbrunnen valley on to Mürren. To this was added in 1912 another cable-operated funicular, a comparatively short one, from Mürren up to Allmendhubel, chiefly of interest to skiers in winter.

Not until 1893 was the project first conceived, by the brilliant engineer Adolf Guyer-Zeller, of adding to this network the Jungfrau Railway proper. A concession was obtained in the following year from the Federal Government, and the work, which was expected to take seven years to complete, was begun in 1896. But owing to the exceptional hardness of the rock which had to be pierced, in the $4\frac{1}{2}$ miles of tunnelling needed, and to the great difficulties (both temperature and rarified atmosphere) of working at so high an altitude, 16 years passed before it was possible, on August 1st, 1912, to open the line to the Jungfraujoch terminus, 11,333 ft. above sea level, on the saddle between the Mönch and the Jungfrau. Even then the line had stopped short of the original intention, which was to proceed to a point immediately under the

Jungfrau, and to finish the journey by a lift to the summit; the curtailment was due to the fact that the cost of the line as far as the Jungfraujoch had vastly exceeded the estimate for the complete plan. For this reason, and also because of the disastrous effect on traffic of two world wars, for a long time the finances of the Jungfrau Railway were badly in the red, but a regular dividend began to be paid in 1949, and ten years later had risen to 7 per cent.

For the Jungfrau line the builders reverted to metre gauge, so compelling a second change of trains for through passengers from Interlaken. With a 1 in 4 ruling gradient, rack-and-pinion working was needed throughout from Kleine Scheidegg to the Eismeer station, under the Mönch, but over the 1 in 16 gradient from there to Jungfraujoch the operation at first was by adhesion. To avoid this mixed rack-and-adhesion working, however, the adhesion section in 1951 was equipped with the rack also.

Each of the railways in the Berner Oberland group still retains its financial independence, but by various successive agreements they have now been formed into a common operating community, with a head office at Interlaken. In 1904 the Lauterbrunnen–Grütschalp–Mürren line became linked with the B.O.B.; in 1932 a joint central administration was formed between the W.A.B. and J.B. lines; and in 1944 these two entered into a joint operating agreement with the B.O.B. The only remaining line in the group is the cable-operated funicular from Interlaken to the Harder, now making a total of six undertakings in the region under one common control. And now for a brief description of each of these railways.

The Bernese Oberland Railway

The journey begins at Interlaken Ost station, where the B.O.B. trains connect with those of the Lötschberg Railway, from the Berne, Thun and Spiez direction, and of the Swiss Federal Brünig line from Lucerne and Meiringen. Most of the B.O.B. trains are worked by eight powerful motorcoaches of 1,120 to 1,270 h.p., and set out from Interlaken with portions for both Lauterbrunnen and Grindelwald, the motorcoach of the rear portion being in the middle of the train. There are also available the nine small 0-6-0 electric locomotives of 400 h.p. which worked all the passenger trains until the advent in 1949 of the first motorcoaches. At Wilderswil, the first stop, connection is made with the Schynige Platte Railway, of which more later, and the railway then enters the deep gorge of the Lütschine, up which it travels to Zweilütschinen, 5 miles from the start. As its name implies this is where the two arms of the Lütschine torrent unite, the Black Lütschine coming down from Grindelwald, and the White Lütschine down the Lauterbrunnen valley.

Soon after leaving Zweilütschinen, where the train divides, the Lauterbrunnen portion encounters the first rack section; the second leads up into Lauterbrunnen station, the busy interchange point with the Wengernalp line and the Grütschalp funicular. Here the cliffs walling in the valley on the west side rise to a height of 1,500 to 1,700 ft.; just beyond the village there is seen the Staubbach waterfall, dispersing like a bridal veil into fine spray before it reaches the bottom of this tremendous drop. The Grindelwald portion, proceeding up the Black Lütschine valley, runs for 2½ miles to Lütschental before taking to the rack; the second rack section leads up into Grindelwald station, 11¾ miles from Interlaken and at 3,392 ft. altitude. The steepest gradient surmounted has been 1 in 11.

The Wengernalp Railway

One of the most scenically spectacular railway rides in Europe is provided by the 12 miles of this small company. It begins with the climb out of Lauterbrunnen up the east side of this great mountain cleft, which is not quite so precipitous as the west side. The original line mounted in a northerly direction at 1 in 4 before curving southwards into Wengen, but in 1910 a second line was completed on an easier inclination of 1 in 5½; the former is now confined to freight operation. On this ascent a magnificent view opens out by degrees of the Lütschine valley, with Lauterbrunnen far below, the Grütschalp funicular soaring up the opposite mountainside with the straightness of an arrow and from this angle looking almost perpendicular, and at the head of the valley a grand amphitheatre of mountains dominated by the cone of the Breithorn.

Wengen is one of the few Swiss mountain resorts without road communication, and so is free from the car and motorcoach invasion of some of its neighbours. It has its *Luftseilbahn*, climbing steeply from the 4,291 ft. altitude of the village to 7,346 ft., near the summit of the Männlichen, from which a fine level walk may be taken along a mountain path to the Scheidegg. The train continues climbing from Wengen, with Mürren now well in view high up above the cliffs on the opposite side of the Lauterbrunnen valley. The Jungfrau is seen dead ahead, over the mountain shoulder of the Lauberhorn, until just before Wengernalp station we round the corner of that shoulder and there is suddenly revealed, at close quarters, the overwhelming prospect of the Eiger, the Mönch and the Jungfrau, towering above the opposite side of the deep Trümleten valley.

Even more impressive is the journey from Grindelwald up to the Scheidegg, which begins with a steep drop to Grindelwald-Grund, where the train reverses, and then mounts at a maximum inclination of 1 in 4, at the base of the north face of the Eiger, with its stupendous precipice, dropping 6,000 ft. sheer from the summit, towering menacingly above the train. I know of few Alpine views that make so extraordinary an impression on the mind as this one.

To reach Kleine Scheidegg the W.A.B. trains have climbed 4,147 ft. from Lauterbrunnen in 6½ miles, and 3,665 ft. from Grindelwald-Grund in 4½ miles. The W.A.B. possesses ten modern motorcoaches of 600 h.p., powerful enough to push two light trailers up the 1 in 5½ gradients from Lauterbrunnen, with a total capacity (including the motorcoach itself) of up to 150 passengers; the 1 in 4 gradients up from Grindelwald, however, limit the load on that section to one trailer. On a fine summer's day patronage is so heavy that any advertised service between Lauterbrunnen and the Scheidegg may need two or three trains, and on the Grindelwald–Scheidegg leg up to four trains, all in sight of one another.

Among developments from 1948 onwards have been the "wye" or triangle of lines at Kleine Scheidegg to permit the turning of trains which may be required to run from one leg of the line to the other, so that the motorcoaches may always be at the lower end of their trains on the gradients. Owing to limited space the two sides of the turning triangle had to be carried into the adjacent mountainside by tunnelling. Also, some extensive avalanche protection work has been carried out on the section below the Eiger north face, so that the important winter sports traffic may be carried on without interruption.

The Jungfrau Railway

The main distinction of the Jungfrau line is both that of reaching the highest altitude of any railway in Europe, and also that it carries passengers to a world of ice and snow that they cannot reach otherwise unless they are competent climbers with guides and full climbing equipment. Moreover, at its middle station they can look out from windows which could only be reached from the outside after one of the most hazardous climbs, which has claimed a number of lives, anywhere in the Alps.

The service is worked entirely by modern two-coach trains, in which, even at the height of summer, it is necessary to provide heating owing to the low temperature in the long tunnel. The train ascends in long curves, partly protected by snowsheds, over the open mountainside until it reaches the western base of the triangle that forms the north face of the Eiger, at the station called Eigergletscher. This takes its name from the much-crevassed glacier of which the toe is immediately below the station. The tunnel is now entered, slanting upwards just inside the Eiger face, until the train stops at Eigerwand. A 5-min. halt here now gives passengers the unique opportunity of looking down, from the centre of that vast precipice, on Grindelwald, some 6,000 ft. below, and over a wide range of view. The line then doubles right round, under the Mönch, and at Eismeer a second stop is made, allowing a view of an icy world of *seracs* and crevasses, backed by the peaks of the Grosse Schreckhorn and the Lauteraarhorn.

Finally, after a journey of 5¾ miles and an ascent of 4,571 ft. from Kleine Scheidegg, the train stops at the Jungfraujoch terminus, 11,333 ft. above sea level, and still, of course, in tunnel. Galleries lead into the substantially-built Berghaus, or hotel, beyond which various diversions await the tourist. A lift to the top storey and a gallery driven through the rock lead to the renowned "ice palace", with its skating rink, garage with motorcars, and music room with piano, all hollowed out of or modelled in solid ice. From here there is an exit on to the ice-cap covering the Jungfraujoch, quite uncrevassed, on which pedestrians can walk without risk over the snow to the Swiss flag on the crest of the pass, with the Jungfrau towering above them to the left, and the Mönch to the right. Another long gallery through rock leads to the glacier on the Mönch side of the hotel, where even in the height of summer there is much skiing, and those so minded can take trips in a sledge drawn by a team of "huskies" imported from Greenland.

A branch from the latter gallery gives access to the lift up to the meteorological station on the Sphinx, which tourists are allowed to visit; from its altitude of 11,723 ft. a prospect of vast extent is obtained. The most impressive part of the view is that looking south down the great Jungfraufirn, or glacier, which continues as the Aletsch glacier, turning round at an angle at the Concordiaplatz, and finishing at Belalp, above Brigue, in a total length of some 16 miles. In all, the passenger from Interlaken to the Jungfraujoch is lifted 9,473 ft. in a journey of just under 20 miles, taking 2¼ to 2½ hours. The usual practice is to make a circuit up *via* Lauterbrunnen and Wengen and down *via* Grindelwald or *vice versa*—necessarily an expensive trip, but one thoroughly worth while provided that the traveller is reasonably assured that the clouds are not down over the higher peaks.

Mürren and the Allmendhubel

In recent years both sections of the transport from Lauterbrunnen to Mürren—the funicular to Grütschalp and the tramway from there onwards—have benefited by the provision of new rolling stock, and Mürren itself has gained by a most handsome new station. The funicular, 1,554 yds. in length, is steep, with an average gradient of 55 per cent., and a maximum of 61 per cent. (nearly 1 in 1½). Each of its two cars can carry 62 passengers. On the tramway the service, at 15 to 18 min. intervals during peak periods, is maintained by three bogie motorcoaches which shuttle to and fro in 15 min. per trip. Along this 3¼ miles, high above the cliffs on the west side of the Lauterbrunnen valley, one of the most renowned of all views of the Eiger, Mönch and Jungfrau is obtained, with the continuation of the mountain chain past Ebnefluh, the Breithorn and other peaks at the head of the valley. The Allmendhubel funicular also has new cars; it is less than ½-mile long, but climbs 847 ft. to a summit level of 6,257 ft. The latest of all the mountain lines here is independent of the Interlaken group; it is the very notable new four-stage *Luftseilbahn* from Stechelberg, in the Lauterbrunnen valley, up through Gimmelwald to Mürren, and then on up past Birg to the summit of the Schilthorn, at 9,740 ft.; but this is described in Chapter 13.

The Schynige Platte Railway

In its equipment this line is somewhat primitive—diminutive 0-4-0 locomotives pushing two-car trains of very light stock, some of the coaches having glazed sides, and others open sides from which any bad weather (together with the view!) has to be shut out by dropping thick curtains. Although it may be granted that the passenger is lifted 4,537 ft., the time of 50 min. for the journey of 4½ miles can hardly be described as speedy, but there is plenty of compensation from what one sees *en route*. Propulsion is rack-and-pinion, with a ruling gradient of 1 in 4.

In the early stages the line mounts through forest high above the Lütschine valley, and then transfers through the short Rotenegg tunnel to the other side of the ridge. Still running largely up forested slopes, the train does not offer much in the realm of scenery until beyond the intermediate passing station of Breitlauenen. Then the line ascends in a wide curve over pastureland, with a very fine view westwards over Interlaken and the whole of the Lake of Thun.

Beyond the Grätli tunnel the great Oberland peaks suddenly come into view, and a fairly startling stretch of the line begins, with the track at the edge of a precipice of unguessed depth. On reaching the terminus, at a vast depth below there is Zweilütschinen, at the junction of the two Lütschine valleys, up the whole length of both of which one can look, to Grindelwald to the left, backed by the Wetterhorn, and to Stechelberg to the right, dominated by the Breithorn. Between the two stretch the stately row of giant peaks—the Schreckhorn, Eiger, Mönch and Jungfrau —a glorious spectacle indeed. Immediately opposite, separating the Grindelwald and Lauterbrunnen valleys, is the Männlichen, which as mentioned earlier can be reached by *Luftseilbahn* from Wengen.

Among the diversions at Schynige Platte are the Alpine garden, which attracts many visitors, and the half-hour's walk to the Daube, a 6,772 ft. peak from which the Lakes of Thun and Brienz can both be seen in addition to the extensive mountain panorama in the opposite direction. The more energetic can set out on foot for the Faulhorn, or for First, upper station of the remarkable four-stage chair-lift, described in Chapter 13, that comes up to that eminence from Grindelwald. One minor thrill of the return railway journey to Wilderswil is when the train conductor nonchalantly works along the footboards of the carriage—on the precipice side of the train—collecting tickets. This is a trip certainly worth making by any visitor to the Bernese Oberland, and easily completed in a morning or an afternoon.

The Harder Railway

The long serrated mountain ridge known as the Brienzer Grat, which reaches its highest point with the Brienzer Rothorn, terminates at its western end with a promontory, thickly wooded, immediately above the town of Interlaken and looking out over the length of the Lake of Thun. Up to this eminence runs the Harderbahn, a rope-worked funicular, 1,569 yds. long, that climbs 2,418 ft. Part of the line is in tunnel, and because of the woods the only view to be seen on the journey is down the length of the railway to Bönigen and the western end of the Lake of Brienz, but the wide range of view from the summit hotel, especially of the great chain of the Bernese Alps, is ample compensation to those who make this 16-min. ascent.

FIVE

The Montreux-Oberland Bernois Railway

THOUGH POSSESSING no more than 47 miles of line, the Montreux–Oberland Bernois Railway, tourist highway between the Lake of Geneva and the Bernese Oberland, can claim a number of records. It was the first line of its length in Switzerland—and, indeed, in Europe—to decide on electrification from its opening in 1901. It has the steepest gradients of any line in Switzerland worked by adhesion, up to a maximum inclination of 1 in $13\frac{1}{2}$. It is the only metre-gauge railway in Europe that has ever boasted a Pullman train, the "Golden Mountain Pullman", which was introduced in 1931.

There were more reasons than one for this Pullman service. The German "Mitropa" company had managed to infiltrate itself into Switzerland with its own restaurant cars on the metre-gauge Rhaetian Railway, and was looking round for fresh narrow-gauge fields to conquer. This was not at all to the taste of the Swiss Dining Car Company (at that time a subsidiary of the International Sleeping Car Company), and the hurried decision was therefore reached to introduce a Pullman service between Interlaken and Montreux. Standard Pullman cars were to be used over the Lötschberg and Spiez–Erlenbach–Zweisimmen lines between Interlaken and Zweisimmen, and four metre-gauge cars were built specially for the M.O.B. journey between Zweisimmen, Gstaad and Montreux. The second reason was that on their "Grand Tour" of Europe many Americans used this route, as they still do, and Americans, of course, are accustomed to Pullman travel.

Two Pullman services were operated daily in each direction between Interlaken and Montreux, with the addition of a restaurant car over the M.O.B. between Zweisimmen and Jor, at the southern end of the tunnel under the Col de Jaman; the reason for the transfer of the latter from train to train at Jor was to avoid having to work the restaurant cars up the long and steep climb out of Montreux. The Pullmans, delightful vehicles with armchair seating and bow windows to each pair of seats, to give better views, were probably the lightest Pullman cars ever built, weighing only 18 tons apiece. Unhappily, however, the weather in the summer of 1931 was deplorably bad, and the new Pullman service proved a dead loss. After no more than a single year's working, the cars were withdrawn and sold to the Rhaetian Railway. On the latter they never functioned as Pullman cars, though for a time they were run as saloons in certain trains, at a small supplementary fare.

The trains of the Montreux-Oberland Bernois Railway start from the

Swiss Federal Railways station in Montreux, with their leading ends pointing eastwards. Immediately they plunge into a helicoidal tunnel, on emergence from which they are travelling in precisely the opposite direction. So, climbing steadily on a gradient which, as mentioned already, is as steep in parts as 1 in 13½, with ever-widening views from this thickly populated mountainside of Montreux and the eastern end of the Lake of Geneva, we reach Fontanivent, and there swing round to due east once again. A mile or so later comes a third swing round, to the north-west, and finally, with another helicoidal tunnel, the last reversal of direction at Chamby, completing four great sweeps on the open mountainside until finally we turn north, high above the deep Gorge de Chauderon. Immediately opposite, at an equally lofty altitude, is Caux, with Glion and Montreux far below.

Still climbing, the M.O.B. passes Les Avants, with its famous narcissus fields; it is here, travelling in the opposite direction, that the traveller gets his first and very dramatic view of the great expanse of the Lake of Geneva. The summit level, 3,542 ft., is reached at Jor; we have climbed 2,246 ft. since leaving Montreux, 7½ miles away by rail. Here we enter a long tunnel, 1½ miles of it, under the Col de Jaman, and thereby transfer from the watershed of the Rhône to that of the distant Rhine. Down the wooded valley of the Hongrin the line winds its way; though some of the curves have been smoothed out in recent years, others still remain of almost incredible sharpness, such as that which leads out of the station at Les Sciernes down to a tunnel far below us on the right, and so into the station at Montbovon.

The M.O.B. is now in the valley of the Sarine—a tributary of the Aar, which in its turn is a tributary of the Rhine, Here it links up with the G.F.M., or Chemins de Fer Fribourgeois Gruyère-Fribourg-Morat, a quite extensive 59-mile system which runs down the Sarine valley to the ancient town of Gruyères and on to Bulle and Palézieux, as described in Chapter 10. But the course of the M.O.B. is up the Sarine valley, first through a very narrow gorge, and then into the wide valley in which lies the pleasant resort of Château d'Oex. This has its two-stage *téléphérique* up to Pra Perron and La Montagnette, an ascent of just under 2,200 ft.; but a much more exciting line is the *Gondelbahn* from Rougemont, a little further along the valley, to La Videmanette. This line, after climbing 3,894 ft., passes through a narrow cleft at the crest of the mountain ridge and reveals a surprise view far down the opposite side. The mountains on this side of the valley, dominated by the 8,075 ft. Gummfluh, at certain points always give me an irresistable impression of looking at the Dolomites.

Passing Saanen the railway reaches Gstaad, beloved of winter sports enthusiasts, and a centre indeed of suspension transport. In and around the village, which itself is at an altitude of 3,450 ft., there are the chairlift to the Wasserngrat, 6,375 ft., and the *Gondelbahn* lines up to Eggli, 5,122 ft., and the Hohi Wispille, 6,270 ft. And not far away, on the main road over the Col de Pillon, at Reusch, there is the lower terminus of the daring three-stage *téléphérique* which ends on the glacial ice-field of the Diablerets mountain, of which more in Chapter 13.

Out of Gstaad the Montreux–Oberland Bernois line sweeps in a half-circle round the village, and begins once again to climb, with a fine retrospective view of the ice-mantled mountains of the Diablerets group, to the left, and the massive Gummfluh across the valley opposite. The summit level of the line is reached at Saanenmöser, 4,173 ft. up, and then begins an abrupt descent which soon opens up a view of the wide Simme valley, with the town of Zweisimmen immediately below us. But our line has to make a big circuit, with a short helicoidal tunnel at the elbow bend, before we run into Zweisimmen station. Across the platform at which we stop there is the standard gauge Lötschberg train which provides the connection to Spiez and Interlaken. Years ago the possibility was seriously examined of laying mixed gauge from Zweisimmen to Interlaken, in order to permit through running between Montreux and Lucerne, using the track of the Swiss Federal Brünig line from Interlaken to Lucerne, but the cost was prohibitive.

Although Zweisimmen is the terminus for the trains from Montreux, it is not the end of the M.O.B. line. As its name implies, it is at the confluence of the two arms of the Simme river; these are separated by the mountain buttress of the Rinderberg, up which, as mentioned in Chapter 13, there climbs the longest *Gondelbahn* in Switzerland, 5,580 yds. all told with a total ascent of 3,481 ft. We have come down the valley of the Kleine Simme, and join in Zweisimmen a branch which proceeds for 8 miles at a much lower level up the Grosse Simme valley to the winter sport resort of Lenk. To the head of this valley the Wildstrubel, 10,665 ft., with its snow fields, provides a grand termination.

It should be added that the rack-and-pinion railway which starts out of the Swiss Federal station at Montreux, and climbs through Glion and Caux to the summit of the Rochers-de-Naye (as described in Chapter 11), together with the connecting funicular railway from Territet to Glion, forms a part of the Montreux-Oberland Bernois system.

Recent improvements to the M.O.B. line, with financial assistance from the Cantons of Vaud and Berne, have included the purchase of four new twin motorcoaches of 1,200 h.p., each just over 109 ft. long and seating 18 first and 86 second class passengers, yet weighing no more than 58 tons apiece. With such power it is no longer necessary to use motorcoaches in pairs on the heavier trains, in order to surmount gradients up to 1 in 13½. But a proposal to change the branch to Lenk from metre to standard gauge, and to turn it over to the Simmental line of the Lötschberg group, so as to permit through running between Spiez and Lenk, has never been implemented.

SIX

The Rhaetian Railway

IN SWITZERLAND's easternmost Canton, the Grisons or Graubünden, we reach a part of the country which is different in many ways from any other. With its 2,774 square miles, it is the largest Canton in Switzerland, but at the same time the most thinly populated, because of its extremely mountainous character. It is historic country; to the Romans, who drove their military tracks northwards from the Lake of Como over the mountain passes, it was known as Rätia, whence the name of its completely independent metre-gauge railway system, the Rhaetian Railway. It has its own language, the dialects of Romansch and Ladin, the nearest approach to Latin in any modern speech. The name "Graubünden" derives from "Graue Bünde", or "Grey League", formed in the early Sixteenth Century when the area was fighting for its freedom, and so named because of the grey garments worn by its men. The equivalent in Romansch was "Grischun", whence the name "Grisons".

From 1818 onwards the tracks over the San Bernardino, Splügen, Julier and Maloja Passes were developed into well-made roads, and carried considerable traffic between Germany and Italy, but the opening of the Gotthard Railway in 1882 from then on attracted that traffic away from the roads, and the Canton realised that the time had now come for the development of a railway system of its own. There was also the considerable attraction of providing the growing resorts of Davos, St. Moritz and Pontresina with railway communication. But the difficulty was the *terrain* through which such railways would need to be engineered, very mountainous and seamed in all directions by profound gorges, and so calling not merely for very long and steep gradients, but also for layout and structures of considerable note.

Davos was the first town to take action. The Swiss North-Eastern Railway, as it then was, had come up the Rhine Valley from Rorschach on the Lake of Constance to Chur, capital of the Grisons, and the Landquart & Davos Railway obtained a concession to build a narrow gauge line from Landquart, 8 miles short of Chur, to Davos; this was opened as far as Klosters in October, 1889, and into Davos by midsummer of the following year. Extensions were put in hand immediately, and by 1896 the line was complete from Landquart to Chur, parallel to the standard-gauge Swiss Federal line, and on up the Hinter-Rhein valley to Thusis.

The stage beyond Thusis, up the Albula valley, was by far the most difficult, and not until July, 1904, did the first Rhaetian trains begin working through between Chur and St. Moritz. A year earlier a branch had been opened from Reichenau, where the Hinter- and Vorder-Rhein streams join, up the Vorder-Rhein valley as far as Ilanz; 1908 saw the completion of the short branch from Samedan to Pontresina; and 1909 the link, through the Landwasser gorge, between Davos and Filisur, on the main Chur–St. Moritz line, was completed. In the year 1912 the continuation of the Vorder-Rhein branch was opened from Ilanz to the historic town of Disentis, to which in later years the Furka–Oberalp Railway (Chapter 7) made its way from Brigue. In 1913 another branch was completed from Bever, on the main line 4½ miles short of St. Moritz, down the Lower Engadine as far as Schuls-Tarasp, a famous spa.

There were hopes in earlier days not merely of extending the latter line across the Austrian frontier to link up with the Arlberg main line at Landeck, but also of continuing the Rhaetian main line in the opposite direction from St. Moritz over the Maloja Pass and across the Italian frontier to Chiavenna, there joining the Italian State Railways, but neither plan ever came to fruition. What did happen, however, was the building of the independent Bernina Railway, which on the Bernina Pass attained the highest level, 7,108 ft., of any through railway in Europe; it then descended rapidly into the fertile Poschiavo valley, finally connecting with the Italian State Valtellina line at Tirano.

The Bernina line, completed in stages between 1908 and 1910, was absorbed by the Rhaetian Railway in 1943. It was worked by electricity from its opening, but the use of current for traction at 1,000 volts d.c., as compared with the 11,000 volts a.c. adopted when the rest of the Rhaetian system was electrified between 1913 and 1922, means that the Bernina section must still have its own motorcoaches. The same applies to the once independent Chur–Arosa Railway, financed by the two towns named and opened in 1914; this the Rhaetian Railway took over in 1942, but its line voltage of 2,000 d.c. also requires separate motorcoaches.

The latest seven Rhaetian locomotives are 2,400 h.p. machines with the unique Bo–Bo–Bo wheel arrangement, able by means of articulation to adjust themselves to the sharpest curves, and to tackle trains of up to 265 *tonnes* (260 tons), that is, 13 bogie coaches of the light Rhaetian rolling stock, up the ruling gradient of the main line, which is 3½ per cent., or 1 in 29. They are named after the principal towns on the system, and in their naming the curious question arose as to whether the generally accepted names, or those in the Romansch dialect, should be adopted. As to Chur, it was the latter, *Curia*, that was chosen; St. Moritz, Davos and Disentis-Mustèr offered no difficulties; but two others are now in the singular position of carrying different names on their two sides. These are *Schuls* and *Scuol*, and *Pontresina* and *Puntraschigna*, respectively. The seventh Bo–Bo–Bo is called *Rätia*, after the kingdom that gave its name to the railway.

There are also ten Bo–Bo locomotives of 1,600 h.p. each, all carrying names that are familiar in the Grisons, which work most of the remaining passenger trains; and a number of earlier C–C and 1–D–1 locomotives

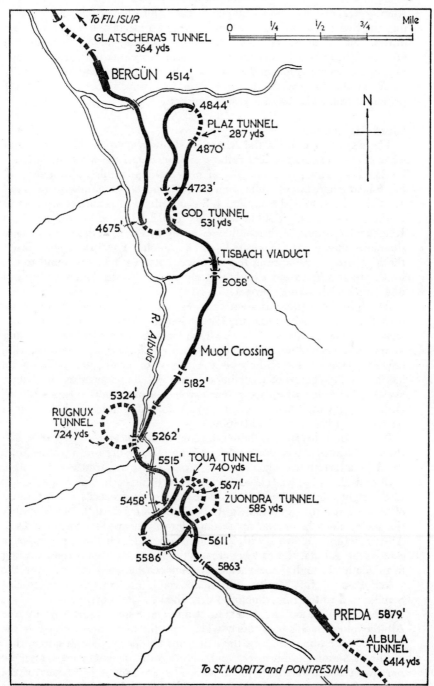

Fig 7. Spiral location of Rhaetian Railway main line between Bergün and Preda.

(the former, double bogie with centre cabs and sloping bonnets, resembling the Swiss Federal "Crocodiles"), which undertake freight and other duties. As to rolling stock, all the main Rhaetian main line trains are now made up of bogie corridor coaches which, despite the narrow gauge, in spaciousness, comfort and *décor*, in the first class particularly, are fully equal to the best of the Swiss Federal Railways' stock. Some of the principal trains also include restaurant cars.

Chur–St. Moritz

The 244 route miles of the Rhaetian Railway provide the tourist with some of the most spectacular railway sightseeing in the whole of Switzerland. The principal main line, of metre gauge as already mentioned, has mixed gauge out of Chur as far as the important manufacturing plant at Domat-Ems, to and from which Swiss Federal locomotives are able to work. Also the only double track of the Rh.B. is the 6-mile stretch to Reichenau-Tamins, at the confluence of the two arms of the Rhine, where the main line diverges from the Disentis branch. The former now climbs the high ground separating the two rivers, and as it bends round to the south presents fine views simultaneously up the Vorder-Rhein valley and down that of the Rhine proper.

At Thusis, a prosperous town 17 miles from Chur, the mountains close round ahead. It is here that the Hinter-Rhein emerges from the profound chasm of the Via Mala, through which runs the important road leading to the San Bernadino and Splügen passes (Chapter 14), The railway, however, bends round and crosses the river in order to enter the but little less forbidding gorge of its tributary, the Albula, known as the Schyn ravine. Climbing steadily, we pass through a succession of tunnels, with glimpses from time to time of the stream foaming along far below, until we come out into the open at Solis.

Just beyond this station there is a remarkable masonry bridge of which the train traveller sees practically nothing when he crosses it, other than the Albula torrent some 300 ft. below him. A narrow stretch of the gorge, with cliff-like sides, was chosen at which to transfer the line from the left to the right bank of the stream. The train then proceeds along the top of the cliff at a tremendous height above the water until, by Tiefencastel, the valley floor has come up to considerably nearer the railway level. At this picturesque town, with its church perched high above the opposite side of the Albula, the railway crosses the important main road leading from Chur through Lenzerheide to Tiefencastel, and thence over the Julier Pass to St. Moritz—the main road, in fact, from north-east Switzerland to the Engadine, also described in Chapter 14.

From Tiefencastel the Rhaetian train continues southwards up the Albula valley, at this point fairly wide, until the line bends inwards to the east. We are about to cross the exit from another profound gorge, that of the tributary Landwasser, and here again the engineers chose the narrowest point at which to do so. The crossing is by means of the famous Landwasser Viaduct, sharply curved, 230 ft. high, and with its

Spiral location on the Furka-Oberalp Railway, near Grengiols. With rack-and-pinion assistance, the trains cross the River Rhône, enter the spiral tunnel on a 1 in 9 gradient, and emerge on the viaduct high above.

More spiral planning, as the Furka-Oberalp Railway and the road climb through the Rhône gorge from Oberwald up to Gletsch. *[Both, Furka-Oberalp Railway*

The unique Steffenbach bridge on the Furka-Oberalp line, dismantled each winter as a protection against avalanches. The inner ends of the side spans are lifted and drawn back, the hinged diagonal supports coming to rest against the abutments, while the hinged centre span moves in the same way to rest against the right-hand abutment.

The Steffenbach bridge as assembled and in use, with a Furka-Oberalp train crossing.   *[All, Furka-Oberalp Railway*

A Furka-Oberalp train beginning the climb from Andermatt to the Oberalp pass. Below is the Urseren valley, with the Furka pass in the distance to the extreme right, and in the far centre is Hospental, where the Gotthard road turns left up to the pass. *[Swiss National Tourist Office*

In the Schöllenen gorge, with the historic Devil's Bridge in the foreground and a train from Andermatt to Göschenen above—a view taken from the modern reinforced concrete road bridge. *[Central Switzerland Tourist Office*

On the Oberalp pass, at 6,720ft altitude—a Furka-Oberalp train emerges from the long avalanche shelter covering both railway and road.   [Central Switzerland Tourist Office

Looking down on the bleak Oberalp pass, with the Oberalp lake in the centre, and a train far below starting down to Disentis.   [Swiss National Tourist Office

One of the handsome corridor buffet car trains of the
Bodensee-Toggenburg Railway between Nesslau and
Wattwil, with the curiously serrated Churfirsten mountain
range in the background.   *[Bodensee-Toggenburg Railway*

A through Lucerne-St. Gallen train on the Südostbahn
section of the route, dropping down to Pfäffikon before
crossing the Seedamm across the Lake of Zürich, in the
centre background, to Rapperswil.
                        [Central Switzerland Tourist Office

A vista of bridges across the Sitter gorge, near St. Gallen, as seen from the air. Far below (extreme right) an old wooden bridge; in the centre the astonishing viaduct of the Bodensee-Toggenburg Railway; then, to the left in sequence, the Swiss Federal Railways viaduct, the former road bridge, and the handsome reinforced concrete structure carrying the present motorway.

[North-East Switzerland Tourist Office]

A nearer view of the Bodensee-Toggenburg viaduct over the Sitter, with its 394ft girder span and masonry piers with a maximum height of 320ft—the highest railway bridge in Switzerland.   *[Brian Stephenson*

A general view of the Sitter gorge, with its many bridges and the wooded Appenzell country beyond, backed by the imposing mountain mass of the Säntis.
[North-East Switzerland Tourist Office

Part of the main station at St. Gallen. On the right is a train
of the St. Gallen-Gais-Appenzell Railway. *[Cecil J Allen*

Alongside the main St. Gallen-Trogen road—a motorcoach
of the Trogen Railway, with the Lake of Constance in the
background. *[North-East Switzerland Tourist Office*

Above: Crossing the Kaubach bridge on its way from Gossau to Wasserauen — the "Ebenalp Arrow" of the Appenzell Railway.

Left: The handsome Pont des Planches bridge carrying the Aigle - Sépey - Diablerets Railway across the gorge of the Grande Eau near Le Sépey.

Below: On the Centovalli Railway, from Locarno to Domodossola — the spidery steel bridge over the Onsernone gorge at Intragna.

The transformation of the former Stansstad-Engelberg Railway—one of the attractive new three-coach train-sets.

The new Hergiswil-Stansstad connection, showing the railway and motorway tunnels under the Lopperberg and the massive Acheregg bridges across the Alpnachersee.
[Both, Luzern-Stansstad-Engelberg Railway

Brienzer Rothorn Railway 0-4-2 rack-equipped tank No. 7
takes water at Planalp on its 5,515ft climb from Brienz to
the summit.   [Brian Stephenson

In the heart of the Brienzer Grat mountain ridge—a Brienzer
Rothorn train on Switzerland's only steam-operated
railway.   [Brienzer Rothorn Railway

In 1971 the Rigi Railway celebrated its Centenary. One of the former steam trains leaving Vitznau on the 4,300ft climb to Rigikulm.

One of Riggenbach's original locomotives of the Vitznau-Rigi Railway—the first in Europe to be operated by rack-and-pinion, and on a ruling gradient of 1 in 4.
[Both, Swiss National Tourist Office

On the final stretch to the summit of the Rigi, with an
Arth-Rigi train on the left and one of the Vitznau Rigi
line on the right.

A Rigi train on the curved Schnurtobel viaduct, rebuilt in
recent years in reinforced concrete.
[*Both, Swiss National Tourist Office*

The oldest type of rack in Switzerland, first introduced by
Riggenbach on the Vitznau-Rigi Railway—a kind of steel
ladder used on gradients up to 1 in 5. This view is on the
Brünig line of the Swiss Federal Railways.

[Swiss Federal Railways

The Abt type of rack, with two parallel rows of teeth,
staggered in pitch, and also suitable for a maximum steepness of 1 in 4. The Furka-Oberalp motorcoach is approaching the Oberalp pass. *[Furka-Oberalp Railway*

Alpnachstad terminus of the Pilatus Railway, showing the Locher rack (with teeth on both outer edges) and the traverser for transferring motorcoaches from one track to the other.

Climbing on a ruling gradient of 1 in 2 from Alpnachstad to the summit of Pilatus—a 60-seater motorcoach crosses Wolfort bridge. *[Both, Pilatus Railway*

The superb prospect from Pilatus to the east. The central portion of Lake Lucerne, with, below, the town of Hergiswil; right centre, the Burgenstock; left, above, the long ridge of the Rigi, with the town of Weggis below its eastern end; faintly in the far distance, left, the Säntis, 65 miles away; the highest peak on the right is Glärnisch.

[Central Switzerland Tourist Office

Switzerland's only rack-and-pinion railway operated with diesel-electric power—a motorcoach on the line from Capolago to Monte Generoso, above the Lake of Lugano.

[Lugano Tourist Office

furthermost arch sprung directly out of the precipice wall into which the train now plunges in tunnel. In this case passengers sitting on the right side of the train do have a fine view of this spectacular masonry structure as they approach it.

Once through the short tunnel beyond the Landwasser Viaduct we are joined at Filisur by the Davos line, of which more later. The next stretch, up to the Albula tunnel, called for outstanding skill in location by the engineer, Hennings. The steepest gradient decided on, up the steeply rising valley, was 3½ per cent, or 1 in 29, and at this figure we now begin to climb; even so, four completely spiral and two partly spiral tunnels have been necessary before we get up to Preda. The first, Greifenstein, is immediately after leaving Filisur; from then on the railway mounts at an ever-increasing height, through many short tunnels and at several points with almost sheer precipices descending from the line, until the longer Bergünerstein and Glatscheras tunnels usher the train into the placid valley basin in which lies the attractive village of Bergün. The valley road, which before these two tunnels was far down below the line, is now almost alongside; it has come by a series of zigzags up through a formidable gorge.

Still sterner engineering measures were necessary from Bergün onwards. Preda lies no more than 3¾ miles ahead in a direct line, but 1,370 feet higher in altitude. To keep the gradient down to the ruling figure of 1 in 29, the line is first carried in two wide sweeps up the pasture land above the village, making the elbow bends by short spiral tunnels. It then mounts higher and higher, through several avalanche galleries, to Muot, where the valley floor has come almost up to the railway level. Still to keep above the stream the line then crosses the Albula, and plunges into the Rugnux spiral tunnel. Emerging, it crosses the stream again, and very shortly enters Toua spiral tunnel, in the opposite mountainside. After this comes the third and highest of the masonry viaducts over the Albula, a wide curve round the opposite bank, the fourth viaduct, and the fourth spiral tunnel, Zuondra. To the uninitiated traveller these constant twists and turns and the sight of the succession of viaducts one above another is quite bewildering. Now, as we approach Preda, the mountains fringing the Albula pass close solidly round ahead.

In the 27½ miles from Thusis a difference in level of no less than 3,590 ft. has been conquered, but the climbing is at an end. From Preda to Spinas the line passes through the 3¾-mile Albula tunnel, the boring of which presented the most serious difficulties because of the irruption of very cold underground springs; at one stage these held up the work for fifteen months, but the tunnel was completed in 3½ years. The maximum altitude of the Albula line, 5,982 ft., is reached in the tunnel, which is dead straight; indeed, from the centre both ends can be clearly seen. After a short downhill run from Spinas we join at Bever, by a very sharp curve, the line which has come up from Schuls or Scuol in the Lower Engadine.

We are now in the wide valley of the River Inn, the tunnel having transferred the train from the watershed of the Rhine to that of the Danube. Away beyond the far side of the valley, which is wide enough to accommodate an airfield and is a noted centre for gliding contests, is the snow-mantled range of the Bernina Alps. From Bever another 1½ miles leads to Samedan, the old capital of the valley and the junction for the short branch to Pontresina; and in a further 3¼ miles, past Celerina, we reach the fine terminal station serving what is now the far more important town of St. Moritz. The journey of 64 miles from Chur, with its tremendous gradients, is completed, according to train and the number of intermediate stops, in from 1 hour 52 minutes to 2¼ hours.

Landquart-Davos-Filisur

The other main arm of the Rhaetian Railway, from Chur to Filisur *via* Landquart, Klosters and Davos, curves out of Landquart to make straight for the mountain wall that hems in the east side of the Rhine valley. Here the Landquart river issues from what is little more than a narrow crack, bordered by immense cliffs between which the railway and road pursued an uneasy course until in recent years a tunnel was bored to give the railway protection from landslides and falling rocks. We emerge into a lovely and fertile valley known as the Prätigau, up which the railway mounts with no engineering of note until it reaches the popular resort of Klosters. The original station here was terminal, but a curved tunnel bored at a later date now permits through running. Continuing, the line has to climb out of the valley, which it does with the steepest gradient, 1 in 20, on any Rhaetian main line. The course is first in the opposite direction, north-westwards, to that in which we have been travelling, and then reversing, by a semi-spiral tunnel, to south-eastwards, with a magnificent view of the valley and of the Silvretta group of mountains at its head. Here the line twice passes under the *Luftseilbahn* from Klosters up to the Gotschnagrat.

There is finally a turn to the south, over the mountain ridge separating the Prätigau from the wide valley in which lies the large town of Davos; the maximum altitude attained between Klosters and Davos is 5,370 ft. at Wolfgang. Beyond Davos, where there is another fine modern station, the river Landwasser begins to drop into the profound gorge which a few miles further on the other main line crosses by the Landwasser viaduct already described. This has necessitated a spectacular stretch of railway construction for the Davos line also, with a number of tunnels and bridges. The most imposing of the latter is the great masonry arch just beyond Wiesen station, with a clear span of 180 ft., carrying the line all but 300 ft. above the Landwasser. After a short stretch along the cliff high above the stream, the line then curves round to join at Filisur the main line which has come up from Chur *via* Thusis.

Davos is one of the most famous skiing centres in Europe, and it is mainly in the interest of skiers. though also of great attraction to summer visitors, that the valley is provided with some of the most extensive mountain transport to be found anywhere in Switzerland, as described in Chapter 13. Including nearby Klosters, these total no fewer than six lines of the *Luftseilbahn* or *Gondelbahn* types, two chairlifts and two funiculars; a near rival is the Upper Engadine, with five *Luftseilbahn* lines, two lengthy funiculars and a chair-lift.

Bever–Schuls–Tarasp

Bever is the junction for the 30½-mile railway which serves the Lower Engadine. This descends the Inn valley past Zuoz, with its ancient mansions, to Zernez, the starting-point for the road which leads over the Ofen Pass to Malles, in the South Tyrol, and with its branch from Santa Maria to the higher Umbrail and Stelvio Passes, as described in Chapter 14. A short distance from Zernez there also branches a road up the Val Cluoza, leading to the heart of the famous Swiss National Park, an area now totalling 54 square miles, set apart in 1909. Here nature is left entirely to herself, all cattle-grazing, shooting, fishing, wood-cutting, and the collection of plants or wild animals, being strictly forbidden.

By the time the railway reaches Schuls, or Scuol (the Romansch name) it has descended 1,610 ft. from St. Moritz, but the River Inn has dropped further still. The town of Scuol is well below the railway station, while the spa, Bad Tarasp, with its Kurhaus and mineral springs, at the bottom of the Inn gorge, is 300 ft. lower down still. High on the opposite side of the gorge is Vulpera, and a little further south the finely situated Tarasp castle, on its rocky knoll. The scenic setting of this group of towns is magnificent and they attract many visitors; through coaches are run on the principal Chur–St. Moritz trains between Chur and Schuls.

Reichenau–Disentis

The other important branch of the Rhaetian system is that up the valley of the Vorder-Rhein to Disentis, where it forms an end-on junction with the Furka-Oberalp Railway. The junction with the St. Moritz line at Reichenau-Tamins, six miles from Chur, is immediately beyond the bridge over the Hinter-Rhein, at the point where the two arms of the Rhine meet. Within a couple of miles the Disentis branch reaches the extraordinary cleft that the Vorder-Rhein has hollowed out for itself through a landslip of vast dimensions which threw itself across the valley in prehistoric times. At a few points the railway has been tunnelled, but elsewhere, alongside the river, it pursues a sinuous course between great cliffs, brownish-white in colour, fringed with trees, and at various points weathered into fantastic shapes and showing large and mysterious cavities. The station at Versam is in the middle of this most sinister stretch.

The gorge extends for a full five miles, before the railway comes out into the open and reaches the historic town of Ilanz, dating back to Roman times, when it was known as Glion, "the first town on the Rhine". Beyond Ilanz the branch, travelling up a very pleasant valley, has few features of note until the great Benedictine abbey at Disentis, founded in A.D.614 by St. Sigisbert and now used as a classical and commercial school, comes into view. We have travelled 36½ miles from Chur, and risen 1,835 ft. in the process. Here, at Disentis, the through coaches of the "Glacier Express" and other trains for Andermatt and beyond are handed over to the Furka–Oberalp Railway.

Chur–Arosa

Formerly, as previously mentioned, an independent company, the Arosa Railway, began its course outside the main station at Chur, as it still does. And the beginning of the line is through city streets, where long trains cause no small obstruction at busy road intersections, such as the crossing of the main Chur–Lenzerheide road at the Plessur Quai. To the outskirts of the city the line borders the Plessur River, and then begins rapidly to climb through thickly forested slopes up the Schanfigg valley. Soon, with the help of a 1 in 16 gradient, the trains are at the vast height above the valley floor which is so common in the Alps; the line winds incessantly, over viaducts and through tunnels, and at times on the edge of great precipices, until it comes out more into the open at St. Peter-Molinis.

The viaducts over lateral valleys now become of larger size, until we reach the Frauentobel and Gründjetobel viaducts, the latter a reinforced concrete arch within sight of the greatest of them all, the Langwies Viaduct. At the time when it was brought into use, in 1914, this remarkable structure, with its main span of 315 ft., also in reinforced concrete, was one of the largest of its kind in the world; with its dark background of trees it presents a most handsome spectacle as we approach it in the train. The most dramatic surprise of the journey, however, is when, after running through a barren valley in the heart of high mountains, we round a curve and suddenly come into view, across one of its two lakes, of the charmingly situated town of Arosa, spread out between 5,715 and 6,070 ft. above sea level. To reach it the Chur–Arosa train has climbed 3,790 ft. in the course of its 16-mile journey.

The Bernina Line

We pass now to the Bernina Railway, which, as previously mentioned, has become a part of the Rhaetian system. From St. Moritz this leads past Punt Muragl, lower terminus of the Muottas Muragl funicular, and parallels the branch from Samedan into the joint station at Pontresina. It proceeds through the woods to Surovas, and then up the valley to Morteratsch, at the foot of the glacier of that name. From here the line curves round, climbing steadily at its ruling gradient, which is 1 in 14 (conquered by adhesion, like the slightly steeper Montreux-Oberland Bernois Railway), with a fine view retrospectively of the glacier and its background of high mountains, particularly the Piz Bernina. A barren upper stretch of the valley is now reached, the line passing, within a short distance of each other, the lower stations of the *téléphériques* up to Diavolezza and the Piz Lagalb.

The train continues past the small Lago Nero and the large Lago

Bianco, separated by a wall which in effect divides the watershed of the
Danube from that of the Italian River Po, the waters flowing respectively
to the Black Sea and to the Adriatic.   On the margin of the latter is the
Bernina Hospice (Ospizio Bernina) station, 7,408 ft. altitude and as
previously mentioned the highest point reached by any through railway
in Europe.   Keeping the line clear of snow at such an altitude is a very
considerable task in winter; in a bad winter trains have been kept working
through a depth of over 20 ft. of it.   Beyond the end of the lake a few
twists and turns of the line through snowsheds bring the train to the
well-known station of Alp Grüm.   High up opposite us is the great Palü
Glacier, streaming down from that peak.   Ahead is the immense depth
of the Poschiavo valley, to which the train must now descend.

Alp Grüm station is located on a kind of promontory of rock.   With
the gradient now continuously at 1 in 14, the train describes a wide
circle beyond the station, above a steep mountain edge, and then descends
the west side of the promontory by two loops, next skirting the base and
doing the same in the deep valley on the east side before coming out into
the open in the glacial basin of Cavaglia.   Leaving this by way of the

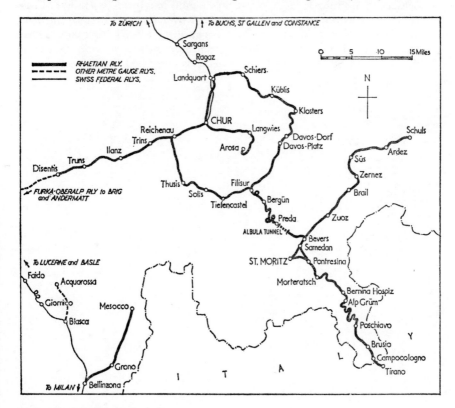

Fig 8. The Rhaetian Railway System.

Cavagliasco gorge, it then makes two immense sweeps on the open mountainside, descending all the time, until it reaches Poschiavo, the chief town in the valley. The direct distance from Alp Grüm to Poschiavo is four miles, but the train travels 10¼ miles, even with a ruling gradient of 1 in 14, in negotiating a difference in level of 3,500 ft. One other piece of spiral planning has been needed, in the Brusio defile—this time entirely in the open—before the Bernina line crosses the Italian frontier and reaches Tirano. From Alpine snows to tropical vegetation we have descended a total of all but 6,000 ft. in a distance of no more than 24 miles from the Bernina Hospice to Tirano.

Bellinzona–Mesocco

Finally, the Rhaetian Railway route mileage of 244 includes a line which is completely isolated from the parent system, but because it is almost entirely located in the Canton of the Grisons passed into the possession of the Rh.B. in 1942. It begins at Bellinzona, capital of the Canton Ticino, parallels the Gotthard main line for two miles to Castione, and then proceeds northwards up the very beautiful valley of the Moësa to Mesocco, climbing some 1,735 ft. in its total length of 19½ miles. From Mesocco runs the main road which went over the San Bernardino Pass, and now passes through the San Bernardino tunnel, to reach Thusis and Chur—one of the important national routes now in course of development by the Swiss Government, as described in Chapter 14.

SEVEN

The Furka-Oberalp Railway

LAST OF ALL the Swiss railways of any length to be completed in Switzerland has been the 60½ miles of the Furka–Oberalp Railway between Brigue, in the Canton of Valais, and Disentis, in the Grisons. From the engineering and operating point of view there could have been few more unpromising fields than this. Separating the valleys of the Rhône and the Rhine there are two high passes, the Furka and the Oberalp, from which the railway takes its name, and between them the deep depression of the Urseren valley, calling for a switchback of immense proportions in the profile of the line. From the operating point of view, while the Rhône Valley is fairly well populated over the 26 miles from Brigue to Oberwald, apart from the towns of Hospental and Andermatt in the Urseren valley the course of the railway beyond Oberwald is largely through completely uninhabited mountain regions, where very little traffic can ever originate.

Then there are the winter conditions to be grappled with at the high altitudes reached by the line. As will be described later, for seven months each winter between October and April inclusive no trains run over the Furka section between Oberwald and Realp, because the traffic offering could never possibly justify the high cost of snow clearance and avalanche protection. In these days of addiction to winter sports, however, the snow brings no small profit to the railway in the Andermatt region, where quite an intensive service is run in winter between Realp, Andermatt and Nätschen for the benefit of skiers, while a normal through service operates over the Oberalp Pass between Andermatt and Disentis.

It was early in the century that a private company obtained a concession for the line, the intention being to link Brigue, on the Simplon main line of the Swiss Federal Railways, with Disentis, terminus of the westernmost branch of the Rhaetian railway system. By 1915 the railway had reached Oberwald in the Rhône valley, and work had begun on the pass sections, but the 1914–18 war had then commenced, and brought the work to a halt because of shortage of labour, materials, and, above all, money. Not until 1923 was work recommenced, under vigorous new auspices, and 1926 saw its completion, with financial help from the communes and cantons concerned, and also from the Swiss Federal Government, in view of the railway's strategic importance. Like the Rhaetian Railway, the Furka-Oberalp was laid throughout to the metre gauge: the final development, carried out by the Visp–Zermatt Railway, was to lay 5½ miles of metre-gauge track parallel to the Simplon main line from Brigue to Visp, linking the two lines together, and providing, with the Rhaetian Railway, the through 168-mile metre-gauge route between Zermatt and St. Moritz which is followed in summer by the "Glacier Express".

We now make our way to where the Furka–Oberalp train is standing in the square outside the main Swiss Federal station at Brigue, headed by a sturdy Bo-Bo 46-ton locomotive, equipped for both adhesion and rack-and-pinion working. The F.O. has some very handsome modern stock, and has created a record in the acquisition of some open second class cars seating 63 passengers but weighing no more than 11.7 tons apiece; weight, of course, is a serious consideration when gradients as steep as 1 in 9 have to be negotiated. Quite possibly among the red F.O. coaches there will be some in the dark green livery of the Rhaetian Railway, for apart from the "Glacier Express" the principal Brigue–Disentis trains have through coaches to and from Chur, capital of the Grisons. Other trains have through coaches between Brigue and Göschenen, and Göschenen and Chur, using for the purpose the Schöllenen line, of which more in a moment.

Leaving Brigue, the Furka–Oberalp train curves sharply round under the Swiss Federal line and crosses the swiftly flowing River Rhône to its right bank. After the stations at Mörel and Betten, from which climb the *téléphériques* to Riederalp and Bettmeralp referred to in Chapter 13, we approach, beyond Grengiols, one of the great steps in the valley floor which are a feature of these glacial regions. Ahead of us is a mountain wall, with our railway carried across its face diagonally at a much higher level, and the mouth of a tunnel below. The tunnel is spiral, and the appearance of the rack in the centre of the track as the train crosses a high viaduct over the Rhône shows how the higher level is quickly reached by a 1 in 11 gradient. In the six miles from Grengiols there are three rack sections in succession, conquering a difference in level of 1,450 ft. in the 8¾ miles between Mörel and Fürgangen.

In the middle of the third stretch the line curves into a lateral valley, past the village of Fiesch, climbing steadily in a wide loop. Whereas up the Rhône valley the mountains that hem it in hide most of the higher peaks, and the glaciers are but rarely visible, up this valley may be seen the proud summit of the Finsteraarhorn, monarch of the Bernese Alps, 14,026 ft. high. Fiesch is the lower terminal of a new *Gondelbahn* line, which as described in Chapter 13 mounts 5,932 ft. in two stages to the summit of the Eggishorn, with its famous view over the great Aletsch glacier. From Fiesch onwards the wide Rhône valley has no very distinctive features; we pass a succession of villages, with their prominent white churches surrounded by clusters of chalets blackened with age, until the train reaches Oberwald, where as previously mentioned the trains from Brigue terminate in winter. Now the mountains close round ahead, and the rack, almost continuous for the next 5½ miles, reappears. Through a rocky gorge the railway and the road climb alongside the foaming river, the railway gaining height by a second spiral tunnel, until we come out again into the open at the village of Gletsch.

High on the mountainside to the left we can see motorcars and motor-

On the way up to Zermatt—a train of the Brigue-Visp-Zermatt Railway in the Matter-Visp gorge, backed by the snowy pyramid of the Weisshorn.   [Cecil J. Allen

Kleine Scheidegg, where passengers for Jungfraujoch change from the Wengernalp to the Jungfrau Railway train. The glittering summit of the Jungfrau is in the background.   [Swiss National Tourist Office

The highest through railway route in Europe—a train of the Rhaetian Railway approaching the Bernina Hospice station, at 7,408ft above sea level.

[Swiss National Tourist Office

The famous Landwasser viaduct on the Rhaetian Railway main line from Chur to St. Moritz.

[Swiss National Tourist Office

Above: Three levels of the Gotthard main line at Wassen with the TEE "Gottardo" seen on the middle level. A view taken from the mouth of the Wattinger spiral tunnel.

[Swiss Federal Railways

Below left: The TEE "Gottardo" crossing the River Reuss by the Intschi bridge, backed by the towering Kleine Windgälle.

[Swiss Federal Railways

Below right: Two of the three levels of the Gotthard main line near Giornico, with the TEE "Gottardo" passing a southbound express.

[Swiss Federal Railways

In fertile southern Switzerland—the Trans-Europe Express "Roland" climbing out of Lugano on its journey from Milan to Bremen, headed by a Swiss Federal class Re 4/4 II electric locomotive.
[Swiss Federal Railways

A typical Swiss station—Wengen, on the Wengernalp Railway. Wengen is one of the few Swiss towns that has no road access, and the railway is thus assured of all-the-year-round traffic.   *[G. Freeman Allen*

Andermatt, road and rail focus of Central Switzerland. In the foreground, postal motorcoaches for the Gotthard, Furka and Susten pass routes: in the background a Furka-Oberalp train climbing to the Oberalp pass.

[Cecil J. Allen

Chair-lift travel—the double chair-lift from Kandersteg up to the Oeschinen Lake. *[Swiss National Tourist Office*

Modern Swiss motorway construction—the concrete viaduct of the motorway which by-passes Vevey and Montreux, seen above the Lake of Geneva.
[Cecil J. Allen

On the 4,870ft descent from the Gornergrat to Zermatt—a
motorcoach on the first stage of the descent from the
10,134ft summit, with the Matterhorn in full view.

[Cecil J. Allen

coaches, descending from or climbing to the skyline by a series of zigzags; this is the Grimsel road, coming down from the 7,103 ft. altitude of the Grimsel Pass to join the road up from Brigue in Gletsch, and then to climb still higher from the 5,773 ft. level of the village to 7,975 ft. on the Furka Pass. Ahead are the windings of the road up to the Furka, and to the left of them the Rhône Glacier, birthplace of the great river. Both roads are described in detail in Chapter 14. Though still a notable spectacle, seen perfectly from the train, the glacier has receded considerably in recent years, and is not quite so imposing as it once was.

Continuing from Gletsch on the 1 in 9, the train climbs a narrow barren valley to the mouth of a tunnel 1¼ miles long, by which the railway engineers saved 900 ft. in altitude as compared with the road. Even so, the 7,088 ft. attained by the railway in the Furka Tunnel is the second highest summit level of any through line in Switzerland; in all, the train has climbed no less than 4,887 ft. since leaving Brigue. We emerge at Muttbach into another lonely and completely uninhabited valley, and with rack once again start to descend, soon passing over a unique bridge.

This spans the gorge of the Steffenbach, subject in the early part of the year to massive avalanches, which in the very first year swept away the permanent bridge erected at this point. The latter was therefore replaced by a bridge designed in most ingenious fashion to be capable of dismantling every autumn and packing away on each side of the gorge until reassembly in the spring; with the tackle used a single day suffices for dismantling, and no more than two days for putting the bridge together again. In view of the suspension of traffic over this section during the winter, the breach in the line causes no difficulty, save to the General Manager and other officers of the Furka–Oberalp Railway. Their head office is at Brigue, and if they require to visit the other end of their system, their only possible route is either via Berne, Lucerne and the Gotthard line to Göschenen, or through the Simplon tunnel to Milan and Chiasso and by the southern stretch of the Gotthard line to Göschenen, where they can join one of their own trains to take them up to Andermatt!

Continuing from the Steffenbach bridge the train passes Realp and Hospental and reaches Andermatt, the centre of the Furka–Oberalp Railway, which has recently opened there a most handsome new station, complete with an attractive restaurant. This mountain-locked town in the Urseren valley is both a railway and a road junction. As to roads, three roads over mountain passes, the Furka, the Oberalp and the Gotthard, converge here, with the road leading down through the sombre Schöllenen gorge to Göschenen. This is paralleled by the Schöllenen Railway, a part of the Furka-Oberalp system, carried through a succession of tunnels and avalanche shelters and at one point crossing the River Reuss where that stream foams over a great waterfall. At Göschenen the Furka–Oberalp trains come to rest outside the Swiss Federal station, which is at the north entrance of the Gotthard tunnel. The Furka–Oberalp line at Andermatt is about 1,100 ft. above the Gotthard tunnel, which passes directly under the village.

From the 7,088 ft. level of the Furka tunnel our train has descended to 4,710 ft. at Andermatt, and has now to tackle the solid wall of mountain that confronts us beyond the station. This is done by a series of wide loops on the open mountainside, with short semi-spiral tunnels at the elbow bends and, of course, rack-and-pinion operation throughout at 1 in 9. Before we finally turn eastwards, Andermatt lies far below us, with the whole wide stretch of the Urseren valley beyond and the notch of the Furka pass in the distance.

Once again the line is in a wild almost uninhabited region, much subject to avalanche visitations in winter, which is the reason for nearly a mile of continuous avalanche shelter over both road and railway where the two border the Oberalp lake. So we reach the summit at Oberalppasshöhe station, at 6,670 ft. above sea level. A little further on is the station at Oberalpsee, where in summer, until recent years, a remarkable marshalling operation was carried out. The westbound "Glacier Express" brings with it from Chur a restaurant car—the only one in Europe to serve meals when on a rack-equipped 1 in 9 gradient!—and after it had provided its passengers with lunch, this car was transferred at Oberalpsee to the eastbound train in order to feed the latter's hungry patrons also. But the transfer is now made at Andermatt.

Of the Furka–Oberalp line all that now remains is the descent through Tschamut and Sedrun to Disentis. Here the through portion of the train is handed over to the Rhaetian Railway for the journey down the valley of the Vorder–Rhein to Chur, the capital of the Grisons—a line described in Chapter 6. So at Disentis we finish a journey which lovers of railways and mountains alike will find it repaying to include in their itinerary. And could a more remarkable switchback than this be found on any railway—2,133; 7,088; 4,710; 6,670 and finally 3,706 ft.—all in one 60-mile stretch of line? It is hardly surprising that even the "Glacier Express" averages no more than 18.3 m.p.h. over this part of its journey.

Such is the importance as a through route of the Furka–Oberalp Railway, from both the tourist and the strategic point of view, that all-the-year round operation is now seen to be a necessity. In June, 1971, therefore the Swiss Government authorised the boring of an 8-mile tunnel between Oberwald in the Rhône valley and Realp in the Reuss valley, which will cut out the rack-and-pinion climbs to the present Furka tunnel, and the parts of the line, including the Steffenbach bridge, which avalanche trouble now makes it necessary to close down in winter. It would not be possible for the railway to finance so costly a project, and the Government is therefore providing a subsidy of about £5,000,000 towards the cost; the work is expected to take some five and a half years to complete. When the tunnel is brought into use, adhesion working will be possible throughout from Andermatt to Oberwald and beyond, and a cut of up to 30 min. in journey times should be possible.

EIGHT

Railways in North-East Switzerland

NOT MANY British tourists find their way into the north-east of Switzerland; the more mountainous parts of the country, with their snowcapped peaks, have a greater appeal. This is a pity, for it would be difficult to find a more pleasant and typically Swiss region than the Canton of Appenzell, which, comprising the two half-cantons of Inner-Rhoden and Ausser-Rhoden, rather curiously is completely enclosed by the larger Canton of St. Gallen. Moreover, the numerous independent railways in the area provide a special and very varied interest for the railway enthusiast.

The region is bounded on the north by the Lake of Constance, with Germany on its north shore and Austria at its eastern end, and on the south by the rocky *massif* of the Säntis group, northern outpost of the Alps proper, visible from all parts of the area. It is intersected by one of the principal main lines of the Swiss Federal Railways, the prolongation of the Geneva–Berne–Zürich line eastwards to the city of St. Gallen, with its 64,000 inhabitants, and on to Rorschach on the Lake of Constance. The same line then continues as described in Chapter 2, past St. Margrethen and Buchs, the junctions with the Austrian Federal Railways, to Sargans and Chur, capital of the Canton of the Grisons. But it is with the interesting minor railways that we are concerned in this chapter.

The Bodensee–Toggenburg Railway

Though owning no more than 35 route miles of line, the Bodensee–Toggenburg is another railway with a considerably greater importance than its mere size might suggest. Bodensee is, of course, the German name for the Lake of Constance, and the Toggenburg is the name of an ancient region, famous for its spinning, weaving and embroidery, of which the centre is the valley of the Thur; it is bounded on the east by the Säntis range, and on the south by the serrated ridge of the Churfirsten, which separates it from the lake known as the Walensee. The B.T. thus starts from Romanshorn on the Bodensee, where its trains use the station of the Swiss Federal line that borders the south shore of the lake; at its western end the B.T. passes through the length of the Toggenburg country. It is single-tracked throughout, but of standard gauge.

The B.T. first climbs through pastoral country to join the Swiss Federal Rorschach main line at St. Fiden, the eastern suburb of St. Gallen, and then passes through the 1,600-yd. Rosenberg tunnel into the main station in that city, 13¾ miles from and 820 ft. higher than Romanshorn. Here its trains use one of the platforms on the north side of the station, and on leaving cross the Swiss Federal line and continue their climb, through the suburb of Bruggen, until they reach the deep gorge through which the River Sitter makes its way down to the Bodensee. Over this the Bodensee–Toggenburg has thrown one of the most remarkable bridges in Switzerland. Short approach masonry viaducts on each side of the gorge lead to the central span, an inverted bowstring truss 394 ft. across, supported on slender masonry piers no less than 320 ft. high. One needs to walk from Bruggen down to the bridge which carried the old main road across the river, and then to make one's way along the stream until one turns a corner and the full height of this astonishing structure suddenly comes into view, for it to make its maximum impression. From immediately underneath, the narrow single line span far above seems almost unbelievable. The four adjacent bridges over the Sitter—the high masonry viaduct carrying the Swiss Federal main line, the old road bridge at the bottom of the gorge, the magnificent reinforced concrete arch of the present main road, and, as the climax, the Bodensee–Toggenburg viaduct, help to explain how the St. Gallen suburb of Bruggen got its name.

Having crossed the Sitter and passed through a few short tunnels we run into Herisau, where the station is shared with the Appenzellerbahn, to be described later. Still climbing, first by a high viaduct over Herisau, which is a town of considerable size, we reach Degersheim, $9\frac{1}{4}$-miles from St. Gallen, and at 2,627 ft. altitude the highest point on the line. From here we are in typical Appenzell country, with rolling hills and deep valleys, largely wooded, passing a succession of viaducts and tunnels until the longest of the latter—the 3,890-yd. Wasserfluh tunnel—leads from the valley of the Necker into the Toggenburg at the picturesque town of Lichtensteig, with its arcaded streets. Here, in a station shaped like a V, the B.T. is joined by a branch of the Swiss Federal which has come up the Thur valley from Wil, an important town on the Zürich–St. Gallen main line. The Bodensee–Toggenburg and Swiss Federal then continue as parallel single tracks for two miles to another junction, Wattwil. From here the Bodensee–Toggenburg runs on up the Thur valley to its terminus at Nesslau, the centre of a very popular winter sport region.

But the more important line out of Wattwil is that of the Swiss Federal, as it forms part of the attractive 94-mile route between Romanshorn, St. Gallen and Lucerne which is operated jointly by the Bodensee–Toggenburg, Swiss Federal and South-Eastern (Südostbahn) Railways. It leads first, on a falling gradient of 1 in 80, through the Ricken tunnel, five miles 608 yds. in length; in the days of steam this single-line bore earned a sinister reputation because an eastbound freight train once stalled in it, with the result that the driver and fireman were asphyxiated by fumes from their locomotive—a casualty impossible of repetition with electric traction. Beyond the tunnel this line joins, at Uznach, the Swiss Federal line from Zürich which borders the north-east shore of the Lake of Zürich to join the main Zürich–Chur line at Ziegelbrücke. The through St. Gallen–Lucerne trains then use the latter in the Zürich direction as far

as Rapperswil, where begins the Südostbahn, to which we come in Part 2
of this chapter.

With the three railways concerned there is considerable interworking
of coaching stock, motive power and train crews.   For the through
services, three daily in each direction between Romanshorn and Lucerne,
and five between Romanshorn or St. Gallen and Arth–Goldau, both the
Bodensee–Toggenburg and the Südostbahn have built some most handsome four-coach trains, each comprising 2,800 h.p. motorcoach, combined
buffet car and second class coach, open second and open composite with
driving compartment; the equipment is equal to the finest in the country,
in the first class especially, and is something of which both companies can
be justly proud.   In addition, there are motorcoaches and independent
locomotives of less power, and a good proportion of modern coaching
stock but little inferior to that of the special trains just mentioned.

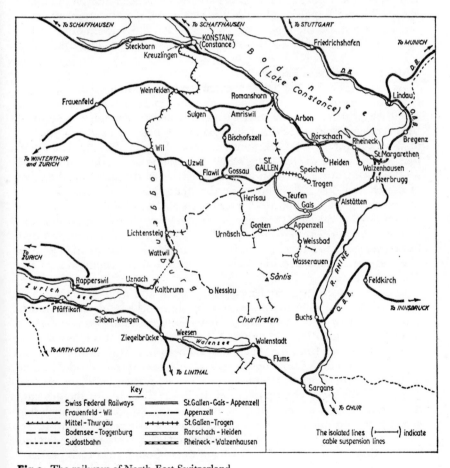

Fig 9. The railways of North-East Switzerland.

Restaurant or buffet facilities are provided on four trains each way daily. Often the coaches of all three participants may be seen in the same train, and just as B.T. locomotives or motorcoaches may work through to Lucerne, so Swiss Federal Re 4/4 locomotives may travel over the B.T. to St. Gallen and Romanshorn. Also, as a matter of convenience, the B.T. line between Wattwil and Nesslau is operated mainly by Swiss Federal trains working through from and to Wil.

By contrast with this modernity the Bodensee–Toggenburg, backed up by a group of railway enthusiasts in Herisau who have formed the first Swiss "Steam Locomotive Club", has kept in working order a 2–6–2 tank locomotive of the Eb 3/5 type which was widely in use by several Swiss railways in former years, the B.T. among them. Since 1966 this loco-motive with a passenger coach converted into a drawing room with easy chairs and sofas, a boudoir and a bar, has been made available to wedding parties over any part of the line between Romanshorn and Nesslau, as a special "Cupid Express". Or the wedding coach may be attached, with-out the steam locomotive, to any ordinary train. A locomotive of this type is now preserved on a pedestal outside the station at Degersheim.

The South-Eastern Railway

As just mentioned, the South-Eastern Railway or Südostbahn begins its course at the junction at Rapperswil, and then makes straight for the Lake of Zürich, which at this south-eastern end is shallow enough to be crossed by an embankment, the Seedamm, 1,024 yards long. At the opposite end of this causeway the S.O.B. joins the Swiss Federal Zürich–Chur main line, and its trains use the latter's Pfäffikon station before diverging to the south-west in order to climb over the high ground separating the lakes of Zürich and Zug. At Samstagern this line is joined by a branch which has come up on a ruling gradient of 1 in 20 from Wädenswil, another station on the Zürich–Chur line; over this branch through trains are run on Sundays between Zürich and the Sattel region, and also to and from Einsiedeln. In their ascents from Pfäffikon and Wädenswil both lines offer extensive views over the Lake of Zürich and the mountains of the Toggenburg area.

Einsiedeln, with its great Benedictine church and monastery, is one of the most famous pilgrimage centres in the world, and brings much profitable traffic to the Südostbahn, both by the ordinary service and by special trains, not a few through from other countries. It is reached by a three-mile branch from the junction at Bieberbrugg, two stations beyond Samstagern. The S.O.B. continues to climb, now through some barren mountain scenery, to Rothenthurm, 1,722 ft. above Pfäffikon and at 3,067 ft. altitude the highest point on the line. Then begins the descent, through pleasanter country, first to Sattel-Aegeri, which to the north has near by the beautiful little Lake of Aegeri and to the south the attractive two-stage chair-lift to Hochstuckli, overlooking the Lake of Lowerz and the town of Schwyz and with the backing of the imposing twin rock peaks of the Mythen. In the train the same panorama also suddenly comes into view as we begin the abrupt 1 in 20 descent to the junction at Arth–Goldau with the Swiss Federal Gotthard line. The last-mentioned is then used through Küssnacht to complete the journey to Lucerne.

Needless to say, the Südostbahn working is now entirely electric, but not a few older readers may remember the familiar sight in the past at Arth–Goldau of the quaint little S.O.B. tank locomotives, with their domeless boilers, which, often in pairs, used to work the S.O.B. trains up their 1 in 20 gradient eastwards.

The Appenzell Railway

One asset of this small metre-gauge railway is that in its brief 21 miles it not only provides the most direct service between Zürich and Appenzell, capital of the half-canton of Inner-Rhoden, but that in addition it gives rail access to all four of the highly important cable suspension lines in this region. Its trains start from the Swiss Federal station at Gossau, 6½ miles short of St. Gallen on the main line from Zürich, and climb to Herisau, diving under the Bodensee–Toggenburg line to share Herisau station with the latter. They then continue climbing until they reach Urnäsch, where those intending to make the *Luftseilbahn* ascent of the Säntis alight and join the motorcoaches for Schwägalp. The line then makes a wide curve round to the east and shortly reaches Jakobsbad, from which runs the *Luftseilbahn* up to the Kronberg, with its record cable span of 7,283 ft. At Gonten the Appenzellerbahn reaches its highest altitude, 2,962 ft., and it then descends to the town of Appenzell.

We are now close to the Säntis *massif*, into the heart of which, turning south once again, the line makes its way. At Weissbad, two miles distant, motorcoaches are waiting to carry passengers to Brülisau, at the foot of the notable *Luftseilbahn* up to the Hoher Kasten; and at the terminus, Wasserauen, 4¾-miles from Appenzell, there is the highly popular suspension line up to the Ebenalp. The railway here terminates in a mountain-locked valley, out of which starts the path used by the most energetic of climbers to conquer the difference in level of 5,350 ft. to the summit of the Säntis. One distinction of the Appenzellerbahn, for so small a railway, is that of possessing a buffet car; this used to make three double journeys daily over the length of the line, but now is kept in reserve for special trips, such as the Sunday "Alpstein Schnellzug".

The St. Gallen–Gais–Appenzell Railway

One end of the station at Appenzell—which has a busy road crossing dividing it into two halves, though it is, of course, laid out for through running—is used by the trains of the Appenzellerbahn, and the other end by another independent company, the St. Gallen–Gais–Appenzell Railway. Both are metre-gauge, but the latter differs from the former in that the S.G.A. trains make parts of their journeys with rack-and-pinion assistance. This line begins its course from a station adjacent to that of the Swiss Federal Railways in St. Gallen. The two lines parallel one another for a short distance from the west end of the station, and the S.G.A. then suddenly turns southwards, and, taking to the rack, goes straight up the steep hillside at a ruling gradient of 1 in 6¼, at the suburb of Reithüsli joining the St. Gallen–Appenzell main road. From here the railway borders the road through Teufen, where the imposing mass of the Säntis comes into view, as far as Gais, 8½ miles, by which point the maximum altitude of 3,077 ft. is attained. The actual amount of climbing is more than the 877 ft. from St. Gallen, for the road has some considerable ups-and-downs, where rack-and-pinion assistance is needed for the trains.

Gais is a junction. The Appenzell trains leave by an extraordinarily sharp curve, turning a complete semi-circle at a radius of not more than three chains, and then, in full view of the Säntis, descending, alongside the road for most of the way and in part with the rack, into the fertile basin in which Appenzell lies. The branch from Gais has a considerably more abrupt descent, after a brief climb to Stoss, which is at 3,130 ft. altitude. With the rack continuously, this is a drop of 1,591 ft. in 2¼ miles into the Rhine valley, of which on the way down a most extensive view is obtained, with the mountains of Liechtenstein beyond. At the foot of the descent the railway reaches the large and straggling town of Altstätten, where it runs in part through the arcaded streets of the old town to terminate at Altstätten station on the Swiss Federal St. Gallen–Chur line. The total length of the S.G.A. is 18 miles.

One or two St. Gallen–Gais–Appenzell trains run through between St. Gallen, Appenzell and Wasserauen, but former through coach workings between St. Gallen, Gais and Altstätten no longer operate. This brings a reminder that for some time past pressure is being put by the Swiss Federal Government on this railway and the Appenzellerbahn to amalgamate or to come under a single management. Since the passing in 1958 of the law described in Chapter 16 which compelled the minor Swiss lines to reduce their fares to the national kilometric standard, and provided Government compensation for any loss of earnings so caused, the Government has had direct interest in the finances of these railways, and strongly favours such groupings as helping to keep down overhead and operating expenses.

The Mittel–Thurgau Railway

As its name implies, this line is located for most of its length through the centre of the Canton of Thurgau. It is of interest as having been almost the last independent company in Switzerland to abandon steam traction, but eventually in 1966, after a period with diesel motorcoaches, electric operation took over. The M.T. trains start from Wil, on the Swiss Federal Zürich–St. Gallen main line, and proceed northwards through fertile country, climbing and then descending to join the Swiss Federal Winterthur–Romanshorn line at Weinfelden. Just beyond this station the M.T. trains diverge again, and climb for the second time over high ground to reveal an extensive view of the western end of the Lake of Constance. Finally the Mittel–Thurgau crosses the Swiss Federal

Schaffhausen main line, and bearing round to the east joins the latter at the junction of Kreuzlingen. From here it is but a short run into the German station at Konstanz, where the M.T. trains terminate. As may be inferred from the use of Swiss Federal tracks, the Mittel–Thurgau is a standard-gauge line.

Other Lines

Of other minor railways in north-east Switzerland, the standard-gauge rack-and-pinion line from Rorschach up to Heiden, and the Rheineck–Walzenhausen line, formerly a rope-worked funicular but now also worked on the rack-and-pinion principle, are mentioned in Chapter 11. The former is unique in that through the main station at Rorschach its trains work over the same metals as such fast trains as the "Bavaria" and the "Rhône–Isar". There is also a small metre-gauge line, only 11 miles long, connecting Wil with Frauenfeld, on the Swiss Federal Zürich–Romanshorn line, though to a separate terminus in the latter town.

The 11-mile Trogen Railway is really an urban electric tramway, starting from the same terminus in St. Gallen as the St. Gallen–Gais–Appenzell trains, running from there through city streets, and after that continuing alongside the main road to Speicher and the historic town of Trogen. The railway or tramway mounts 890 ft. to its maximum altitude of 3,090 ft. at Vögelinsegg, but after that is fairly level. Over much of this short journey a fine view is obtained of the eastern end of Lake Constance, backed by the Austrian mountains behind the town of Bregenz.

F

NINE

The Lucerne-Stans-Engelberg Railway

NEW RAILWAY CONSTRUCTION in Western Europe is so comparatively rare in these days that any such development is bound to attract attention. Such has been the case with the recent transformation of what formerly was the Stansstad–Engelberg Railway. This little line, with its somewhat antiquated equipment, was the sole railway communication with the town of Engelberg, which has become so immensely popular, both as a summer resort and above all as an easily reached centre for winter sports, that improved access became vitally necessary. Rail passengers from Lucerne required to take a lake steamer to Stansstad before boarding the train, and the Lucerne–Engelberg journey by lake and railway took an average of just over two hours. Any improvement of the railway would also be of considerable value to Stans, capital of the Canton of Nidwalden, and to other towns in the vicinity, such as Buochs. There was certainly a good road up to Engelberg, but there were points along it where traffic could get held up, especially the Acheregg swing-bridge over the south-western arm of the lake.

The project was therefore conceived of linking this metre-gauge line with the Swiss Federal Brünig line, of the same gauge, to permit through running from Lucerne to Engelberg. It would be no easy task. The junction with the Brünig line was to be effected at Hergiswil, from which a tunnel 1,925 yards long (over a mile) would have to be bored through the length of the south-eastern buttress of Pilatus known as the Lopperberg, and this would have to be followed by a substantial reinforced concrete bridge at Acheregg over the narrow entrance to the Alpnachersee, the arm of the Lake of Lucerne leading to Alpnachstad. It was decided to combine this bridge with a dual carriageway for the road (which also would require a lengthy stretch of approach tunnelling), replacing the former narrow swing-bridge which carried the latter; and both rail and road bridges would require to give sufficient headroom for the lake motorships to pass underneath.

Then, up the length of the Aa valley some quite expensive realignment of the railway, as well as track reconstruction with heavier material, would be needed to smooth out the sharpest curves and to permit the raising of the speed limit from 40 to 75 km.p.h. (25 to 46 m.p.h.). Near its southern end the railway is lifted 958 ft. into the Engelberg valley basin by a rack-and-pinion section at 1 in 4, nearly a mile long, from Obermatt up to Gherst. Here it was necessary formerly to provide and man a number of small locomotives at Obermatt to push the motorcoaches (which had no rack equipment) and their trailers up, and at so low a speed—3½ m.p.h.—that with the attachment and detachment of these bankers the time taken to negotiate this stretch was 20 minutes.

A number of new and handsome three-coach train-sets therefore were to be acquired, with 1,000 h.p. motorcoaches so equipped as to do away with this assistance, and to make possible an increase in speed up and down the rack section to 12 m.p.h., cutting the time between Obermatt and Gherst from 20 to 7 minutes, in addition to the acceleration along the length of the valley. New and handsome stations were planned, especially those at Stansstad and Stans. Finally, the current system of the former Stansstad–Engelberg Railway, 850 volts 3-phase a.c., was changed to the standard Swiss Federal 15,000 volts a.c. in order to make it possible for the Engelberg trains to run over the Brünig line between Hergiswil and Lucerne.

It would have been impossible for the small railway itself to finance so costly a scheme, and we have here an interesting example of how railway development is assisted nationally, and if necessary subsidised, in a country which has such faith in its railways as Switzerland. Two-thirds of the cost was found by the Swiss Federal Government, half of this contribution being an outright gift, and the other half ranking as preference stock. The remaining one-third was provided by the two cantons affected—Nidwalden and Obwalden—all their contribution ranking as preference stock.

Incidentally, this ensures that these two cantons will be keenly interested in the prosperity of their railway, which, as previously mentioned, provides much quicker and more comfortable communication than before between Lucerne and Stans as well as Engelberg, as also, by postal motorcoach connection from Stans, to Buochs, Beckenried and other towns in the vicinity. Stansstad has assumed a new importance as a lakeside resort, and a considerable fillip has been given to the prosperity of the Aa valley as a whole. As compared with the former two hours or so by steamer and rail, the fastest train from Lucerne to Engelberg now takes 54 minutes, and most of the stopping trains need no more than an hour, or very slightly over. The reward for the railway and its backers has been more than to double the passenger patronage. Up to 3,200 persons in one day have been handled at Engelberg by the new service.

One feature of the Lucerne–Stans–Engelberg Railway, as it is now called, is the number of mountain lines, most of them of the cable suspension type, to which it gives access. At Stans is the lower station of the three-stage funicular to the summit of the Stanserhorn. A little further on, at Dallenwil, up the west side of the valley there are two small *téléphériques*, one, recently rebuilt with new and more capacious cabins, up to Wiesenburg, and the other to Wirzweli. Up the opposite mountainside there is the line to Niederrickenbach, also recently modernised, which finishes with an exciting swing across a deep gorge. From the upper station of the latter a walk of about a mile leads to a new chair-lift, up the ridge known as the Haldigrat, in a fine skiing area.

Then, when the railway reaches Engelberg, from the middle of the town there soars the Brunnibahn—a substantial *Luftseilbahn* carrying its passengers up to a sunny terrace commanding a fine view of the Engelberg valley and of the Titlis, immediately opposite. A short walk from the railway station brings one to the lower terminus of the short Gerschnialp funicular, from the upper station of which there are now two parallel *téléphériques*, the later and higher capacity one with its 6,266 ft. cable span across a deep valley, and both very fully occupied during the winter sport season. They terminate at the Trübsee, from which further cable transport is available, by the older chairlift to the Joch Pass, and by the recently completed *Luftseilbahn* which climbs in two stages to the glaciers at the western end of the Titlis range, known as the Kleintitlis. So there has been plenty of justification for the remarkable transformation of the former railway from Stansstad to Engelberg.

TEN

Other Minor Railways

As HAS BEEN stated earlier, 57 per cent of the railway route mileage of Switzerland is owned by the national system, the Swiss Federal Railways, all the remainder being the property of a large number of independent railways. Of these the most important have been dealt with in the preceding chapters, the largest of them, the Rhaetian Railway, in Chapter 6; the Lötschberg group in Chapter 3; the Bernese Oberland group in Chapter 4; the Montreux–Oberland Bernois in Chapter 5; the Furka–Oberalp in Chapter 7; and the Lucerne–Stans–Engelberg in Chapter 9. The collection of independent railways in North-East Switzerland were described in Chapter 8, while the following chapter, 11, on Mountain Climbing by Rack-and-Pinion, brings in a number of lines grouped round the Rhône valley, such as the Brigue–Visp–Zermatt, the Martigny–Châtelard, the three lines radiating from Aigle, and several others.

There still remain, however, a number which deserve mention. I have described earlier how the Swiss Federal Government, since the passing in 1958 of its law compelling minor lines in general to reduce their fares to something near the national kilometric standard and making up by subsidy any loss of net revenue so caused, favours the grouping as far as possible of the minor lines under centralised management, in order to cut down overhead costs and make possible more economical working. From its inception the Bern–Lötschberg–Simplon Railway has formed such a group, and the various railways in the Bernese Oberland have operated for a number of years past under common management at Interlaken, as described in Chapter 4, although in both cases each individual company concerned retains its financial identity, and possesses its own rolling stock. Some later groupings have now to be described.

One of the most important of these is the Emmental–Burgdorf–Thun group, which is managed from a central office at Burgdorf. It comprises the railway of that name, with a main line from Thun to Solothurn which intersects the Swiss Federal Berne–Lucerne line at Konolfingen and the Berne–Zürich main line at Burgdorf; the Solothurn–Moutier line, which extends the former to Moutier, on the Swiss Federal Delémont–Biel main line; and the Vereinigte Huttwil or Huttwil United Railways, these latter consisting of three railways—the Langenthal–Huttwil (Langenthal also being on the main Berne–Zürich line of the Swiss Federal), Huttwil–Wolhusen (terminating by the junction at Wolhusen with the Swiss Federal Berne–Lucerne line), and the Ramsei–Sumiswald–Huttwil. The entire group controls exactly 100 route miles of line, with 47 stations, possesses

34 locomotives and motorcoaches, 91 coaches and 305 wagons, and so is of some substantial importance. So much so, indeed, that in 1962 the Confederation and the three cantons concerned—Berne, Solothurn and Lucerne—granted the group substantial credits for track and station improvements and new rolling stock.

The E.B.T. system is standard gauge throughout. The most interesting journey that it offers is from Moutier through to Thun, which usually involves a change at Solothurn and in most cases at Burgdorf also, but on Sundays in summer and daily through the winter season boasts one through working from Solothurn to Thun, with reversal at Burgdorf. Three miles after leaving Moutier the S.M.B. plunges into a 2-mile tunnel under the Weissenstein, the 4,220 ft. high summit of the eastern-most ridge of the Jura with the most celebrated of all views of the distant Alpine chain, across the wide plain of the Aar. The line emerges at Oberdorf, lower terminus of the highly popular two-stage chair-lift to the Weissenstein. Commanding much the same view, though from the lower level, it then descends in a very wide arc, joining the main Swiss Federal Biel–Olten line at Solothurn West, and using it into the main Solothurn station. Here the E.B.T. trains from Burgdorf normally use an independent station on the south side, with a subway connection, though it is possible for trains to run through.

At Biberist, 3 miles from Solothurn, the E.B.T. serves a large and important industrial plant, and then continues over flat country, though with the Bernese Alps almost continuously in view in clear weather, to Burgdorf. Here also the E.B.T. trains have their own station, for the trains to and from Thun; those from Solothurn enter the Swiss Federal station at the west end, and if running through to Thun require reversal here across the Swiss Federal tracks. Between Burgdorf and the junction at Hasle-Rüegsau, 5½ miles away, there is an intensive service of over 50 trains each way daily; the line branching north-eastwards at the junction runs to Ramsei and Langnau, on the Swiss Federal Berne–Lucerne line, and it also links at Ramsei with the Huttwil–Sumiswald–Ramsei branch of the Huttwil system.

From Hasle-Rüegsau onwards the E.B.T. main line, which incidentally is equipped throughout with modern Integra colour-light signalling, passes for some distance through a wooded valley, the Bigental, emerging after two short tunnels into the open at Grosshöchstetten, with the Bernese Alps once again in view, now much nearer and more impressive. From here it is a short run down to the junction with the Swiss Federal Berne–Lucerne line at Konolfingen, and then, still on a downgrade, into the joint Swiss Federal-Lötschberg station at Thun. The whole journey from Moutier to Thun is one of a little over 50 miles, and carries the traveller through what one might regard as a cross-section of Switzerland —the wooded Jura, with its deep valleys; the flat central plain of Switzerland, intensively cultivated; the rolling hills of the Emmental region; and finally the Lake of Thun, with the backing of the High Alps.

Another influential minor railway group is the Chemins de fer

Fribourgeois Gruyères–Fribourg–Morat, or G.F.M., which comprises three lines, the metre-gauge Gruyères Railway, running from Montbovon, on the Montreux–Oberland Bernois line, through Gruyères to Bulle, and from Bulle through Châtel-St. Denis to Palézieux, on the Swiss Federal Berne–Lausanne main line; the short standard gauge line from Bulle to Romont, also on the Berne–Lausanne line; and, completely separated from the other two, the Fribourg–Morat–Anet standard gauge line, from Fribourg to the ancient walled town of Murten (or Morat), where it intersects the Swiss Federal Lyss–Payerne–Palézieux line, and Ins, or Anet, on the Berne–Neuchâtel section of the Lötschberg group. All these railways, 61 miles in all, are worked by electric motorcoaches, which include some very modern examples; there are 19 all told, with eight electric tractors, and a considerable number of coaches and wagons.

The G.F.M. is also unique among the private Swiss lines in the possession of 75 road motorcoaches, which provide a busy road service by two routes between Fribourg and Bulle, and others between Fribourg and the spa of Schwarzsee, Schwarzenburg, Schmitten and several other destinations, in a network covering the entire area. In recent years a good deal of money has been spent on modernising the G.F.M. lines and equipment also.

A smaller group which similarly has undergone a transformation with aid from the Confederation and the Cantons of Berne and Solothurn comprises the Solothurn–Niederbipp and Oberaargau–Jura lines. On leaving Solothurn, the S.N.B. crosses the River Aar and proceeds along its north side, whereas the Swiss Federal Biel–Olten main line keeps to the south side until not far short of Niederbipp, where the two use the same station. From the opposite side of this station the O.J.B. then turns south-west to run into a terminal alongside the Langenthal station of the Swiss Federal Berne–Zürich main line. Out of this terminal the remaining section of the O.J.B., reversing direction, parallels the Swiss Federal for a short distance, and then swings over it to reach a terminus at Melchnau. The S.N.B. and O.J.B. have a physical connection at Niederbipp which permits through running, and eleven pairs of trains, composed of new rolling stock, circulate daily in each direction between Solothurn and Langenthal. This is a much smaller group, with no more than 22 route miles of line all told.

In addition to the Swiss Federal and the minor S.M.B., E.B.T. and S.N.B. lines, a fourth independent railway makes its way into Solothurn. It is the Solothurn–Zollikofen–Berne, with a busy 22½-mile line which formerly terminated in the Bahnhof-Platz, outside the main station at Berne, but now, with the help of a new reinforced concrete bridge over the Aar and a fairly lengthy tunnel, possesses a four-platform station under the Hauptbahnhof. This is a metre-gauge line.

The Jura region has three associated railways, the Porrentruy–Bonfol, the Chaux-de-Fonds–Glovelier and the Tavannes–Noirmont, the first of standard gauge and the other two of metre gauge. The 8-mile Bonfol line, detached from the remainder of the group, runs north-eastwards

from Porrentruy, on the Belfort–Biel–Berne main line to the French
frontier at Delle; formerly it continued across the frontier to Pfetterhouse
in Alsace.   The other two constituents, however, provide a continuous
route from Glovelier, also on the Porrentruy–Biel main line, through
Saignelégier to the important watchmaking centre of La Chaux-de-Fonds,
skirting the French frontier for the whole distance.   The Tavannes–
Noirmont section starts from Tavannes, on the Swiss Federal line between
Moutier and Sonceboz, and achieves distinction by climbing to an
altitude of no less than 3,250 ft. at Breuleux-Eglise, between Tramelan
and the junction with the line from Glovelier at Le Noirmont.

With 46 miles of metre-gauge and eight miles of standard gauge track,
all electrified, the Jura Railways form a by no means negligible group,
and thread some highly attractive country through the heart of the Jura
Mountains.   A delightful description in detail of a journey over this
system is found in the chapter entitled "Exploring the Jura" in the book
Railway Holiday in Switzerland, by George Behrend, a keen observer not
only of railways but also of the people, manners and customs of the regions
that he visits.   Various other Swiss railway byways, off the beaten track
of the tourist, find a place in this book.

In the extreme south of Switzerland there is a railway which is unique
in being located half in another country, and because its trains appear to
take two hours longer to travel in one direction than they do in the other.
This is the 24-mile Centovalli Railway, from the Swiss resort of Locarno
on Lake Maggiore to Domodossola, on the Simplon main line in Italy.
The difference in time is because the Italians now elect to adopt
European Oriental time, which is one hour earlier than the Central
European time of most countries in Western Europe—a change made in
1966 which has caused considerable timetable complications in handling
the traffic exchanged with neighbouring states.   Actually the Centovalli
line is jointly owned, by the Swiss Ferroviarie Regionali Ticinesi, which
controls all public transport in the Locarno area, and the Italian Società
Subalpin di Imprese Ferrovie, the initials F.A.R.T. and S.S.I.F., with
the national flags of both countries, appearing on all rolling stock.   In
recent years some handsome new three-car articulated trains have been
introduced carrying names such as *Lemano*, *Varese* and *Vigezzo*, and calling
only at principal stations these make the run in about $1\frac{3}{4}$ hours.

The forerunner of the Centovalli Railway was a line which started
from San Antonio, $1\frac{1}{4}$ miles south of the Swiss Federal terminus in
Locarno, and ran up the Maggia valley to Bignasco. From this in later
years the Centovalli took off westwards at Ponte Brolla to cut through the
mountain country of the "Hundred Valleys"—Centovalli—and so to
cross into Italy and reach Domodossola. The parent, however, is now
defunct, and it is the child that has prospered. Moreover, at the Locarno
end the railway has been extended through the town to terminate
outside the Swiss Federal station. At the Italian end it finishes in a tunnel
under the main station at Domodossola, with direct access to all the
platforms.

The Centovalli throughout has a route of great beauty. From Ponte Brolla it climbs high above the densely wooded Melezza valley, with incessant windings of the metre gauge track and innumerable tunnels long and short—32, by my count—and this is its most spectacular stretch. It is particularly so as the line curves sharply round over a spidery steel arch spanning the Onsernone stream to reach Intragna, a large village perched on a rocky eminence. The Swiss-Italian frontier is at Camedo, with the two customs houses a stone's-throw apart on both sides of a narrow gorge, but the customs formalities are of the simplest kind and are soon completed.

Continuing up the Melezza gorge, the line emerges into a wide mountain valley, and reaches its maximum altitude of 2,677 ft. at Santa Maria Maggiore, the principal town of the region and a favourite Italian holiday resort. Snowclad mountains above the Diveria valley have now come into view ahead, and soon we find ourselves high up on the north side of that valley, looking down on the large town of Domodossola. A series of wide sweeps on the open mountainside lead down over the wide valley to the terminus under the main station. Holidaymakers wishing to connect Swiss resorts on the Lake of Geneva or in the Valais with Locarno, Lugano or other centres in the Italian Lakes region will, with the help of the Simplon tunnel, find the Centovalli Railway a most attractive link.

Finally, there is one minor line in Switzerland which is unique in operating on the narrowest gauge in the country—0.75-metre or 2 ft. 5½ in. It is the Waldenburgbahn, which runs from Liestal on the Basle–Olten main line up to Waldenburg. A reminder of the past which will delight the heart of every railway lover is one of the former little steam locomotives now mounted proudly on a pedestal at Liestal station. It would be impossible to find space to describe many other of the minor lines in this entrancing country, which is certainly a paradise for all those enthusiasts who are in search of railway variety.

ELEVEN

Mountain Climbing by Rack-and-Pinion

IT WAS IN the year 1863 that a Swiss engineer named Niklaus Riggenbach took out a patent for a method of operating trains up gradients far steeper than any which had been thought practicable up to that time; his idea was to carry passengers up to one or more of the famous mountain viewpoints in his country. The plan was to anchor between the running rails of the track a kind of steel ladder, or rack, and for his locomotives, instead of using driving wheels of the ordinary kind, to be equipped with vertical toothed wheels, or pinions, driven by steam cylinders and engaging with the rack, whence the title "rack-and-pinion". This locking of the locomotive to the track, as it was in effect, gave the necessary grip for climbing, and safeguard from running away when descending.

Nothing was done until 1869, when Riggenbach heard that an American, Sylvester Marsh, had built a "cogwheel railway", as he called it, up Mount Washington in New Hampshire. Riggenbach hurried over to the United States to see Marsh's line in successful operation, and on his return formed a company without delay and obtained a concession from the Canton of Lucerne to build a rack-and-pinion railway from Vitznau, on the Lake of Lucerne, up the sloping strata on the west side of the Rigi, with a gradient of 1 in 5, to Kaltbad, at the north-west corner of the Rigi ridge, from there turning north-east to Staffel and Rigi-Kulm.

But at Staffel an unexpected obstacle was encountered. The line here had to pass from the Canton of Lucerne into that of Schwyz, and the Schwyzers refused to grant the necessary permission. So the railway, opened in 1871, stopped short at Staffel until the following year, when the Federal Government assumed the authority to grant all concessions for new mountain railways. The citizens of Arth, on the Schwyz side, then decided to build their own railway up the Rigi, but first completed the section from Staffel to the summit, which they turned over to the Vitznau–Rigi Company at a rental that is still paid for its use. Two years later the Arth–Rigi Railway, climbing the near-vertical face of the Kräbelwand, continued up a deep cleft of the mountain past Klösterli to join the rival line at Staffel. From there the Arth-Rigi Company built its own independent line to Rigi-Kulm, which explains why this last mile of the ascent is double-tracked today.

Riggenbach's first locomotive, a primitive machine with vertical boiler and sharply-inclined chassis—to keep the boiler in a vertical position on the 1 in 5 gradient—may still be seen in the Swiss Transport Museum at Lucerne. It pushed a light passenger coach up the 4,301 ft.

difference in level between the lower and upper terminals in a journey taking 80 minutes. Today capacious electric motorcoaches cover the distance of some 4½ miles in 35 minutes, and the electric motorcoaches of the Arth–Rigi line reach the summit from the junction at Arth-Goldau in exactly the same time. The Vitznau–Rigi Railway offers the finer views of the two, as the central section of the Lake of Lucerne is in full view all the way up to Kaltbad, with the Bürgenstock opposite, and eventually the distant Bernese Alps; then, as the line turns north-east towards the summit, a vast prospect opens up of Pilatus, the town of Lucerne and all the country to the north.

In earlier years the Vitznau–Rigi line had a branch running along the whole length of the Rigi ridge to one or two big hotels at Rigi-Scheidegg, at its western end. This was level enough to be worked by ordinary steam locomotives without any rack assistance. Rather regrettably the hotels have gone and the line is no longer in use, but the abandoned track formation, with a viaduct and a tunnel, now provides a very fine high level walk, which can be ended by swinging down in a small cable car from Scheidegg to Kräbel, a station on the Arth–Rigi Railway, within 6 minutes of Arth-Goldau. But what a magnificent opportunity that abandoned track would offer to some railway enthusiast to start up a miniature line like our own Romney, Hythe & Dymchurch, scale model locomotives and all!

Riggenbach was followed by another engineer, Locher, who decided on the far more difficult task of building a railway to the summit of Pilatus, on the opposite side of the lake, a little over 1,000 ft. higher. He envisaged a route from Alpnachstad, on the south-western arm of the lake, to a summit terminus just below the peak known as the Esel, climbing 5,344 ft. in a distance of 2⅝ miles. This ascent thus required an average gradient of about 1 in 2½, and a ruling or steepest gradient of 48 per cent., or almost exactly 1 in 2. At such an inclination operation with the Riggenbach rack would not have been safe, and Locher therefore patented a design of his own which is unique. His rack consists of flat bars of steel with teeth machined in both outer edges; instead of vertical pinion wheels his locomotives were equipped with horizontal pinions, gripping the rack from both sides.

With the modern electric motorcoaches this method of operation continues unchanged; each coach has two pairs of pinions, which help to provide protection against derailment by centring the coach on the track; they are supplemented by flanges on the *outside* of the ordinary carrying wheels. It would also be unsafe to attempt to transfer motor-coaches from one track to another by ordinary switches and crossings; electric traversers are used for this purpose at the upper and lower terminals, and also at the intermediate crossing-loop at Aemsigenalp. Electricity, of course, has made all the difference to the working of the Pilatus Railway; at first a journey of 85 min. with steam and never less than 70 min., it is now no more than a 30 min. climb from Alpnachstad.

The most exciting part of this journey is near the summit, as the line winds its way round the limestone crags of the Esel, on the face of a sheer precipice. The Pilatus Railway authorities have made extensive use of some ingeniously doctored photographs, showing the distant summits of the Bernese Alps as though they were visible from this breath-taking stretch of line. But this is impossible, for the solid bulk of the Matthorn ridge is in the way; it is not until one has climbed the last 300 ft. to the summit of the Esel, or has taken the attractive path to the Tomlishorn, 6,995 ft., the highest of the Pilatus peaks, that the full extent of a most glorious view, from the Säntis, 65 miles away to the east, to the ice-mantled peaks of the Bernese Oberland, between 30 and 35 miles to the south-west, is fully revealed. From Pilatus back to Lucerne the journey can be varied by taking the daring *Luftseilbahn* from the summit down to Fräkmüntegg, and the *Gondelbahn* from there down to Kriens, in the Lucerne suburbs, by the lines described in Chapter 13.

One Swiss rack-and-pinion railway of considerable age is unique in being still steam-operated. This is the line from Brienz, on the lake of that name in the Bernese Oberland, to the summit of the Brienzer Rothorn, the highest peak of the Brienzer Grat, a serrated ridge that borders the lake on its north side. The first purely mountain railway in the Bernese Oberland, opened in 1892, this little railway has passed through many vicissitudes; indeed, it was out of action from 1915 to 1931 because of the effects of the First World War. Several years ago there was a proposal to replace it by a cable suspension line, but there was such an outcry in Switzerland from parents whose children might never again be able to see steam locomotives in action if such a substitution were to take place that the project was abandoned.

So the sturdy little Brienzer Rothorn locomotives still noisily push their two carloads of passengers up through 5,515 ft. of altitude—the greatest difference in level surmounted by any individual Swiss rack-and-pinion line—and up gradients as steep as 1 in 4, to the Brienzer Rothorn terminus, 4¾ miles from Brienz. The line first climbs through the woods high above the lake, and then through a mountain buttress in the middle of which great openings like windows in the rock give a spectacular view downwards.

Then we climb into a lonely mountain valley where at the midway station, Planalp, the thirsty locomotive takes water. In this vicinity there was a structure rather like a Bailey bridge, dismantled in winter because of avalanche risks, but since abandoned with the help of a track deviation. The line, climbing steadily, then makes a wide circuit round the contours of a barren alp until a short tunnel leads to the upper terminal, 7,378 ft. above the sea, with the tourist left to climb on foot the final 337 ft. to the summit of the peak. For the energetic two fine walks may be made from here, one to the railway station of Brünig-Hasliberg, on the Swiss Federal Interlaken–Lucerne line, and the other to Schönbüel, the upper terminus of a suspension line up from Lungern, the next station beyond Brünig-Hasliberg in the Lucerne direction. Also a new *Luftseilbahn*, opened in 1971, now makes it possible to descend in a cabin holding 80 for some

3,412 ft. to Sörenberg, on the north side of the mountain, but the lower terminal is accessible only by road.

The other rack-and-pinion railways in the Bernese Oberland area have Chapter 4 to themselves, including the ascent to Jungfraujoch, at the record altitude of 11,333 ft. So we come now to the chief rival of the Jungfrau line, which is found in the Canton of Valais, close to the Swiss-Italian frontier; it is the railway climbing from Zermatt to the Gornergrat, opened in 1898. Though not reaching so great an altitude by 1,200 ft. as the Jungfraujoch, the Gornergrat line has the major advantage, apart from four very short tunnels, of being out in the open the whole way up from the 5,262 ft. altitude of Zermatt to the 10,134 ft. of its upper terminus, during the whole 5¾ miles of its ascent offering incomparable views, particularly of the mighty Matterhorn.

The rocky eminence of the Gornergrat commands one of the most famous glacial panoramas in Europe, with the great peaks of Monte Rosa, the Lyskamm and the Breithorn immediately opposite, their glaciers draining into the Gorner Glacier far below; westwards the Matterhorn and other peaks round to the dazzling cone of the Weisshorn; to the north the deep cleft of the Zermatt valley; and to the north-east the twin Mischabel peaks, Dom and Täschhorn. In earlier years the Gornergrat Railway operated only in summer, as a scenic attraction; but in recent years the increasing popularity of winter sports has made winter working even more profitable. This in its turn has compelled the building of more than a mile of continuous snowshed between Riffelalp and Riffelberg, and a glass-sided waiting room at the Zermatt terminus in which a maximum of 500 passengers can be accommodated for orderly mar-shalling on to the capacious electric cars.

Access to Zermatt is by one of the various Swiss lines which, like the Berner Oberland described in Chapter 4, use the rack on their steeper sections only. This is the Visp–Zermatt, or, as it has become since the 5½-mile extension to Brigue was brought into use to link with the Furka–Oberalp Railway (Chapter 7), the Brigue–Visp–Zermatt Railway. This prosperous line, opened in 1891 and until 1929 steam-operated, has four rack sections, the steepest of them at 1 in 8 past Stalden, where the Saaser–Visp and Matter–Visp valleys, from Saas-Fee and Zermatt respectively, unite. For most of its course, up past St. Niklaus, the Visp–Zermatt line is in a narrow valley hemmed in by high mountains, with no more than an occasional glimpse of glaciers and the white cone of the Weisshorn, but from Randa onwards the Breithorn comes into view at the head of the valley. Not until the last half-mile into the Zermatt terminus, however, is the great pyramid of the Matterhorn suddenly revealed.

In recent years the Visp–Zermatt line has undergone a high degree of modernisation. The former Bo–Bo electric locomotives have been largely displaced by powerful motorcoaches, each of 1,600 h.p., and comprising twin cars seating 12 first and 100 second class passengers. Even up gradients as steep as 1 in 8 and 1 in 9, these motive power units are capable of hauling five or six bogie coaches of lightweight stock, in trains providing up to 370 passenger seats. The "Glacier Express", with its through coaches from St. Moritz, now covers the 21¾ miles from Visp to Zermatt, conquering a difference in level of 3,130 ft., in 67 minutes; after the line was first electrified, in 1929–1930, the time taken was over 1½ hours, and in its earliest days, with steam traction, as much as 2½ hours was needed. Recently the whole length of the line has been equipped with colour-light signals, controlled from a panel at Brigue.

Further down the Rhône Valley we come to Martigny, where the valley, until then almost straight, suddenly decides to turn through a complete right-angle towards the Lake of Geneva. Here is the terminus of the Martigny–Châtelard Railway, to which title the management likes to add the word Chamonix, for this line provides direct access, with through coaches, to that famous French resort. The Martigny–Châtelard trains start on the level, alongside the Simplon main line, as far as Vernayaz, and then suddenly shoot upwards at 1 in 5, partly through tunnels, until high above the Rhône; next they turn inland into the gorge of the Trient, above which, on a sunny terrace, lies a string of attractive villages—Salvan, Les Marécottes, Le Trétien and Finhaut.

At one point, just short of Finhaut, the railway winds its way round a sheer precipice, 1,400 ft. above the Trient torrent. The line then descends to the valley floor at Châtelard, the last Swiss station, and passing across the frontier reaches the French station of Vallorcine. Here the through coach is transferred to a metre-gauge train of the French National Railways, to pass through the mile-long tunnel under the Col des Montets into the magnificent scenic spectacle offered by the Chamonix Valley, the long line of the Aiguilles, to the left, leading the eye up to the snowy dome of the monarch of the Alps, Mont Blanc, with the glittering Glacier des Bossons cutting diagonally across the wooded slopes below it—a notable spectacle indeed.

Also out of Martigny there runs a standard-gauge railway which, though not rack-operated, may conveniently be mentioned here. It is the 12-mile Martigny–Orsières, which throws off at Sembrancher a short branch to Le Châble, in the Val des Bagnes, the station for Verbier. Following the custom of many railways which name their motive power after the towns and districts they serve, with pictorial representations on their insignia, the M.O. now has a motorcoach named *Bagnes*, which has the unique distinction of carrying on its sides a picture of two nude ladies relaxing in a bath-tub! The M.O. also operates a thriving service of motorcoaches, from Orsières up to Champex. and also over the Grand St. Bernard to the Italian town of Aosta.

Continuing westwards from Martigny we come next to Bex, lower terminus of the line which gives access to the well-known resort, both winter and summer, of Villars, or Villars-sur-Ollon. Climbing at 1 in 5 begins after the railway has passed along the main street through Bex to the suburb of Bévieux; at Gryon the rack comes to an end, and a tunnel through a mountain ridge transfers the train from the valley of Les Plans on to the open mountainside above the Rhône Valley. A viaduct 165 ft.

high across the Gryonne, carrying both railway and road, leads into Villars. The total climb has been 2,762 ft. It is possible to go considerably higher, by a rack-operated branch of the Bex–Villars–Bretaye line from Villars to the 5,932 altitude of the Col de Bretaye.

Five miles west of Bex we reach the old town of Aigle, where three independent railways, two of them of the rack-and-adhesion type, converge in the square outside the Swiss Federal station. One is the quite lengthy Aigle–Ollon–Monthey–Champéry line or A.O.M.C., under which we have passed midway between Bex and Aigle. As far as the town of Monthey the line for most of the distance borders the public road; then, after backing to a junction outside the town, the train starts up the first of three rack sections, climbing above the deep Val d'Illiez, on the opposite side of which is the massive bulk of the Dents du Midi.

Also starting out of the station square at Aigle, and proceeding in the opposite direction, is the line up to the famous curative resort of Leysin, a continuous rack-and-pinion ascent of 3,252 ft. (with a steepest inclination of 1 in 4½, once the town of Aigle has been cleared), which terminates with a tunnel leading into the Grand Hotel. The brown-and-cream motorcoaches of the Aigle–Leysin line are precisely the same colour as those of the former Great Western Railway in our own country.

In addition to the dark green motorcoaches and trailers of the A.O.M.C. already described, the third railway whose motorcoaches and trailers, grey and white in colour, are ranged in Aigle station square are those of the Aigle–Sépey–Diablerets line, which though not rack-and-pinion, may conveniently be mentioned here. With the help of a ruling gradient of 1 in 16½, its train climbs rapidly out of Aigle up the opposite side of the Ormont Valley from Leysin, at one point at a great height on a precipitous slope above the Grande Eau stream. This has to be crossed for the trains to reach Le Sépey, which they do over a massive and very handsome reinforced concrete bridge; from Le Sépey they reverse back over the bridge and continue up the Grande Eau valley to reach the town of Les Diablerets, facing the impressive face of the Diablerets mountain.

The Simplon main line now reaches the eastern end of the Lake of Geneva, and starting from Montreux we find another rack-and-pinion railway, heavily patronised both in summer for its scenic interest, in winter by skiers, and all the year round by the communities that it serves. This is the 6½-mile line up to the Rochers-de-Naye, mounting with a ruling gradient of 1 in 4½ from the 1,296 ft. altitude of the Swiss Federal station in Montreux up to the 6,460 ft. of the summit terminus. The ascent is first up wooded slopes to Glion, a populous suburb of Montreux; then from one side to the other of a mountain buttress up to Caux; and finally, high above the Chauderon Gorge, making direct towards the great rock pillar known as the Dent de Jaman. Burrowing under this, the railway comes out into a mountain-locked alp, passing through several snowsheds and finally tunnelling under the summit ridge to curve in an almost complete circle into the upper terminus. On a clear day the summit itself, 275 ft. higher, commands much of the Lake of Geneva as well as the mountains of the Bernese Oberland, the Valais and the Savoy.

To reach another small rack-and-pinion railway in this area it is necessary to take a train of the Veveysans electric network from the Swiss Federal station at Vevey up to Blonay, from which the same company's rack-and-pinion line climbs 2,388 ft. to the summit of a mountain known as Les Pléiades, also commanding a fine view over the Lake of Geneva.

Still further west, at Lausanne, is a railway which is of interest in that for many years it was a rope-worked funicular, but has now been converted to rack-and-pinion operation. Connecting Lausanne's port of Ouchy with the centre if the city, even as a funicular this line was unique in running four-car trains; the practice continues with rack operation, which has considerably speeded up the service. Running at 7½-min. intervals the trains complete the one-mile journey in six minutes, including two intermediate stops. Another railway formerly rope-operated and now worked by rack-and-pinion, but with single motorcoaches, is in the north-east of Switzerland, a ¾-mile line from Rheineck in the Upper Rhine Valley to Walzenhausen. Not far away is yet another rack-and-pinion line, from Rorschach up to Heiden, one of the only three rack-and-pinion lines laid on the standard gauge of 4 ft. 8½ in.

I have left almost to the end the description of one well-known rack-and-pinion railway which has a claim of an entirely different kind to be unique. This is in the matter of motive power, which is no longer steam, nor is it electric; diesel locomotives and motorcoaches are used for the climbing. The line concerned is on the Lake of Lugano, and in the course of a 5½-mile journey climbs 4,327 ft. from Capolago to the summit of Monte Generoso. For much of the way up the view is tantalisingly hidden by the forest through which the line makes its way, but at last the train comes out into the open at Bellavista, and from there an exciting stretch round a great precipice leads finally to the colony just below the summit at Generoso Vetta. On a clear day it is possible to see southwards across the plain of Lombardy to Milan and its cathedral; and away to the west, Monte Rosa and it neighbouring peaks present a superb spectacle, as also does the long line of the Alps across the northern horizon, as far east as the Ortler group in the south Tyrol.

Of railways which use rack-and-pinion traction only on their steeper sections I have already mentioned the Berner Oberland, the Visp–Zermatt, the Martigny–Châtelard, and the lines which radiate from Aigle. The Furka–Oberalp Railway has a chapter (7) to itself, and descriptions are given elsewhere of the Brünig line of the Swiss Federal, the Lucerne–Engelberg, and certain small lines in the Canton of Appenzell. Some of these lines employ a fourth variation of the rack itself, that devised by Roman Abt. The Abt rack consists of two parallel rows of vertical teeth, staggered, with a corresponding double pinion under the locomotives or coaches for engagement. This is regarded as a safer type of rack than the Riggenbach for gradients as steep as 1 in 4.

Climbing through a wilderness of rock the 5,344ft from
Alpnachstad to the summit of Pilatus—a Rigi motorcoach
on the 1 in 2 ascent. *[Pilatus Railway*

Pilatus summit station, at 6,678ft altitude. The railway
terminus is to the right of the circular cafeteria and hotel
building, and to the left of it is the terminus of the cable
suspension line down to Fräkmüntegg. *[Martin Mengelt*

Left: Climbing from Zermatt to the Gornergrat — the cantilever bridge of the Gornergrat Railway across the Findelen gorge.

Right: Nearing the end of the 4,872ft climb from Zermatt— a motorcoach of the Gornergrat Railway. Up the rocky ridge in the background, just below the glacier, there now runs the cableway to Trockener Steg.

Left: In midwinter — a Gornergrat Railway train mounts the 1 in 5 gradient with rack-and-pinion, with the Matterhorn as an impressive background.

Right: Another view near the summit of the Gornergrat Railway, backed by the snow-clad summit of the Breithorn. To the spiky peak on the extreme right, the Little Matterhorn, a cableway is now planned from Trockener Steg.
[*All, Swiss National Tourist Office*

Climbing from Montreux to the Rochers-de-Naye, an ascent of 5,164ft. The conical peak behind the motor-coach is the Dent de Jaman.

The summit station of the Rochers-de-Naye line, at 6,460ft altitude, looking north. Note the snowsheds, to permit operation throughout the winter.
[Both, Montreux-Oberland Bernois Railway

Left: A striking impression of a motorcoach of the Martigny - Châtelard Railway mounting the 1 in 5 gradient from Vernayaz, in the Rhône valley.

Above: Approaching the point, near Finhaut, where the Martigny - Châtelard train rounds a sheer precipice above the Trient gorge.

Left: The abysmal Trient gorge, as seen from the railway at Finhaut, with the Glacier du Trient in the distance.

[*All, Martigny-Châtelard Railway*

The passing loop on the Chanterella-Corviglia funicular railway. St. Moritz is seen below the cars, and Pontresina in the distance beyond the woods. *[Tourist Office of St. Moritz*

Climbing a gradient of 1 in 1½ on the two-stage funicular from Mülenen to the summit of the Niesen, an ascent of 5,390ft. Above the car is seen the Kander valley.
[Niesen Railway

On the edge of a precipice—the terminus of the Monte Generoso Railway, above the Lake of Lugano, at 5,223ft altitude.

One of Switzerland's steepest funicular railways, the Stoos terminus of the line from Schlattli, near Schwyz, finishing at 1 in 1¼. In the background are the twin peaks of the Mythen.

The Weissfluhjoch terminus of Switzerland's second longest funicular railway, the 4,490yd Parsennbahn from Davos, at 8,737ft altitude.

Nearing the 8,031ft summit of the funicular from Punt Muragl to Muottas Muragl, in the Engadine, backed by the great peaks of the Bernina group.
[Both, Grisons Tourist Office

A single chair-lift familiar to holidaymakers in the Engelberg area; it climbs from the Trüb lake, or Trübsee, to the Joch pass. The Trübsee hotel is seen at the bottom right of the view.   [Central Switzerland Tourist Office

A striking view of the four-stage double chair-lift from Grindelwald to First, with the Fiescherhorn in the background.   [Swiss National Tourist Office

Above: Gondelbahn travel. Two of the curious little two-seater cabins of Switzerland's longest *Gondelbahn*, the 5,529yds from Zweisimmen to the Rinderberg. The mountain in the distance is the Wildstrubel.

Below: The first *Gondelbahn* in Switzerland was that from Crans, near Montana, to Bellalui, with cabins of the more usual four-seater type. Across the Rhône valley are the mountains of the Valais.

Right: Another *Gondelbahn* with cabins seating two passengers only, that from Grächen, a modern winter sport centre above the Zermatt valley, to Hannigalp.

[*Swiss National Tourist Office*

The *Luftseilbahn* from Surlej (Silvaplana, near St. Moritz) up to Piz Corvatsch, 10,843ft altitude. To the right is the Lake of Sils, bordered by the Maloja pass road.

On the opposite side of the same valley is the line from Corviglia up to Piz Nair, 9,941ft. The peaks in the background are Piz Palü (left), Piz Bernina (below cabin) and the pyramid of Piz Roseg (right).

[Both, Tourist Office of St. Moritz

The two parallel suspension lines from Gerschnialp, above
Engelberg, to Trübsee. The main cables of the earlier, on
the left, were carried on six pylons; the later, on the right,
has two only, with a cable span of 6,266ft between them.
[Central Switzerland Tourist Office

Climbing the face of a sheer precipice—the *Luftseilbahn*
from Brülisau to the Hoher Kasten, in North-East Switzerland. *[North-East Switzerland Tourist Office*

The daring *Luftseilbahn* from Leukerbad up to the crest of the cliffs fringing the Gemmi pass — a clear span to the pylon just seen above the precipice to the extreme left.

[Bern-Lötschberg-Simplon

A recently - opened *Luft - seilbahn* above the Engelberg valley, in two stages from Trübsee to the Kleintitlis, finishing at 10,030ft altitude.

[Central Switzerland Tourist Office

Also among the newest *Luft-seilbahn* enterprises is the four-stage line from Stechelberg in the Lauterbrunnen valley to the summit of the Schilthorn, at 9,734ft altitude; this is the first stage, to Gimmelwald, notable for the use of cabins accommodating 100 persons apiece.

The end of the third stage, from Mürren, is at Birg, perched on the summit of the rock in the centre. The final stage completes a journey of $4\frac{1}{4}$ miles, with a total lift of 6,866ft — easily a Swiss record for a line of this type. [Both, *Schilthorn Bahn AG Mürren*

One of a string of small suspension lines serving high-laying villages on the north side of the Rhône valley—the *Luftseilbahn* from Mörel to Riederalp.

[Bern-Lötschberg-Simplon

The highest *Luftseilbahn* in Switzerland, from the Gornergrat to the Stockhorn, above Zermatt. In the centre background is Hohtälli, where a change is necessary, and the last pylon on the extreme right adjoins the Stockhorn terminus, at 11,178ft altitude.

TWELVE

Mountain Climbing by Funicular

EARLY IN the history of Swiss mountain railways there came a demand in certain localities for lines which, by the use of gradients steeper than any which could be negotiated safely with rack-and-pinion, could make more direct ascents. Such was the genesis of the funicular or cable-operated railway, of which there are 50 examples in all in Switzerland, 37 of them ranging in length from 577 to 4,601 yds. The longer of these have two, and in one case, three independent sections, with change of car intermediately.

The principle, familiar in Great Britain in the short lines up the cliffs at some of our seaside resorts, is that of two cars, connected by a common haulage cable passing round a winding wheel at the upper terminus, which are thus balanced against one another, one moving upwards as the other moves downwards. By this system of balance, the amount of power needed to keep the cars in motion is kept to a minimum. A single track only is required, apart from the central loop at which the cars pass one another. The wheels on one side of each car are double-flanged, so gripping the rail-head, while the wheels on the other side have no flanges; one car has its double-flanged wheels on the right-hand side, and the other on its left, so that without any moveable switches at the two ends of the passing loop, each car, whether travelling up or down, automatically takes its own side of the loop. The haulage cable rides on grooved pulleys in the centre of the track, which are arranged at sufficiently close intervals to permit limited curvature on a funicular railway without any risk of the cables jumping out of the grooves in an attempt to straighten themselves.

Electric power is the normal method of operation, but there are three examples, notably the line from Territet up to Glion, that use the weight of water in a tank under the car to provide the necessary motion; time must be allowed to fill each tank at the upper station and to empty it at the lower on each trip. The funicular from Cossonay Station, on the Lausanne–Neuchâtel line, to Cossonay, uses the same water-balance principle. The third water-balance funicular is the short 190-yd. line from Lucerne up to the Gütsch, the operation of which is now entirely automatic; at predetermined intervals the car doors close, the cars move up and down, and the doors reopen, the only member of the staff on normal operational duty being the one who collects the fares at the lower station turnstiles. The 1,343-yd. line from Cossonay station up to Cossonay now has similar automatic operation.

The longest single section of any Swiss funicular is the lower stage of the

97

line running from Sierre up to the popular resort of Montana; this is 2,597 yds. in length, or almost exactly 1½ miles. A second section of 2,004 yds., from St. Maurice-de-Laques to Montana, brings the total length to 4,601 yds. in the course of which there is an ascent of 3,054 ft. The journey, with five intermediate stops, takes just over half-an-hour. Next comes the Parsenn line, from Davos up the Weissfluhjoch, with successive sections 2,034 and 2,393 yds. long respectively, making up a total length of 4,427 yds.

The Parsenn line has several considerable distinctions. With its lower terminal at 5,106 ft. above the sea, the ascent of 3,631 ft. makes the Weissfluhjoch terminal, at 8,737 ft., easily the highest reached by any funicular railway in Switzerland. The line also was the first (other than the far shorter and less steep Ouchy–Lausanne line) to use cars in pairs, coupled together, accommodating no fewer than 140 passengers per pair on one section and 168 on the other. Still more remarkable, perhaps, is that in these days of dwindling railway fortunes the Parsennbahn, mainly because of its heavy patronage in the winter sports season, is able to pay a dividend of no less than 12 per cent. per annum. Mainly in the interest of skiers, all the three lines mentioned have been extended still further upwards in later years by means of cable suspension transport.

The only three-section Swiss funicular is one of considerably earlier vintage, that up the Stanserhorn, a pointed peak on the Lake of Lucerne, commanding what by not a few is regarded as an even better view than that from its more distinguished neighbour, Pilatus. The total length of the Stanserhorn line is 4,280 yds., but it is steeper than either of the three lines already mentioned, because it climbs 4,593 ft. in all. But the two-section Niesenbahn in the Bernese Oberland, mounting to another peak that commands a magnificent view, of the entire Bernese Alps as well as of the Lake of Thun far below, conquers a difference in level of no less than 5,390 ft. in a journey of 3,842 yds. On the uppermost of the three sections of the Stanserhornbahn, just as the line passes through the base of the summit hotel into the terminus, the maximum inclination of 63 per cent.— all but 1 in 1½—is attained. No part of the Niesen line, however, is steeper than 55 per cent. In steepness both these railways are handsomely beaten by the line from Schlattli, near Schwyz in Central Switzerland, up to Stoos, whose ascent of 2,306 ft. in a length of 1,488 yds. requires an average gradient of 61 per cent. and a maximum steepness of 78 per cent.

Yet even this last cannot claim the record. For the record two lines closely compete; both were built to carry materials up to the site of great dams which were built in the mountains to provide storage lakes for the hydro-electric power-stations of the Swiss Federal Railways, by which they are owned, and both parallel the pipe-lines. One of them, climbing from Châtelard–Giétroz, a station on the Martigny–Châtelard Railway, up to the Barberine Dam, has a maximum gradient of 87 per cent., though its ascent of 2,300 ft. in 1,432 yds. demands an average inclination of no more than 63 per cent. Even steeper is the funicular which can be seen from the Gotthard main line when passing Ambri-Piotta, the second station after emergence from the south end of the

Gotthard tunnel. It is the Ritom line, which in the 1,485 yds. from Piotta to Piora mounts 2,566 ft., with an average grade of 71 per cent. and a maximum of 89 per cent.—very nearly 45 deg. This line is unusual in that it has a single car only, raised and lowered from the upper station.

Another funicular that is unique in its design is the one which ascends from Paradiso, a suburb of Lugano, to the summit of Monte San Salvatore, a conical peak which offers one of the finest viewpoints round the Lake of Lugano. This has its two cars, but each is confined to one-half only of the line. The cars are connected in the ordinary way by a common haulage cable, but this simultaneously pulls up the lower car and lowers the upper car until they meet at the middle station, where the passengers cross a central platform from one car to the other.

There are one or two funiculars other than the Parsennbahn at Davos which have equipped themselves with cars, single or double, of high capacity. Some serve what, in effect, are the high-lying suburbs of large cities, such as those from Biel up to Macolin and Evilard, in the Jura region, carrying up to 140 and 100 sitting or standing passengers respectively. The capital city of Berne also has a remarkable funicular which leads up to the summit of the Gurten, a ridge on the south side of the city commanding a magnificent view, of the Bernese Alps particularly, and a favourite playground for the citizens. This has recently been completely rebuilt, and now is the most up-to-date in the country. Some 1,143 yds. in length, it can be operated at either of two speeds, 3.50 or 5.70 metres per second; the latter is used when the traffic is heavy, and reduces the journey time from five to three-and-half minutes. At the latter speed, the highest of any funicular railway in Europe, up to 1,400 passengers an hour can be moved up or down in cars carrying up to 100 passengers apiece.

In the Engadine, St. Moritz has its two-section funicular up to Chanterella and Corviglia, with a capacity of 140 passengers in each of its new cars, which run up to an altitude of 8,156 ft. A short distance away is the older line from Punt Muragl up to Muottas Muragl, with its 2,390 yds. the second longest single-section Swiss funicular. From its upper station, 8,031 ft. above the sea, a glorious view is obtained of the Upper Engadine, with the chain of lakes from St. Moritz up to the Maloja. It also gives access to one of the finest walks in the entire region, fairly level and all at or near the 8,000 ft. contour, to Alp Languard, from which one may descend to Pontresina by chair-lift.

Of other Swiss funiculars the briefest mention must suffice. The 2,287-yd. line from the Neuchâtel suburb of La Coudre to the Chaumont is one of several (Ligerz–Tessenberg and St. Imier–Mont Soleil are others), leading to eminences in the Jura range from which, across the lakes of Biel and Neuchâtel and the broad central plain of Switzerland, a distant view is obtained on any clear day of the entire chain of the snowclad Alps, from the Säntis in the north-east past the easily recognisable peaks of the Bernese Oberland to those of the Valais and across the French frontier to Mont Blanc.

Heavily patronised funiculars all the year round include that from Kehrsiten, on the Lake of Lucerne, to the big hotels on the Bürgenstock; the short line from Engelberg to Gerschnialp has its capacity strained to the utmost in winter, when the traffic in skiers has increased to such an extent as to demand the doubling of the *Luftseilbahn* from Gerschnialp up to Trübsee, as mentioned elsewhere. In the Bernese Oberland the line from Lauterbrunnen up to Grütschalp, referred to in Chapter 4, hitherto has provided the only means of access to Mürren, though now supplemented, as described in Chapter 13, by the new and remarkable *Luftseilbahn* from Stechelberg to Mürren and the Schilthorn. On the Lake of Lucerne another funicular, the old-established line from Treib up to Seelisberg, gives the same service to that attractively situated village.

As mentioned in the previous chapter, there are two lines of modest inclination in Switzerland which originally were of the funicular type, but in recent years, to increase their capacity, have been converted to rack-and-pinion traction; one is the busy line from the port of Ouchy, on the Lake of Geneva, up into Lausanne; and the other is from Rheineck in the upper Rhine Valley to Walzenhausen.

THIRTEEN

Mountain Climbing by Cable Suspension

FOR MANY years past, even well before the beginning of the present century, cableways for the transport of minerals have been a familiar sight, most of them pursuing a fairly level course. But not until the middle 1900s was the principle first applied to passenger transport in the Alps, and in particular to travelling upwards at a considerable inclination by this means. At about this time there was brought into use in Colorado, U.S.A., what was advertised as the "Sunrise Peak Aerial Railway—the World's Grandest Scenic Route", and the additional slogan "To the Clouds in a Bucket" gave some indication of the method employed. This line, climbing from roughly 9,000 ft. above sea level at Silver Plume to 12,500 ft. on the Sunrise Peak, was carried on timber supports, spread over its length of 1½ miles, and passengers were carried in pairs in bucket-shaped cars, a primitive foreshadowing of the chair-lift of today.

But the initial Swiss experiment in the same direction was very far from primitive in design and equipment. It is generally thought that the first Swiss *Luftseilbahn* or *téléphérique*—the German and French names respectively for the suspension lines with large cabins—was at Engelberg, from Gerschnialp up to Trübsee, opened in 1927, but this is not the case. In 1908 the engineering firm of Von Roll, in Berne, who today are probably the best known of all Swiss builders of this type of line, completed at Grindelwald what was known as the "Wetterhorn Aerial Railway". In a single span this climbed 1,380 ft. from a station just below the foot of the Upper Grindelwald Glacier to a point 5,502 ft. above sea level, at the western corner of the Wetterhorn's north face, there giving access to a high level path leading to the Gleckstein hut of the Swiss Alpine Club, and so of considerable assistance to climbers.

Although no accidents attended the working of this line, it was found to be subject to damage from avalanches, and by 1914 had ceased to operate, never again to be brought into action and later dismantled. Then came the 1914–18 war, in which very considerable use was made of aerial transport in the mountains, especially by the Italians and Austrians in their fighting in the South Tyrol, and it is not surprising that the experience so gained led after the war to its adaptation on an extensive scale to mountain passenger transport. So it was that by 1927 the Swiss had brought into use the line at Engelberg from Gerschnialp to Trübsee, already mentioned, in 1935 the daring line from Schwägalp up to the summit of the Säntis, in North-Eastern Switzerland, in 1939 that from Champéry to Planachaux, and in 1942 the line from Riddes in the

Rhône Valley to Isérables. Not until the 1950s, however, after the 1939–45 war, did the flood tide of *Luftseilbahn* construction set in.

The development of the chair-lift, or *Sesselbahn* (*télésiège* in French) began later, in 1944, with the line from Trübsee to the Joch Pass, above Engelberg, followed in 1945 by that from Flims to Foppa, in the Grisons; many more lines were opened in the years immediately following. The Joch Pass line was of the single-chair type, and the Flims–Foppa line had double chairs. The next development was of what is known as the *Gondelbahn*, worked on the chair-lift principle, but with two-seater or four-seater enclosed cabins instead of open chairs. The first Swiss line of this type was from Crans, near Montana, up to Bellalui, high above the Rhône Valley, opened in 1950–51.

In first cost, the cable suspension line has many advantages over any type of railway. Whereas a rack-and-pinion railway or a funicular requires a track, which to preserve a fairly even gradient needs to be carried round the mountain contours and often through tunnels or over viaducts (in addition to the cost of the track itself), the suspension line is subject to no such restrictions. If a valley lies in its path, the line can be swung straight across it, and the spans between pylons on some of the most recent lines have increased to over a mile in length. Over some of the deeper valleys, also, the cabins of certain lines move at more than 1,000 ft. above the valley floors, though open chair-lifts are never carried at more than 20 to 30 ft. above the ground. The only limit to the planners of cable suspension lines is that the cables, unlike those of the funicular railways, must be kept dead straight throughout their length; any change of direction requires independent cableways for the two or more sections of the line.

The rack-and-pinion railway has an advantage over the suspension line in that a succession of trains can follow one another to cope with peak traffic; the same is true up to a point, of course, of the chair-lift or *Gondelbahn*, except that the carrying capacity of each unit, from one to four passengers, is only a tiny fraction of that of a rack-and-pinion motorcoach or train. But several of the double chair-lifts or *Gondelbahn* lines can move up to 500 passengers an hour up or down. Like the funicular railway, however, the *Luftseilbahn* has no more than its two balanced cars, one moving up and the other down, though many lines have cars accommodating 60 passengers, and one or two of the latest lines have cabins holding 125 (and their skis as well!). In addition to much lower constructional cost, the operating costs of a suspension line are relatively low. A single-section chair-lift, for example, can be operated by three men, one to work the motive power, and two to assist passengers into and out of the chairs. The busier lines, however, need independent ticket-sellers.

The extraordinary proliferation of aerial transport in Switzerland since the Second World War has been due in the main to two causes. One has been to provide access to highlying villages, a journey of minutes having thus been exchanged for laborious hours up and down the former steep mule tracks. The other is the vast expansion of winter sport activity, from which many of the lines derive the major proportion of their annual revenue. Up to the end of 1970—the latest figures available at the time of writing—Swiss lines of the *Luftseilbahn* type had increased in number from 6 in 1948 to 87 (with 109 independent sections). The corresponding figures for chair-lifts were 16 (24 sections) and 85 (103 sections) respectively. Though the first *Gondelbahn* was not in existence by 1948, twenty years later 56 such lines, with 65 sections, had come into operation. This has brought the total of cableways up to 228, comprising 277 independent ropeways, and these are only the lines of sufficient importance to be included in the Swiss official *Kursbuch*, or timetable. There are also many smaller lines of the *Luftseilbahn* type that have been built under Cantonal concessions, not to mention hundreds of *teleski* or ski-lift installations. It should be added that a number of former chairlifts have proved so successful that they have now been replaced by cableways of the *Gondelbahn* type.

Construction of new lines is still proceeding, and it is quite clear that as yet the saturation point is far from having been reached with this aerial transport. By the end of 1964 the investment in Swiss cable suspension lines had attained a total of over £180 million. As to comparative cost, figures show that whereas the average cost per metre of rack-and-pinion lines had been Sw.fr.899, and of funicular railways Sw.fr.816, that of suspension lines of all kinds had averaged only Sw.fr.622 per metre. Moreover, as all the latter were built in much later years than the former, with the cost of labour and materials far higher, the actual difference in cost has been still more in favour of the suspension lines, not to mention their lower operating costs. Many of these lines are mentioned in other chapters, in the description of the railway and road routes that give access to them, but the more outstanding of them now need description.

The Chair-Lift

Chair-lifts are of two types. The simplest and least costly are those in which a single cable provides for both the support and the movement of the chairs, which are permanently attached to it at regular intervals. In general these are single chairs only, arranged to face the direction of travel, and into and out of which passengers must get while they are in motion. The rate of travel is, of course, quite slow, but there are always attendants to assist the passengers in getting on and off. The earliest of this type was the line, mentioned previously, from Trübsee, above Engelberg, to the Joch Pass, 1,583 yds. in length, and climbing 1,440 ft. to an altitude of 7,260 ft. The longest single-section line is above the upper Rhine Valley—the upper stage of a line from Bad Ragaz which finishes at Laufböden, 7,295 ft. up, after a run of 2,671 ft. and an ascent of 1,944 ft.

The building of lines with open chairs to operate at very high altitudes has not usually been encouraged, but an exception is the short chair-lift which runs from the Great St. Bernard Pass up to La Chenalette, and in its 799 yds. reaches an altitude of no less than 9,095 ft. At Champex, the delightful resort high above Orsières, there is a single chair-lift which has the distinction of finishing at La Breya with the steepest gradient of all chair-lifts in the country, 89 per cent.; this climbs 2,224 ft. in its length of 1,356 yds. In winter some of the chair-lifts in locations where winter sports are carried on are converted into ski-lifts, the chairs being temporarily replaced by hooks to which the skiers attach themselves, and with their skis on the snow thus are drawn up from the lower station to the upper. Also in such regions there are, of course, innumerable ski-lifts or *télé-skis* which are exclusively of this latter type and are in operation in winter only. When used as a ski-lift, a chair-lift is worked at a higher speed and thus can move passengers at a greater frequency than in the chairs.

The double chair-lift carries its passengers in pairs. A certain number of these lines have the chairs permanently attached to the moving rope, with passengers entering and leaving while the chairs are in motion, but on 16 of the more important ones there are more elaborate measures to permit passengers to get in and out while the chairs are stationary, and also to regulate the frequency of the chairs in accordance with the traffic demand. At each terminal there is a semi-circular runway round which the pairs of chairs move. After loading, each pair is released, and runs down a gentle incline to the exit, where grips at the top of the uprights by which the chairs are carried engage automatically with the moving rope; the greater the weight in the chairs, so much the firmer the grip.

At the terminal there is automatic disengagement as the chairs reach the runway, and after helping the passengers out, the attendant then works the chairs round the runway ready to go down or up again, as the case may be. Each station can store a number of chairs in what, in effect, are "sidings", and the chairs can be run on to the rope at any frequency the traffic may demand, provided always that a certain minimum distance is kept between each pair.

Whereas with any single chair-lift that has more than one section a change of chair at the junction is necessary, this is not the case with four of the lines using double chairs. Ingenious junction stations have been devised, where it is possible by a switch arrangement to move a pair of chairs from one ropeway on to the next, so permitting through running.

The most remarkable line in this category with little doubt is the one familiar to all holidaymakers in the Bernese Oberland, from Grindelwald up to First. This has four independent sections, with three junction stations, and a 30-min. through journey can be made in the same pair of chairs through the entire 3,625 ft. difference in level. In length its 4,762 yds. (2¾ miles) easily creates a record for a Swiss chair-lift, as also does its possession of no fewer than 220 pairs of chairs, which are run on to the rope at a minimum distance of 130 ft. apart, that is, at about 16 sec. intervals. The line carries passengers up to a level at which many great peaks of the Bernese Oberland that are invisible from down below in Grindelwald all come into view in a most magnificent prospect. Also from First there are a number of highly attractive mountain paths, as for example to the Schynige Platte or the Grosse Scheidegg, or to the summit of the Faulhorn, with an even more impressive view.

The longest double chair-lift with one section only is from Nods in the Jura region, not far from Neuchâtel, up to the Chasseral; it is 3,226 yds. in length, and has no fewer than 160 chairs in pairs attached to its moving cable. Of double-section lines five in addition to that from Grindelwald to First exceed 3,000 yds. in length, but one only, that from Flims to Foppa and Alp Naraus, has through running of its chairs from the lower to the upper section.

An unusual type of double chair-lift is found at the new Moléson mountain village, near the historic town of Gruyères. Here, in addition to the *Gondelbahn* up to Plan Francey and the continuation *Luftseilbahn* to the summit of the Moléson, there is a cableway up to La Vudalla on which passengers travel in pairs, not sitting but standing, in what look like large buckets. At the terminals they have to swing themselves in and out through the side doors while the buckets are in motion. Even at their slow speed this is quite an exciting exercise, as I have proved by experience!

The Gondelbahn

While to many, myself included, chair-lift travel on a fine day is about the most delightful form of mountain climbing imaginable, because of the completely unobstructed view from the chairs, it is a different matter in adverse weather. In such conditions the single chair-lift offers no protection whatever, and the double chair-lift nothing more than a canopy over the chairs. It is this fact which has encouraged the development of the *Gondelbahn*, which is worked on the same principle as those chair-lifts on which the chairs are detached from the moving cables at the terminals, but with completely enclosed two-seater or four-seater cabins instead of chairs. As the cabins are enclosed, the planners of *Gondelbahn* lines have had a great deal more freedom in the matter of length of span and height above ground than with a chair-lift, and without any sacrifice of safety. Gay colours for the cabins also add to the attraction of the Gondelbahn.

The first of these lines, completed in 1950/51, was from Crans, just west of Montana, to Bellalui, climbing 3,335 ft. in three sections which totalled in length 4,883 yds. (2¾ miles), but it differed in design from those built subsequently. As with a *Luftseilbahn*, the two lower sections have independent supporting and operating cables, whereas in a normal *Gondelbahn* a single cable serves both purposes. The third section, however, was unique in having a moving cable to which hooks were attached at regular intervals, engaging with eyes above the cabin roofs, each cabin thus being swung out from the runway on engagement by a hook. But this arrangement had certain defects, and a *Luftseilbahn* has since been substituted.

Another *Gondelbahn* of unusual design is that at the Valais resort of Saas-Fee, which climbs 2,142 ft. to Spielboden, at 8,057 ft. altitude, adjacent to the great glaciers of the Mischabel group. This has its four-seater cabins permanently attached to the moving cable, which stops momentarily at both upper and lower stations as each cabin reaches the loading platform, to enable passengers to get in and out. It is not entirely encouraging to many users, however, when on the journey their cabins are constantly coming to a stand while they are high up in mid-air. Adjacent to its lower terminus is that of the *Gondelbahn* up to Plattjen, 8,438 ft., which pampers its passengers by seating them in little armchairs.

Record for length among the *Gondelbahn* lines is that running from Zweisimmen in the Bernese Oberland up the Rinderberg ridge, which separates the two arms of the Simme valley. In two sections, with change between the two-seater cabins at the intermediate station, this climbs 3,481 ft. in a journey of 5,529 yds., that is, nearly 3¼ miles. A close rival, and one a good deal better known, because it forms part of one of the ascents from Lucerne to Pilatus, is the 5,433-yd. line from Kriens to Fräkmüntegg, an ascent of 2,950 ft. This is in two sections, with transfer of the four-seater cabins from one ropeway to the other at the intermediate station. The Crans-Bellalui line has been mentioned already; from its terminus, 8,297 ft. above the sea, a magnificent view is obtainable over the Rhône valley to the great peaks of the Valais, and westwards as far as Mont-Blanc. So there is also from the Cabane des Violettes, 7,546 ft. up, reached by a 2,783 yd. *Gondelbahn* from Zaumiau, a mile east of Montana. The latter has now been extended further up to the Plaine Morte glacier of the Wildstrubel, to 9,844 ft. altitude.

Two closely adjacent lines of note, each with two sections but without through running, are those in the Upper Rhine valley from Bad Ragaz to Pardiel, and from Wangs to Furt, 3,822 and 3,542 yds. long, and with ascents of 3,677 and 3,232 ft. respectively. Both are prolonged by chair-lifts to the skiing grounds in the Pizol region. The record for altitude is reached by the *Gondelbahn* which starts from the Swiss portal of the Great St. Bernard tunnel and climbs 2,764 ft. to the Col de Menouve, at 9,068 ft. above sea level.

One Swiss *Gondelbahn* which had but a short life was unique in that it did not climb. Built in connection with an exhibition, it was for some time a familiar sight as one looked along the length of the lake from the city of Zürich. It crossed the width of the lake, near the city end, between the Seefeld Quay and the Belvoir Park, in a single span of 1,552 yds. The cars were run up inclines from the two ends of the line to high towers on both sides of the lake, like those of a suspension bridge, and between the towers the supporting cables stretched in a shallow curve across the water, at a height sufficient to clear the masts of ships passing underneath. From this altitude a fine survey of the great city was possible, and one cannot but regret that the line did not remain in permanent use.

The only similar line in Switzerland was one which was built at Lausanne, at the time of the great national exposition or "Expo" of 1964, to connect the exhibition grounds with the steamer pier at Ouchy, but this also has since been dismantled. One or two very short lines of this type may be found at certain of the Butlin camps round the coasts of Great Britain.

The Luftseilbahn or Téléphérique

A great deal might be written of this modern form of aerial travel, of which many most remarkable examples are to be found in the Swiss Alps. Whether in the matter of enormously long rope spans, or maximum height above ground, or the altitudes reached, or the capacity of the cabins, the *téléphériques* calling for special comment are numerous indeed, and it is difficult to know to which of them to give pride of place.

Few could be more notable, however, than the *Luftseilbahn* from Stechelberg, at the head of the Lauterbrunnen valley in the Bernese Oberland, to Mürren and the Schilthorn, the final stage of which was brought to completion in 1967. The total lift over the four stages is no less than 6,869 ft., achieved in a total length of 7,580 yds., or just over 4¼ miles. The two stages from Stechelberg up to Mürren are of interest in that the cabins meet at the intermediate station of Gimmelwald, but do not pass one another. The principle of balance is maintained by the one cabin moving down from Mürren as the other moves up from Stechelberg; this combined operation is carried out despite the sharp angle at which the two lines meet at Gimmelwald. Each of these cabins holds a maximum of 100 passengers; on the two upper sections, which are independent of each other, cabins holding 80 are installed. From the Schilthorn terminus, a view of unparalleled grandeur is now obtained of the Oberland peaks, of Mürren and the Lauterbrunnen valley far below, and of the Blümlisalp and beyond to the west.

A notable group of lines is that which in recent years has been built to carry passengers up to the Diablerets glacier, not far from Gstaad. As the lines concerned are in two cantons, two companies were formed to carry out the work. One arm starts from Reusch, on the road from Gstaad over the Col de Pillon to Diablerets village, and climbs in two stages to the Cabane de Diablerets. The other begins at the Col de Pillon itself, as a *Gondelbahn*, to Pierres-Pointes, from which there is an exciting *Luftseilbahn*, finishing at an angle of 1 in 0.8 (steeper than 45 deg.) to the top of the cliff on which the Cabane de Diablerets is located. The latter company built the final stage, a single span over a deep valley to the summit station, 9,665 ft. above the sea, on the margin of a great uncrevassed glacier affording wonderful skiing all the year round. The longer and bigger ascent of the two is that from Reusch, 6,114 yds. with a total lift of 5,210 ft.

The distinction of reaching the highest altitude of all the suspension transport in Switzerland belongs to the *Luftseilbahn* from the Gornergrat, the summit terminus of the rack-and-pinion railway from Zermatt, to the Stockhorn. This starts, of course, at 10,212 ft. above the sea, but it finishes at 11,196 ft. As yet the French still hold the ascendancy in altitude with their daring line from Chamonix to the summit of the Aiguille du Midi, 12,467 ft., but this is shortly to be challenged by the plans to extend another of Zermatt's *téléphériques*.

This is the three-stage line that climbs from Zermatt to the Trockener Steg, at 9,603 ft. altitude. The terminus is just short of the Theodul Pass, which heads the Zermatt valley between the Breithorn and the Matterhorn. From the other side of the pass the Italians have come up in the same way from the village of Cervinia to a station called Testa Grigia, at 11,414 ft. altitude, and it is possible to be transported over the glacier between Trockener Steg and Testa Grigia by "Sno-cat". But the Swiss now propose an airy swing from Trockener Steg to the spiky little peak on the western flank of the Breithorn, called the Little Matterhorn, which will finish just short of the latter's 12,815 ft. summit, and so will beat the present French record. Zermatt has a third *Luftseilbahn*, paralleling the first stage of the Trockener Steg line, up to the Schwarzsee, and a chair-lift up to Sunnegga, which has been extended by yet another *Luftseilbahn* to the Unter-Rothorn, 10,170 ft.

For a group of suspension lines of great note we need to repair to the Engadine. Of these the most remarkable is the two-stage line from Surlej, across the Inn valley from Silvaplana, four miles from St. Moritz, to near the summit of Piz Corvatsch; here the terminus, at 10,843 ft. (where a most delightful restaurant has been built, with picture windows round a half circle), gives immediate access to grand ski slopes that find considerable use in summer, and much more, of course, in winter. This line climbs 4,685 ft. in a distance of 4,850 yds.

On the opposite side of the Silvaplana Lake from Piz Corvatsch there is the Piz Nair, which has been made similarly accessible by a suspension line. This, however, though it attains an altitude of 9,941 ft., is much shorter, for one travels from St. Moritz up to its lower terminus at Corviglia, 8,189 ft., by the two old-established funicular railways which connect at Chanterella. The Piz Nair, commanding the whole length of the Upper Engadine on the one side, and a wide prospect of mountains and glaciers on the other, is one of the finest viewpoints in the region.

Then, on the way from the neighbouring village of Pontresina to the Bernina Pass, there are two more *téléphériques*. One, so popular in summer and winter alike that it is able to pay a dividend of 15 per cent., and which in the first seven months alone of 1966 carried a million passengers, has its lower terminus at Bernina Diavolezza station of the Bernina Railway. Its length of 3,947 yds. makes it the second longest single section *Luftseilbahn* in the country, during the course of which its passengers are lifted 2,897 ft. to the terminus on the Diavolezza, 9,790 ft. up, immediately opposite the dazzling snows of Piz Palü and its neighbours in the Bernina group. It is quite an exciting trip, especially as one is carried by a 3,090 ft. rope span high above the dark green Diavolezza Lake. A short distance beyond the lower Diavolezza line terminus is that of yet another *Luftseilbahn*, up to the Piz Lagalb, 9,520 ft. altitude, on the opposite side of the valley, the glory of which is the view southwards, over the depths of the Poschiavo valley to the mountains of Italy some 20 miles distant.

A further great centre of suspension transport is Davos, simply explained by the fact that this is one of the finest areas for skiing in the entire country. Mention has been made in Chapter 11 of the notable Parsenn funicular; some years ago this prosperous line was extended by a short *Luftseilbahn* from its Weissfluhjoch terminus, at 8,756 ft. altitude, to the summit of the Weissfluh, 9,262 ft. In quite recent years a further line has been run down diagonally from the Weissfluhjoch through 1,525 ft. to the Parsennhütte. This is on the glorious path which runs high above the Davos valley from the Gotschnagrat (upper terminus of another *Luftseilbahn* that climbs 3,600 ft. up from Klosters, in the neighbouring valley), past the midway Höhenweg station on the Parsenn funicular to the Strela Pass. Here we are at the top of the *Gondelbahn* coming up from Schatzalp, immediately above Davos. Then on the opposite side of the valley there is the two-stage *Gondelbahn* soaring up past Ischialp to the Jakobshorn, 8,455 ft., with its branch chair-lift from Ischialp to Brämabüel. Yet another Davos *Luftseilbahn* is from Dörfji, on the Flüela pass road, up to Mitteltälli, with a climb of 2,241 ft. to 8,173 ft. altitude.

A second Valaisian *téléphérique* centre of note is Verbier, a town towards the western end of the canton, which, set in a mountain amphitheatre perfect for the purpose, has mushroomed into existence almost solely as the result of winter sport activity. Access to Verbier, 4,920 ft. above the sea, is by road only, from the terminus of the Le Châble branch of the Martigny–Orsières Railway. One company now operates no fewer than 15 cable lines round Verbier—five of the *Gondelbahn* type, with a *Luftseilbahn* on up to Les Attelas and another from there to the summit of Mont Gelé, 9,872 ft. From these there are eight connecting chair-lifts to the Tête-des-Vaux, the Lac-des-Vaux and the Col-de-Chassoure, all helping to create a skiers' paradise. The same company also works the chair-lifts at Champex and the Col-de-la-Forclaz, together with 19 ski-lifts.

The north-east of Switzerland was early in the field with its *Luftseilbahn* from Schwägalp to the summit of the Säntis, opened in 1935. This isolated peak, 8,215 ft. high, offers one of the most extensive views in the entire country, and the line, used to capacity on any fine day in the summer, is equally popular with skiers in winter. In length, 2,359 yds., its initial cable span of 3,860 ft. carries the cars to the crest of the precipitous north face of the mountain, and the terminus is reached at 8,146 ft. Parallel to the Säntis range is the rather lower Kronberg, and in recent years this has been conquered by a *Luftseilbahn* up from Jakobsbad, a station on the Appenzellerbahn, which boasts the longest cable span in the country without any intermediate support—a truly staggering 2,220 m., or 7,283 ft. (1⅜ miles). The total length of the line is 3,525 yds. and the climb 2,533 ft.

In an adjacent valley is the popular *Luftseilbahn* from Wasserauen, the terminus of the Appenzellerbahn, in the heart of the Säntis range, to the Ebenalp, mounting 2,552 ft. in 1,644 yds. To this has been added yet another line in the immediate vicinity, from Brülisau to the Hoher Kasten, a peak which overlooks both the Appenzell basin and its bordering mountains, and, on the east, all the upper Rhine valley from Lake Constance up to Sargans and beyond. As with the Säntis, this 2,970-yd. ascent finishes up the face of a sheer precipice to the 5,877 ft. terminus.

A few other notable lines need mention. One of the most outstanding is found at Andermatt, and it climbs in two stages to the summit of the Gemsstock, 9,695 ft. above the sea, an ascent of 4,954 ft. in a length of 4,396 yds. which entails a considerable gradient. As with certain other of the latest lines, control of the cars, both in accelerating and in slowing down to stop, is automatic. This brings a reminder of a *téléphérique* which is entirely automatic in operation; it is a short line on the Lake of Lugano, from Brusino Arsizio up to Serpiano. The only staff consists of two at the lower station; at the upper the car doors are automatically operated.

Not far from Lucerne there is the single-section *Luftseilbahn* which in length nearly approaches that to the Diavolezza—the 3,631-yd. line from Stöckalp to Melchsee Frutt, with an ascent of 2,713 ft. Also in the same vicinity, in the Engelberg valley, there is the second longest cable span between pylons; it is the 1,910 m. (6,266 ft.) of the second line which has been run from Gerschnialp to the Trübsee. This line has now been extended further up to a terminus on the glaciers at the western end of the Titlis range, known as the Kleintitlis, at an altitude of 9,950 ft. Incidentally, by taking the chair-lift from Trübsee to the Joch Pass, walkers have at their disposal a most attractive expedition down to the beautiful little lake at Engstlenalp, and then on to Melchsee-Frutt.

Another walk that attracts many can begin and end with two *Luftseilbahn* experiences which will not readily be forgotten. From Kandersteg the line up to Stock, when it passes over the cliff that heads the valley, is at a height of more than 1,100 ft. above the valley. At Stock, 5,988 ft. up, the invigorating 6½-mile walk begins, through the heart of the Bernese Alps, that leads to the 7,697 ft. crest of the Gemmi Pass. From the frowning cliffs above the village of Leukerbad a small cabin holding 20 is then launched down a single cable, in a clear span of 4,430 ft. on the initial stage of which the height above ground must be considerably more than 1,000 ft. However, this breathless experience is preferable to making one's apprehensive way, as I did once, by the zig-zag path down the face of the sheer precipice into Leukerbad, just over 3,000 ft. below. Incidentally, a wonderful circuit for a fine day is to take this route from Kandersteg to Leukerbad, then by road the motorcoach down to Leuk, in the Rhône valley, and the Swiss Federal up to Brigue, returning to Kandersteg by the Lötschberg line. Or, if one wishes the walking to be downhill, the tour can be made in the opposite direction.

A similar good test for nerves, with which I have experimented, is in a cabin holding ten (and no conductor!) from Rhäzüns, on the Rhaetian Railway main line between Chur and Thusis, to Feldis. An enormously high cliff fringes the opposite side of the Hinter-Rhein, and the little line swings straight up to the top of it, again with considerably more than 1,000 ft. of space below the car before the cliff pylon is reached. This line mounts 2,628 ft. in a length of 2,518 yds. Elsewhere in the Grisons, in addition to the *téléphériques* already mentioned, Lenzerheide has its substantial two-stage line from Canols to the summit of the Parpaner Rothorn, 9,405 ft., just over two miles long with a total climb of 4,455 ft. In the same canton, Arosa has a two-stage line climbing 2,919 ft. to the summit of the Arosa Weisshorn, at 8,687 ft., from which one can look right down the Schanfigg valley to Chur, some 6,750 ft. below, as well as at a vast range of mountain scenery in all directions. There is also the finely equipped new *Gondelbahn* from Klosters Dorf, 2,510 yds. long, up to Albeina, on the opposite side of the valley from Gotschnagrat. This finishes at 6,191 ft. altitude.

The Lake of Lucerne was so well provided with rack-and-pinion and funicular railways in earlier years that not many additions by suspension lines have been needed, but there are two which are well known to all visitors to this area. One is the daring descent from the summit of Pilatus to Fräkmüntegg, two spans of 1,501 yds. in all falling 2,135 ft., and linking the rack-and-pinion railway up the mountain with the *Gondelbahn* from Fräkmüntegg down to the Kriens suburb of Lucerne. The other is the popular ascent of 3,747 ft. in a single section 3,393 yds. long (over two miles) from Beckenried on the lake to Klewenalp, starting-point in summer for some attractive mountain walks and a great skiing centre in winter. To these there has now been added a direct *Luftseilbahn* from Weggis up to Rigi-Kaltbad, and a more adventurous one is planned from Brunnen to the summit of the Fronalpstock, which will cut to a mere fraction the time now spent in the circuit by way of motorcoach to Schwyz and Schlattli, funicular to Stoos and two stages of chair-lift to the top.

The greatest concentration of lines that have been built to give access to highlying villages, in many cases at the expense of the communes themselves, is on both sides of the Rhône valley, where a whole succession of lines climb 2,000 to 3,000 ft. to the villages on the sunny terraces round which a great deal of agricultural activity is carried on. The only approach to a fair-sized village like Isérables, for example, is by the 2,174-yd. line that mounts 2,024 ft. from Riddes, on the Simplon main line, and earns special distinction in that under each cabin provision is made for slinging a jeep—driver and all!—carrying the town's produce over an airy swing to the valley below. East of this point one can count seven lines in succesion climbing the south side of the valley two from Haute Nendaz and Veysonnaz, near Sion; one from Chalais, near Sierre; and two from Turtmann and two from Unterbach, stations on the Simplon line. In the Rhône valley eastwards from Martigny and as far as Fiesch with the lateral valleys, there is a total of nearly 30 cableways of various types.

On the north side of the valley we have the lines from Gampel to Jeizinen, above the Lonza valley; from Gamsen, near Brigue, to Mund; and a string east of Brigue, three from Mörel to the Riederalp and Greicheralp area, those from Betten to Bettmeralp and Fürgangen to Rosswald, and, the most recent, the two-stage line from Fiesch, just over 1¾ miles long, to a terminus 9,442 ft. above the sea just below the summit of the Eggishorn. From here we can overlook the great Aletsch glacier and beyond it in full view the Eiger, Mönch and Jungfrau, while a short climb brings us to the summit of the Eggishorn itself, looking down on the famous Märjelensee with its icebergs and their fantastic colours. The intermediate station of Küboden is on the grand high level path that extends from the well known Hotel Jungfrau–Eggishorn, in the west, to Bettmeralp, Riederalp and Riederfurka in the west.

Many new cableways have been brought into use since the first edition of this book was published. Saas-Fee has its new *Luftseilbahn* up to Felskinn, in the heart of the glaciers at an altitude of 9,833 ft., which eventually may get extended to the crest of the glacial ridge separating the Saas–Fee and Zermatt valleys, at over 12,000 ft. Another new line at Saas-Fee, in this case a *Gondelbahn*, carries you up to Hannig, at 7,677 ft., with a superb view over the valley. A short distance to the west Zinal has its new *Luftseilbahn* to Sorebois, all but 8,000 ft. up, looking across at the Zinal Rothorn and other ice-mantled peaks, and starting-point for some fine mountain walks. Further west the up-and-coming resort of Anzère, north of the Rhône valley, has a new *Gondelbahn* up to the 7,748 ft. Pas de Maimbré.

In Central Switzerland a new *Luftseilbahn* from Weglosen to Seebli, in the Hoch–Ybrig region south of Einsiedeln, breaks a record with cabins holding up to 125 occupants. An even more astonishing record is that which has been set up by the *Luftseilbahn* from Mulania, near Flims Waldhaus in the Grisons, which not only operates with cabins holding 125, but also over a single-section line with a record length of 4,545 yds. (just over 2¾ miles) and a total climb of 3,711 ft. This means that when the line is in action the two cabins are connected by no less than 5½ miles of moving haulage cable. Elsewhere the Stockhorn in the Bernese Oberland has been conquered by a two-stage *Luftseilbahn* which starts near the village of Erlenbach, on the Spiez–Zweisimmen railway, and climbs 4,626 ft. in 2½ miles to the 7,037 ft. summit station of this isolated peak, a magnificent viewpoint.

As we have seen, the vast proliferation of cable transport in Switzerland, though partly to carry passengers up to famous viewpoints and partly to give access to highlying villages, has been mainly in the interests of winter sports. So the major developments have been in and around the principal winter sports centres, in particular the Engadine, Davos, Zermatt, Saas-Fee, Montana–Crans, Villars, Verbier and Flims–Waldhaus. In recent years former lines which have reached high altitudes have been extended still further, to glacial areas at between, 9,000 and 10,000 ft. altitude, to facilitate skiing all the year round. Moreover, the process of development still continues, and all over Switzerland many further cableways are planned or already in construction. In view of the success of cable transport in the Alps it is quite astonishing that, apart from one or two modest chair-lifts to assist skiers in the Highlands, nothing of the kind has been attempted in the mountain regions of Great Britain.

The thrill of *Luftseilbahn* travel—nearing the end of the airy swing from Kandersteg up to Stock, with the cabin some 1,150ft above the ground. Behind is the ice-mantled summit of the Balmhorn. *[Bern-Lötschberg-Simplon*

Left: Vertical transport—the famous lift, 540ft high, carrying passengers to the Hammetschwand, on the Bürgenstock, with its extensive view over the Lake of Lucerne. *[Tourist Office of Central Switzerland*

Above: One of a series of *Luftseilbahn* lines on the southern shore of the Walensee, much used in winter by skiers. This line climbs from Unterterzen to Tannenbodenalp. *[North-East Switzerland Tourist Office*

Some magnificent reinforced concrete bridges have been
built by the Swiss to carry their roads. This one, just west
of St. Gallen, carries the motorway to Zurich across the
Sitter gorge.

The even greater Hundwilertobel bridge, between Hundwil
and Waldstatt, in the Appenzell country. The span of the
main arch is 312ft, and the maximum height of the road
above the Urnäsch stream is 240ft.

[Both, North-East Switzerland Tourist Office

One of the new Swiss national motorways. This example is passing Rheineck, in the upper Rhine valley, on its way to Chur, and is the main approach to the San Bernardino road to Bellinzona. The railway is the main line from St. Gallen to Chur; in the centre (below) is the rack-and-pinion line to Walzenhausen.   [Swiss Federal Railways

Difficult road location in mountainous country—a bridge over a narrow gorge on the road up the Val d'Anniviers from Sierre to Zinal.   [Swiss National Tourist Office

One of the most recent mountain roads in Switzerland—
a postal motorcoach climbing past the Stein glacier to the
Susten Pass, 7,411ft above the sea.
[Swiss National Tourist Office

The windings of the modern Gotthard motorway in the
Schöllenen gorge, mounting from Göschenen to Ander-
matt. On the left is the avalanche shelter over the Schöllenen
Railway. *[Central Switzerland Tourist Office*

By the operation of the ramified Swiss postal motorcoach network no community in Switzerland is without adequate transport. Some of the coaches negotiate extremely steep and sinuous mountain roads, such as this one from Meiringen up to the mountain village of Rosenlaui. In the background is the Wetterhorn.   *[Swiss National Tourist Office*

Protection is needed by many mountain roads against the
danger of avalanches. Here is the lengthy avalanche shelter
on the Oberalp Pass over the Furka-Oberalp Railway and
the Disentis-Andermatt Road.   [Furka-Oberalp Railway

Inside the Great St. Bernard tunnel, showing one of the
light signals controlling the traffic and various instructional
signs.   [Swiss National Tourist Office

Above: Some of the innumerable windings of the old Gotthard road in the Val Tremola on the abrupt descent from the Gotthard Pass to Airolo.
[*Central Switzerland Tourist Office*

Left: How many motorists avoid climbing with their cars to mountain passes — a motorcar train of the Lötschberg Railway working through the Lötschberg tunnel between Kandersteg, Goppenstein and Brigue.
[*Bern-Lötschberg-Simplon*

Above right: Some of the amazing construction of the new Gotthard road, bracketed out from the steep mountainside above the Val Leventina in order to avoid an unduly sharp curve.

Right: The striking road curve as seen from below, with its concrete supporting pillars.
[*Both Swiss National Tourist Office*

Meeting - place of two fa-mous mountain pass roads. In the foreground is the Grimsel road, leading down to Gletsch, and up the opposite mountainside is the Furka road, with its final windings to the Furka Pass in the extreme left background. Below the Furka road can be seen the Furka - Oberalp Railway.

The crest of the Furka Pass, 7,975ft above the sea, with the Furka Hotel.

[Both, Furka-Oberalp Railway

Flagship of the Lake of Lucerne steamer fleet—the S.S.
Stadt Luzern, with oil-fired boilers, licensed to carry up
to 1,200 passengers. In the background is seen the Uri-
Rotstock peak.

By contrast, the latest Lake of Lucerne motorship, the
Gotthard, with seating for 750 passengers and a total
capacity of 1,200, built by the Lake of Lucerne Ship
Company and introduced in 1971.
[Both, Lake of Lucerne Ship Company

Past and present at Lucerne—the paddle-steamer *Wilhelm Tell* and the motorship *Pilatus*. In the background is the Rigi.

Among the high mountains at the southern end of the Lake of Lucerne—the S.S. *Gallia* calls at Tell's Chapel.

[Both, Lake of Lucerne Ship Company

The *Jungfrau*, one of the magnificent motorships of the Lötschberg Railway, at speed on the Lake of Thun.

A happy summer scene at Neuhaus, Interlaken's "Lido" at the eastern end of Lake Thun, with the Lötschberg motorship *Stadt Bern*.   *[Both, Bern-Lötschberg-Simplon*

At Oberhofen Castle, on the Lake of Thun—the *Niederhorn*, one of the smaller Lötschberg motorships.

[Bern-Lötschberg-Simplon

A striking view of the Lake of Lugano—one of the motorships passes Morcote, beloved of artists, with its church and houses clinging to a precipitous mountainside.

[Swiss National Tourist Office

Top: On the Lake of Geneva—the *Vevey,* one of the graceful paddleships of the Compagnie Générale de Navigation du Lac Leman, or C.G.N.

Above: C.G.N. paddleship *Italie* approaches Montreux in preparation for calling there.

Below: And then proceeds towards the head of the lake for its terminal call at Villeneuve.

[All, *Swiss National Tourist Office*

The Lake of Zürich has its heavily-patronised steamer service. Refreshments and light meals can be enjoyed on the open deck on fine days. Approaching is the S.S. *Stadt Rapperswil*.   [*Swiss National Tourist Office*

The only ships owned by the Swiss Federal Railways are those plying on the Lake of Constance, from and to the ports of Romanshorn and Rorschach. This is the recently-built M.V. *Romanshorn*, which carries railway wagons between Romanshorn and the German port of Friedrichshafen.   [*Swiss Federal Railways*

FOURTEEN

The Mountain Pass Roads

WHILE THE SWISS have developed their railways in a remarkable way, from both the engineering and the operating point of view, through such difficult country as their own, they have by no means neglected their roads. And whereas the main railways penetrate the great Alpine chain by means of some of the longest tunnels in the world, the boring of which has been an epic in itself, many of the main roads carried at a far higher level over the principal passes are but little less noteworthy from the engineering point of view. This engineering reaches its climax in the way in which a perfectly even gradient has been preserved when the roads are being lifted, by a whole series of elbow bends, up veritable mountain walls where the mountainsides of narrow valleys have left very little room for manoeuvre. Moreover, many roads themselves are now being improved by tunnelling on a considerable scale.

Most holidaymakers in Switzerland have some of their most enjoyable and spectacular excursions by means of motorcoaches traversing one or more of these passes. While many such trips may be made in privately-owned coaches or private cars, the most familiar means of transport is the admirable service provided by the yellow motorcoaches of the "P.T.T.", or the Department of Posts, Telegraphs and Telephones of the Swiss Federal Government. From the earliest days all the licensing of road motor vehicles has been in the hands of the P.T.T., which with rare exceptions permits no motorbus services between towns in Switzerland. No village or commune in the country that has road access is without adequate transport by this highly efficient yellow network, but it is all focused on the railways, so that, apart from private cars, town-to-town transport is entirely by rail; as a result, closure of any railway line or station is a rare occurrence. In addition, the P.T.T. motorcoaches deal with a large proportion of the excursion traffic by road, and this leads many of them over the mountain passes.

No passenger in one of the P.T.T. motorcoaches can fail to be impressed with the exceptional competence of the driver, and this is not surprising when the conditions of his service are known. The driver-to-be must have had preliminary training as a mechanic or a fitter, which is the subject of a technical examination by the P.T.T., as well as a medical check-up, before he is accepted as a candidate. Then follows a year in one of the workshops of the Swiss Postal Motorcoach Service to perfect his technical knowledge before he is allowed to drive, and driving for the first year is confined to trucks before he is given a test for driving a bus or a motorcoach. In addition to these two years of training, other requisites are a knowledge of at least one language other than the driver's own, and the stipulation that from taking out his vehicle in the morning to returning it to the garage at night he must not touch a drop of alcohol.

And what about the coaches themselves? The latest modern types seat 36 and 26 passengers respectively, and are of 150 and 115 h.p., which is adequate for the stiffest and longest Alpine climbs. Internally, foam rubber cushions provide comfortable seating throughout the longest runs, and during the journey the inside seats can be moved a few inches into the central gangway to provide more elbow-room. The broad windows are firmly set in rubber to provide draughtproof conditions in cold weather, when each bus is thoroughly heated by the engine exhaust; in the summer sliding upper panels to the windows provide adequate ventilation. A public address system is installed to enable the driver to tell his passengers points of interest about the run. There is ample space for heavy luggage in waterproof compartments below the passenger deck, and on runs which have to deal with any amount of parcels traffic trailers are attached to the bus.

What is of maximum importance to the passenger, however, is safety. If he is seated just behind the driver he may well be amazed, when the coach is making one of those tremendous descents from a mountain pass round a whole series of hairpin bends, at the dexterity with which these are negotiated, often, it might appear, with no more than a foot or less of clearance round some mountain wall or precipice edge, and with very little reduction of speed. It has to be remembered, of course, that the driver is making the same run day after day, in all probability; but at the same time it is good to know that he has at his command motor, foot and hand-brakes, and, in addition, an independent mechanically-operated emergency brake. Moreover, by Swiss law he must have his coach under such control as to be able to bring it to a stand, on the steepest gradient, in a distance of not more than 20 feet.

It may be added that also, by law, the postal motorcoaches have the right of the road, all other traffic having to give way if necessary on any mountain road that is shown in the timetable as "Bergpoststrasse" when is heard the imperious three-tone horn of one of these coaches approaching. This sound the three notes of the common chord of A—C sharp, E and A— and no other vehicle is allowed to have a horn making the same sounds. The postal motorcoaches are designed with a relatively short wheelbase for their length, and with a considerable overhang at the rear end, which is a great help in manoeuvring them round the hairpin bends already referred to. So no passenger need have the slightest apprehension when travelling in a Swiss Alpine Postal Motor Coach over one of the mountain roads; the record of safety of the postal service has always been extremely high and still so remains.

Not only does one admire the competence of the drivers of the Swiss postal motorcoaches, but the condition of the roads themselves also excites admiration. This is particularly the case over the high passes, when one considers the weather conditions to which these roads are exposed, especially the snows and frosts of winter. Hitherto snow has been responsible for the closure in winter of most of the pass roads, but as already mentioned some major road tunnelling has now been begun—the Great St. Bernard tunnel already is in use and that under the crest of the San Bernardino Pass now is also—in order that the roads concerned may be usable by motor traffic throughout the year. Even so, the approaches to these tunnels require to be kept clear by snowploughs, and motorists need to provide themselves with chains. The same applies to the few passes over which it is generally possible for motor traffic to pass in winter, such as the Julier, Maloja, Ofen, Brünig and one or two others.

As to the passes closed in winter, very efficient arrangements exist for conveying motor vehicles through the Gotthard, Simplon and Lötschberg railway tunnels; and these facilities have become so popular that they are extensively used in summer also. And now for a brief description of some of the principal pass routes.

The Simplon

For many centuries the Simplon Pass has been a trade route between the Rhône valley and Northern Italy. It is associated with the name of Kaspar Stockalper, who in the Seventeenth Century dominated the traffic over it, which he protected with a guard of 70 men. It must have been a profitable business, as is witnessed by the palace which he built in Brigue in 1642, and which with its three massive towers and onion domes is still the most prominent building in that town. Near the Simplon Pass and at Gondo on the Swiss-Italian frontier, also, there still remain the eight-storey buildings which he erected as shelters for travellers. Not until the beginning of the Nineteenth Century, however, was a proper road built over the pass, by the order ¡of Napoleon I; it was begun in 1800 and finished in 1807. Over its length nine evenly-spaced refuges were built, for the protection of travellers in bad weather; numbered in consecutive order from Brigue some of these are still recognised stages along the route, though now with such modern equipment as telephones.

Scenically, it is better to travel the Simplon road from east to west. Leaving the Italian town of Domodossola, the road parallels the Simplon railway up the Diveria Valley past Varzo and Iselle di Trasquera, where the railway disappears into the 12¼-mile Simplon tunnel. After crossing the frontier, the first Swiss village reached is Gondo, and the entry to Switzerland is sensational. A great cliff overhangs the village, and the road then passes into what *Baedeker* well describes as "One of the wildest defiles in the Alps". It is the sombre Ravine of Gondo, which the Diveria stream has carved out between precipitous sides anything up to 2,000 ft. high. On emergence the road is carried upwards in a wide circuit, from which one can look down on the beginning of this remarkable cleft, before reaching the village of Simplon, the only place of any importance on the route, from which the pass has taken its name.

Climbing steadily until above the tree line, and now with snow-capped mountains on all sides, the road comes out on to a barren upland, first passing the old Hospice—a church-like building in the valley below—and then the uncompromising square block of the present Hospice, before reaching the large Hotel Bellevue. This is on the crest of the pass, at 6,578 ft. altitude, 3,763 ft. above Gondo. Ahead now can be seen the mountains of the Bernese Oberland, with the Finsteraarhorn and Aletschhorn prominent, and these remain in view for much of the descent to Brigue. From the summit we first encircle the head of a very deep valley by a stretch of road which lately has been widened and in part tunnelled for avalanche protection. High above the valley the road descends, rounding a mountain buttress and curving a long way into the Gunterthal to reach the small village of Bérisal. Again, after crossing the Gunter bridge and taking to the other side of the valley, there is a long stretch of road high above the gorge of the Saltine, which the Gunter stream has now joined. From here onwards the town of Brigue is in full view below, and beyond it many miles of the Rhône Valley, the whole backed by the Bernese Alps—a fine view indeed. So through the suburb of Ried we reach Brigue, having descended a total of 4,363 ft. from the Simplon Pass. As already mentioned, a regular service for motorcars is run through the Simplon tunnel between Brigue and Iselle, but in winter, when the pass is usually blocked by snow from November to March inclusive, the tunnel provides the only way through.

The Julier

It is believed that as far back as the time of the Emperor Augustus the Romans constructed a road from Clavenna (the present Chiavenna) over the Maloja pass into the Engadine, which, four miles short of the present St. Moritz, continued over the Julier pass to what is now Tiefencastel, and on to Cuera, the present Chur. Today on the crest of the Julier Pass, at an altitude of 7,500 ft., there are two stumps of round pillars which it is thought may have been Roman milestones. But the name of the pass is derived from the Celtic sun-god Jul. Between St. Moritz, Tiefencastel, Lenzerheide and Chur this today is a well-used route, open even in winter, and in summer boasting five daily motorcoach services in each direction over its entire length, and additional ones between Chur and Lenzerheide.

Out of St. Moritz the coaches take the Maloja road as far as Silvaplana, and then climb into the mountains between the Piz Julier and Piz Lagrev. On this side of the pass, as we have begun the ascent at 5,955 ft., the ascent is comparatively short, for the difference in level to be surmounted is no more than 1,545 ft., and it seems little more than a matter of minutes before we have exchanged the verdure of the Engadine for wild mountain scenery, fringed by jagged peaks. A level stretch leads to the Julier Hospice, 7,349 ft. up, and 150 ft. short of the crest of the pass, which is at an altitude of 7,493 ft. Then begins a long series of downward sweeps, leading in 5 miles to the village of Bivio, and the beginning of forested slopes. Shortly beyond this there comes into view a large and attractive lake, but like many others in the canton its origin is artificial, as is obvious when we reach the dam at its northern end. This is of the type that consists of a solid and very broad mass of soil faced on the water side with masonry; its outer side has been terraced and very effectively sown with grass, so presenting a perfectly level stretch of green across the valley which from the north has an odd appearance with its mountain background.

The next stretch of the valley is wide and fertile, and is dotted with many villages. Of these the largest is Savognin, capital of the Ober-halbstein region. This possesses a two-section chair-lift just over 2 miles long and mounting to a terminus called Somtgant, 3,061 ft. above the 3,852 ft. altitude of its starting-point; but the use of this is mainly in winter by skiers. Passing through some fairly deep gorges the road now makes its way down to the Albula valley at the village of Tiefencastel; from here it climbs up to the railway station, on the Chur–St. Moritz main line, which is also quite an important postal motorcoach staging-point.

Continuing towards Chur another climb of just over 2,000 ft. is needed by the St. Moritz–Chur coach to reach the summit level of 4,955 ft. at Parpan. Three miles before this we pass Lenzerheide, a very important winter sports centre, and one of the very few towns of any size in Switzerland that is without railway communication. Needless to say, both summer tourists and winter skiers have suspension transport here at their disposal—a two-section chair-lift just over $1\frac{3}{4}$ miles long to the 7,625 ft. altitude of Piz Scalottas on the west side of the valley, and on the east a massive two-section *téléphérique* from Canols, midway between Lenzerheide and Parpan, to the 9,405 ft. summit of the Parpaner Rothorn, which commands an extensive view of the whole of the Valbella region. After Churwalden there begins the long descent into the Plessur valley, with a drop in level of 3,070 ft. in $8\frac{3}{4}$ miles before the road reaches Chur. The entire journey of $48\frac{1}{2}$ miles from St. Moritz to Chur takes three hours by the faster coaches, with limited stops only. It is in the opposite direction that they are put to the hardest test, because the total difference in level to be overcome, out of Chur and from Tiefencastel up to the Julier Pass, is no less than 7,750 ft.

The Maloja

As mentioned in Section 2 of this chapter, the Maloja road forms part of a historic route between Switzerland and Italy dating back to the Roman Emperor Augustus; today it connects St. Moritz and the Upper Engadine with Chiavenna and the Italian Lakes region. Over it there runs a regular postal motorcoach service in each direction between St. Moritz and Lugano, four times daily each way during the height of the summer season and once each way in winter, throughout which the pass remains open, taking 4 to $4\frac{1}{2}$ hours for the run. The road is also heavily used by motorists and private motorcoach operators. One unique feature of this pass route is that from the north its immediate approach for 15 miles or more is practically level; from 5,830 ft. altitude at St. Moritz station in 11 miles to Maloja Kulm there is a difference in level of no more than 124 ft. But it is a different matter altogether on the south side, where, as almost throughout the Alps, the descent southwards is far more abrupt than the ascent from the north.

The start from St. Moritz, past the chain of lakes—those of St. Moritz, Champfèr, Silvaplana and Sils—is very beautiful, with forested slopes rising to some 7,200 ft. altitude and more, and the shapely Piz della Margna gracing their opposite shores. The great Palace Hotel at Maloja, somewhat shorn of its former glory, dominates the village, and immediately beyond there begins the descent, with its twelve hairpin bends, that in four miles lowers the road by 1,160 ft. We have entered the attractive Grisons valley known as Bergell, or in the Italian, Val Bregaglia, one of the few fairly populous areas of Switzerland that has no railway communication. In former years there was some talk of extending the Rhaetian Railway from St. Moritz to link up with the Italian railway system at Chiavenna, but eventually it was the Bernina Railway, from St. Moritz to Tirano by the Poschiavo valley, that won the day.

There are six successive stages in the descent of the Val Bregaglia, four of them on Swiss soil. Villages are passed with attractive names, such as Vicosoprano; by Promontogno, now down to a level of 2,685 ft., a warmer climate is evidenced by the appearance of walnut, chestnut and other fruit trees. Yet up the lateral valleys glaciers are still visible high above us, such as the Bondasca glacier at the head of the valley of that name. But the finest glacial prospect in the area is from Soglio, reached by a road which branches westwards just short of the frontier, and climbs 885 ft. from Promontogno to give a magnificent prospect of the jagged peaks and their enveloping glaciers in the Bondasca *massif.* Three ancient palaces also add to the interest of Soglio, which is the destination of many motorcoach trips from St. Moritz during the summer.

Two miles beyond Promontogno the Maloja road reaches the frontier post of Castasegna, where the usual formalities are conducted. This is 25 miles from St. Moritz, and 7 miles further on is the Italian town of Chiavenna, where the Maloja and Splügen roads join one another, and continue to the Lake of Como and beyond.

The San Bernardino and the Splügen

One of the major Swiss plans for road improvement today concerns what is eventually to be one of the nation's super-highways, affording the most direct road communication from North-Eastern Switzerland—St. Gallen, the Upper Rhine valley and Chur—to North Italy. Already work on this fine highway, with dual carriageways over considerable distances and a number of massive reinforced concrete bridges, has been completed from the Lake of Constance past Chur to Thusis, and from here onwards, through the heart of the Alps, some very costly improvements are now approaching completion. Most costly of all is the San Bernardino Road Tunnel, just over 4 miles in length, which cuts out much of the climb to the 6,774 ft. pass and now makes the route usable by motor traffic throughout the winter. In the deep recesses of the Via Mala, south of Thusis, also, much new tunnelling has been necessary in order to straighten and widen the road as far as possible. Some spectacular engineering, with massive viaducts, has been carried out to ease the gradients and curvature south of Mesocco.

We leave Thusis at an altitude of 2,369 ft., and almost immediately enter the formidable gorge of the Via Mala, with its precipitous limestone walls towering to a height of some 1,600 ft. above the stream, seen far below the road at the bottom of what appears not much more than a crack. At least, it was thus seen from the old road, but is now largely out of sight because of the tunnelling. After about 3 miles, however, the gorge widens to the pleasant Schamsertal, up which it proceeds past Zillis to Andeer. We have not yet finished with gorges, however, for beyond Andeer the road has to climb through another quite spectacular one, the Roffla ravine; on emergence from this we find the Hinter-Rhein flowing once again through a broad and barren valley, which leads the road to the village of Splügen, at an altitude of 4,429 ft. Here the Splügen road diverges to the south, and in 4 miles climbs to the Italian frontier on the summit of the pass, 6,945 ft. above the sea. As previously mentioned, this road then descends to join the Maloja road at Chiavenna, 21 miles further on. The twice-daily motorcoach service between Thusis and Chiavenna is suspended in winter.

The San Bernardino highway has now been provided with a bypass on the east side of Splügen village. The road continues, climbing steadily, until it reaches the hamlet of Hinter-Rhein, not far from the source of that river. It is here, 5,330 ft. above the sea, that the new tunnel begins, finishing just short of the town of San Bernardino. The road, however, now attacks the steep mountainside below the Mittaghorn, climbing with sixteen reverse bends into a bleak mountain valley, and eventually reaching the lonely inn and hospice on the summit, 6,774 ft above the sea. Many more windings lead down to San Bernardino, which is itself at the considerable altitude of 5,720 ft., at the head of the Mesocco valley. At Mesocco, 9 miles further on, we find the terminus of the completely detached section of the Rhaetian Railway, which the road accompanies down to Bellinzona, capital of the Canton Ticino and 62 miles from Thusis. Unlike the Maloja and Splügen pass roads, the San Bernardino road is thus on Swiss territory throughout its length. There is now a regular postal motorcoach service between Thusis and Bellinzona throughout the year.

The Great St. Bernard

First of the Swiss mountain pass roads to be prepared for all-the-year-round motor traffic by tunnelling, the Great St. Bernard road starts from Martigny in the Rhône valley. As far as Orsières it parallels the small independent Martigny–Orsières Railway—a standard-gauge line which distinguished itself a few years ago by throwing off a new branch, from Sembrancher to Le Châble, in the valley leading up to the great Mauvoisin hydro-electric barrage. In Le Châble also is the station from which postal motorcoaches climb out of the valley to the increasingly popular winter sport resort of Verbier. A distinctive feature of this branch is the graceful concrete viaduct by which its trains cross the Drance valley.

From Martigny road and railway make their way up the winding gorge of the Drance, with thickly wooded sides of immense height, which continues, apart from a temporary widening at Sembrancher, as far as Orsières, the railway terminus. Here the valley forks again, the western branch being the Val Ferret, and the eastern, the continuation of the Drance valley, leading up to the St. Bernard. As the road sweeps up in wide curves above Orsières, high on the mountainside opposite, reached by another road in a succession of zigzags, is seen the opening of the valley leading to the delightful village of Champex, with its little lake, in full view of the snows of the Grand Combin.

The St. Bernard road continues to climb steadily, past the villages of Liddes and Bourg-St. Pierre, and a high dam enclosing the storage lake of a hydro-electric power plant, until just beyond Bourg it reaches the beginning of an avalanche shelter, open on the outside, which extends for no less than $3\frac{1}{2}$ miles to the northern entrance to the tunnel proper. Tunnelling was first proposed in the last century, but not until 1936 were detailed plans made, and 22 years more were to pass before work was actually put in hand in 1958 on the Swiss side, and in 1959 on the Italian. Drilling began from both ends, and on April 5th, 1962, the two bores met; in March 19th, 1964, the tunnel, 3.66 miles long, was opened for traffic. With the protective gallery beginning at an altitude of 5,400 ft., accessibility throughout the winter has been reasonably assured. The tunnel itself, 6,230 ft. above sea level, saves nearly 2,000 ft. of the climb up to the St. Bernard Pass, which at the hospice is 8,110 ft. above sea level. A total of $10\frac{1}{2}$ miles of new approach roads was required.

After running through barren mountain scenery, it is no small surprise to run into the very large concrete building which houses the Swiss and Italian passport and customs staffs, and various facilities for motorists. The latter, of course, have the choice of "tunnel" or "col", the old road to the latter branching just before the tunnel is entered; in summer motorcoaches connecting with the through coaches are run over the pass from here to the summit and down to Bosses on the Italian side. The tunnel is level, brilliantly illuminated, provided with colour-light signals and with telephones at frequent intervals. During its passage the frontier is crossed, and at the Italian end a massive concrete bridge over a deep gorge leads into another large building for frontier formalities. These are conducted at one end of the tunnel only, on the Swiss side for those entering from Switzerland, and on the Italian for those in the opposite direction. Beyond that, to preserve the evenness of gradient, the road makes a great sweep down into a lateral valley covered for $2\frac{1}{2}$ miles with avalanche protection and continuing with a long curved reinforced concrete viaduct leading out into the main valley once again. At Bosses the new road joins the old, and from there down to the important town of

Aosta, where the motorcoach finishes its journey, there are no engineering features of note. From Martigny the climb to the summit of the col is one of 6,580 ft., and from Aosta 6,210 ft., but as previously mentioned this height is reduced by 1,880 ft. if the tunnel route is followed. The postal motorcoach service between Martigny and Aosta is operated by the Martigny–Orsières Railway with Italian cars.

The Gotthard

It is recorded that as early as 1775 an Englishman named Greville succeeded in driving a coach from Altdorf to Giornico over the Gotthard Pass by what was little more than a rough track, and 18 years later another Englishman performed a similar feat between Flüelen and Como with the aid of four horses and half-a-dozen men, taking a week in the process. As to what were the perils suffered by coach, horses and passengers in these proceedings we have no record. But at last, between 1827 and 1830, the old track was converted to a well engineered road, which carried all the traffic, save when blocked by snow in the winter, until the Gotthard Railway was opened in 1882. Since then many improvements have been made to the road, and these are still continuing.

From Switzerland the road approaches to the Gotthard Pass, like those of the railway, are chiefly from Lucerne and Zürich. As yet, both parallel the railway. The road motorist from Lucerne has to follow the same circuitous course *via* Küssnacht, Arth-Goldau and Schwyz (where the Zürich road is joined) to Brunnen, or to take the equally roundabout though scenically superior lakeside road from Küssnacht through Weggis, Vitznau and Gersau to Brunnen. Then follows the famous Axenstrasse, access to which from the Arth-Goldau and Schwyz direction is now possible by a tunnel which bypasses Brunnen. But as already mentioned the future route from Lucerne is to be by the motorway over the new Acheregg Bridge to Stans, and then by way of Buochs, Beckenried and a long tunnel under the Seelisberg peninsula to Flüelen, that is, throughout along the west instead of the east side of the Lake of Lucerne.

Up the Reuss valley much costly engineering work is in progress, including tunnelling, to improve the road, and above Göschenen the ascent through the Schöllenen gorge, with its incessant loops to and fro, its big single-span reinforced concrete arch replacing the former Devil's Bridge, and its lengthy avalanche shelters, is most spectacular. So the road reaches Andermatt. At long last a bypass has been provided at Andermatt, where a narrow hump-backed bridge, immediately followed by a right-angled turn into an equally narrow street, was formerly a constant hold-up to traffic.

Out of Andermatt the same road as that over the Furka Pass is used as far as Hospental, where the Gotthard road branches to the south. The climb from here to the pass, through barren mountains, has no special features; these are reserved for the descent southwards, begun almost immediately after we have passed the small colony on the summit. Down the narrow Val Tremola the engineering of this road has few rivals in

Switzerland. We face a succession of turns and twists, almost endless, down the face of something not far short of a sheer precipice. As the coach or car successfully negotiates one series of spirals, another and yet another burst into view far below, until at last the road emerges into the Val Leventina, and makes its final wide loop to reach Airolo, at the southern portal of the Gotthard tunnel. It is small wonder that so many motorists seek the hospitality of the tunnel in order to avoid the punishment of their car engines involved in climbing 3,185 ft. in a distance of no more than 8 miles; indeed, the direct distance is a bare 4½ miles. The summit of the pass is 6,916 ft. above sea level. But from here a new road has been constructed high above the precipitous west side of the Val Tremola, thence tunnelling under the ridge separating this valley from the Val Leventina; above this it emerges at a tremendous height, and then descends with two long wide sweeps on the mountainside, so cutting out almost the whole of the endless succession of elbow bends in the Val Tremola.

Down the Ticino valley the road once again keeps company with the railway, and here again many improvements have been made to ease the curvature. One in particular, near Giornico, has altered the famous view of the three levels of the Gotthard line as seen from above the entrance to Piano Tondo tunnel, near Giornico; a new concrete road viaduct has now appeared alongside the middle level of the three. The remainder of the road calls for no special remark. It is possible to make the journey over the pass between Andermatt and Airolo by postal motorcoach four times daily each way from mid-June to the end of September, but the service is suspended in winter, and the pass is usually snowbound from mid-October until the end of April. But construction is now under way of a road tunnel from Airolo to Hospental, roughly parallel to the railway tunnel, which will permit all-the-year-round road transport.

The Grimsel, Furka and Susten

For many years past the road tour of the Grimsel and Furka Passes has been a great attraction to holidaymakers in Switzerland, especially those in the Bernese Oberland; this pleasure has been greatly enhanced by the opening of the Susten Pass road, which makes possible the highly popular "Three Passes Tour". For this the normal starting-point, if the postal motorcoach facilities are used, is Meiringen, though private coach operators, of course, make the circuit from many other centres, particularly Interlaken and other Bernese Oberland towns; even from as far away as Lucerne it is possible to make the round trip, with the Brünig thrown in as a fourth pass.

From Meiringen there is first a short climb over the Kirchet, a vast prehistoric cliff fall through which the River Aar has bored a profound crevice—the Aareschlucht, open to sightseers—on its way down the valley. Beyond this, in a more open valley, is the village of Innertkirchen, where the Susten road diverges. As the Grimsel road mounts steadily, we have more than one reminder of the effect that the increasing demands for hydro-electric power have made on scenery. In earlier days one of the sights on the upper part of this road was the great Handegg waterfall, 150 ft. high; but this is now little more than a trickle.

Instead, we first pass the great Handegg power-station, and then come into sight of a high dam across the valley, which has made necessary a diversion of the road. No sooner have we climbed to the level of the lake so formed than two further dams come into view—a straight dam dead ahead and a curved one to the right, separated by a rocky outcrop. When we have climbed above these, it is seen that they impound a much larger lake, extending well back into the mountains, and backed by the imposing cone of the Finsteraarhorn, the highest peak in the Bernese Alps. In the commanding position offered by the lake-girt rock the Grimsel Hotel has established quite an extensive range of buildings. But not so extensive as the veritable colony that we find on the summit of the pass— as with so many other passes the fruit of the motor age in which we live. Here is fourth and smaller lake, natural in its origin.

Immediately beyond the pass, where the road crosses from the watershed of the Rhine to that of the Rhône, the Rhône valley comes into view, far below the road. High up to the left is the river's source—the Rhône glacier. From it flows the infant Rhône, through the village of Gletsch, and then down a gorge in which we can see the spiral course of the Furka-Oberalp Railway and the road to Oberwald and beyond. Looking to the left again, the railway and the Furka road are seen climbing the opposite mountainside, the railway on its 1 in 9 rack-operated gradient, considerably steeper than the 1 in 15 of the road. The whole is a most impressive panorama. By great sweeps to and fro on the steep mountainside, the road descends 1,330 ft. in 6 miles from the 7,103 ft. altitude of the Grimsel Pass to Gletsch—a village which consists mainly of a large and elderly hotel and some extensive barracks.

After pausing for breath in Gletsch, the coach begins the climb of just under 2,200 ft. to the Furka Pass, at first with a big elbow bend above the village, then sweeping eastwards to cross the Furka-Oberalp Railway just before the latter enters the Furka tunnel, and finally to and fro up the steep mountainside at the head of the valley to reach the hotel established many years ago by the Seiler family from Zermatt. And it is of interest that, looking down the Rhône valley from the hotel on a clear day, it is possible to see the great ice-mantled peaks of the Valais, including the Weisshorn and the Mischabel group, and, peeping over the right shoulder of the latter, the tip of Zermatt's Matterhorn. But the principal attraction of the hotel stop, which is made by all the coaches, is the immediately adjacent "snout" or lower end of the Rhône glacier.

A little more climbing brings the road to the crest of the Furka Pass, 7,975 ft. above sea level. Here the road crosses back from the Rhône to the Rhine watershed, and begins the long and sweeping descent into the Urseren valley. The emergence of the Furka-Oberalp Railway from the Furka tunnel is in view more than 800 ft. below, but we do not reach the

railway level until the village of Realp. Road and railway then keep
company through Hospental, where the Gotthard road comes in from the
south, into Andermatt, the great mountain pass centre of Switzerland.
This also is an invariable stop for motorcoaches.

For the continuation over the Susten Pass motors and motorcoaches
leave Andermatt by the Gotthard road, down through the Schöllenen
gorge to Göschenen, where connection can be made with trains over the
Gotthard main line, and then, further, to Wassen; here the Susten road
proper begins. From the engineering point of view the latter, completed
between 1941 and 1946 mainly for strategic reasons, in my judgement is
the most notable of all three passes negotiated on this circuit. It begins
with some thrills, as between two tunnels the road crosses the deep chasm
of the Meienreuss between the upper and middle Meienreuss bridges of
the Gotthard Railway. We then ascend the barren Meien valley into the
heart of the High Alps, with a serrated mountain ridge ahead until the
road winds round its base to face the imposing cone of the Sustenspitz.
Then, after further windings on the mountain face, the road tunnels for
½-mile under the crest of the Susten pass to reach its summit level, 7,296 ft.
above the sea.

It would take too much space to describe the brilliant engineering by
which the road is carried from this tunnel portal down to Gadmen. We
first descend, in face of the Stein glacier, backed by the snowy dome of
the Sustenhorn, to the Steingletscher Hotel. The road then continues
downwards, with the gradient steepening in places to 1 in 11, and with
constant elbow bends and a succession of tunnels, to Gadmen. From
here an older road has been modernised, leading through a deep mountain
valley to Innertkirchen, where the Grimsel road is rejoined, after which
a short run to Meiringen completes one of the finest road circuits in the
whole of the Alps.

As a switchback also it could have few equals; indeed it would be
difficult to imagine a more exacting test for a motorcoach or motorcar
engine than this tour. Think of the differences in altitude *en route*—
Meiringen, 1,960 ft.; the Grimsel Pass, 7,103 ft.; Gletsch, 5,783 ft.; the
Furka Pass, 7,975 ft.; Wassen, 3,050 ft.; the Susten Pass, 7,460 ft.; and,
finally, Meiringen once again at 1,960 ft. Including the short climbs
over the Kirchet, between Meiringen and Innertkirchen, the motors or
motorcoaches have to mount a total of all but 12,000 ft. in the course of
the "Three Passes Tour"! Snow generally closes all three passes from
mid-October to mid-June.

The Klausen

Another of the Swiss mountain passes which, like the Susten, is more
modernly strategic than historic is the Klausen, the road over which
provides direct communication between the eastern end of the Lake of
Zürich and the southern end of the Lake of Lucerne. The Klausen road
really begins at Linthal, which is reached by a branch of the Swiss
Federal Railways from Ziegelbrücke, on the Zürich-Chur main line,

through Glarus, the prosperous capital of the canton of that name, in its striking setting at the base of the snowmantled Glärnisch. Linthal is a finely situated village; looking up the valley are the snowy peaks of the Tödi group, and an even finer view is obtained by taking the funicular railway up to Braunwald, a delightful mountain resort, and the further chair-lift to Kleiner Gumen, 6,247 ft. altitude.

A regular postal motorcoach service plies in summer between Linthal and Flüelen, on the Lake of Lucerne. On leaving Linthal, the road first makes the inevitable zigzag climb up the mountainside on the west side of the valley until, after an ascent of nearly 2,200 ft., it is able to turn westwards into a grassy valley known as the Urnerboden, 4½ miles in length, bounded by high mountains, in particular the snowfields of Clariden. After the village of Urnerboden stiff climbing begins again, with the road winding through the rocky cauldron of the Klus, with its waterfalls—to me very reminiscent of the Cirque de Gavarnie, in the Pyrenees—to reach the summit of the Klausen Pass. In 14½ miles we have climbed from 2,135 ft. altitude at Linthal to 6,391 ft.

Three-quarters of a mile further on we reach the Hotel Klausenpasshöhe, and a breathtaking prospect opens up ahead. It is the vast depth of the Schächental, into which we have now to descend. Above the opposite side of the valley rise the ice-mantled summits of the Clariden, Windgälle and other peaks. The head of the valley is walled in by a sheer precipice; and nearly 3,000 ft. below, looking like tiny toys, are the châlets of a prosperous farming community. At first the road makes a lengthy slant down the precipitous north wall of the valley until eventually we come to another series of loops and elbow bends, and passing the pleasant village of Irigen reach the valley floor at Unterschächen, 3,130 ft below the crest of the pass, and 7 miles by road from the pass hotel. Continuing down the valley, high above the Schächenbach stream, we run finally through Burglen and Altdorf to complete the 32½-mile run to Flüelen, which takes about 2½ hours. The Klausen pass normally is open only from mid-June to mid-October.

Other Mountain Pass Roads

The roads over mountain passes described in the preceding sections of this chapter are not an exhaustive list, though perhaps the most important; one or two others deserve mention. In the Grisons a pass over to Italy additional to the Maloja, Splügen and San Bernardino is the Lukmanier, further to the west; on its modernisation a good deal of money has been spent in recent years, including tunnelling, avalanche galleries, and a concrete surface over much of its length. The Lukmanier road starts from the upper end of the Vorder Rhein valley, at Disentis, at 3,760 ft. altitude. Running due south, it enters the Val Medel, the valley of the tributary Mittel Rhein; in the first 4 miles, high above the valley, there are a number of tunnels, between which fine views of the gorge are obtained.

There are no other engineering features of particular note as the road climbs past Platta and the old hospices of St. Gall and Santa Maria to the summit, 6,826 ft. above the sea and 13 miles from the starting point, hemmed in by high and barren mountains. On the subsequent descent many avalanche tracks are crossed; by Olivone, 24½ miles, we are into wooded country once again, and by Acquarossa, 30½ miles, and at 1,740 ft. altitude only, into the populous part of the Brenno valley. From here down the remaining 8½ miles to Biasca, on the Gotthard main line, we have the company of the independent metre-gauge Biasca-Acquarossa Railway. This pass is usually open from mid-June to the end of October.

In the eastern area of the Grisons there is the road over the Bernina Pass, which for most of its length parallels the Bernina Railway; in fact over certain sections in the Poschiavo valley the railway actually runs along the roadside. The only divergence between the two is at the summit of the pass; from the Bernina Hospice station the railway bears westwards towards Alp Grüm and descends from there through the Cavaglia glacial basin, whereas the road bears eastwards into the Valle Agone, the head of the Poschiavo valley, and continues through La Rösa to that town. The summit level of the road, 7,621 ft., is only 218 ft. higher than that of the railway. Snow usually closes this pass from November till the end of May, though the railway is kept open with snowploughs.

The highest road summit on Swiss soil is the Umbrail Pass, 8,205 ft. up, in the extreme east of the Canton of the Grisons. The Umbrail road starts from Zernez, in the Lower Engadine, and in its early stages is of note as it skirts the famous Swiss National Park, in which Nature holds undisputed sway, and rare animals and plants abound; the wild Val Cluoza, the entrance to which is passed by the road, is the principal means of access. The road climbs first to Il Fuorn, or the Ofen Pass, 7,060 ft. up and open throughout the year, where the snowclad Ortler mountain group comes into view; it then descends to Santa Maria, the capital of the Münstertal, or Val Müstair, from which it is possible to proceed through Müstair itself across the Italian frontier into the South Tyrolese Vintschgau valley and so to Merano and Bolzano.

But the Umbrail Pass road diverges due south from Santa Maria, and in 8½ miles climbs, with many windings, from 4,555 ft. altitude to 8,205 ft., and immediately afterwards joins the Stelvio road, which 2 miles later crosses the Stelvio Pass, or Stilfserjoch, 9,049 ft. above the sea, and the former meeting-place of three countries—Switzerland, Italy and Austria. Since the First World War, however, the Austrian frontier has been pushed back a considerable distance to the north, and the summit of the Stelvio Pass is therefore Italian. This pass has the distinction of being the highest road summit in Europe. From it the road drops in an endless series of windings, in full view of the towering peaks of the Ortler, to Trafoi, Spondigna, Merano and Bolzano. Between July to September inclusive there is a daily service between St. Moritz and Bolzano over the Ofen, Umbrail and Stelvio Passes, taking about ten hours for the run. It may be added that a connecting postal service operates three times daily in summer between Davos and Zernez over the Flüela Pass, 7,818 ft. up, which separates the Davos valley from the Lower Engadine. This road reaches the latter at Susch, 4 miles down the Inn valley from Zernez. The Umbrail, Stelvio and Flüela Passes are all generally snow-blocked from mid-October to mid-June.

While we are in the Lower Engadine, it is worth while to mention the fine road from St. Moritz that continues from Zernez and Schuls—the terminus of the Lower Engadine branch of the Rhaetian Railway—to Martinsbruck or Martina, on the Austrian frontier. Here the principal road crosses the Inn over a bridge that has the customs posts at both ends, and then climbs with innumerable windings for over 1,100 ft. up the steep mountainside above the right bank to pass into a neighbouring valley in which lies the considerable Austrian village of Nauders. From Nauders the road passes through the Finstermünz gorge suddenly to emerge, at Hoch Finstermünz, at an enormous height above the Inn valley, and on the face of an almost sheer precipice—a breath-taking prospect indeed. Through a succession of tunnels we then make our way down the precipice, eventually joining the road which has pursued a far easier course alongside the Inn from Martinsbruck and reaching the town of Pfunds. The remainder of the coach journey is in Austrian territory, and leads to the town of Landeck, on the Arlberg main line of the Austrian Federal Railway. There are regular motorcoach services between St. Moritz, Schuls and Landeck over this highly spectacular road, and the trip is certainly one to be commended.

Among the remaining pass roads one which is considerably used in summer by motorcoaches and is open throughout the winter, is over the Col de la Forclaz, 5,009 ft. altitude, between Martigny and Le Châtelard; from the latter the road continues across the French frontier to Vallorcine, and from there over the Col des Montets into the Chamonix valley. In recent years an entirely new road, well graded, has been built out of Martigny, in a great loop high above the Drance valley, and higher up there are many more windings before the summit of the pass is reached. From here a single chair-lift may be taken to the Mont d'Arpille, all but 6,700 ft. above the sea. An abrupt descent then is made, in full view of the Glacier du Trient, to the village of Trient, beyond which the road emerges into the Trient valley. At the angle here is the Tête Noire Hotel; immediately opposite is the high-lying village of Finhaut, on the Martigny-Châtelard Railway; but between the two is the abysmal gorge in which the river flows. A road has now been constructed across the valley between the Tête Noire and Finhaut, which hitherto has been without road access.

Further west the Col de Pillon, 5,073 ft., has been mentioned in Chapter 13, in connection with the Diablerets cable lines; it has no features of note. Another pass in the same vicinity is the Col des Mosses, 4,740 ft.; this is on the road which from Aigle, in the Rhône valley, ascends the valley of the Grande Eau, high above its right bank, to Le Sépey, and from there climbs over the pass to descend on the far side to Château-d'Oex. This road also has its own *Gondelbahn*, a recently constructed line which climbs in two stages to the Pic Chaussy—an ascent of 2,812 ft. in a length of 4,416 yards (all but 2½ miles)—yet another attraction to skiers in this renowned winter sporting area. Both the Col de Pillon and Col des Mosses roads are kept open throughout the year.

Three other passes only require mention. One is the Oberalp, which leads from the most notable mountain pass centre in Switzerland—Andermatt—eastwards towards the Canton of the Grisons. This is, in effect, a continuation of the road up the Rhône valley from Brigue to Gletsch and from there over the Furka Pass to Andermatt, which has been joined at Hospental by the Gotthard Pass road, and also by that which has come up through the Schöllenen Gorge from Göschenen. Like the Furka road, so the Oberalp road parallels the Furka-Oberalp Railway; both wind to and fro up the mountain wall east of Andermatt until they can turn inland, where railway and road share a lengthy avalanche shelter because of the prevalence of avalanches in this bleak pass region. The summit level is at 6,706 ft. The road then descends past Sedrun to Disentis, in the Vorder-Rhein valley. It is usually negotiable only from mid-June to mid-October.

Then the year 1970 saw the opening of a new pass road of note. This is from Ulrichen, in the upper Rhône valley, over the Nufenen Pass at 8,005 ft. altitude, and down the lengthy Val Bedretto past All' Acqua to Airolo, at the southern end of the Gotthard tunnel. The most breathtaking section is where this finely engineered road is carried in windings eastward up the face of an almost sheer precipice from Ladstafel to the summit. In summer the Furka-Oberalp Railway operates a daily motorcoach service between Ulrichen and Airolo.

The third pass is the Brünig, at the fairly modest altitude of 3,316 ft., on the highway between Lucerne and the Bernese Oberland. No postal motorcoaches use this route, as it parallels the Brünig Railway, but in the summer season it sees an endless procession of motorcars and motorcoaches. In winter there is no difficulty in keeping this pass road open.

Future Developments

Many costly projects are envisaged for the development of the national highways in Switzerland, and as the previous sections of this chapter have indicated, certain of them already have reached or are near completion. In many cases the planning includes tunnels, some of considerable length. As yet a beginning only has been made in building bypasses round the towns and villages through which important motor roads pass, particularly those through the mountains, and negotiating the narrow streets of many of these places is no small problem, especially for motorcoaches and other lengthy vehicles, but this handicap no doubt will be dealt with in due time. Elsewhere some remarkable road construction both has been and still is being carried out, with clover-leaf junctions, extensive reinforced concrete viaducts, astonishing locations on precipitous mountainsides, and the tunnelling already mentioned. The programme looks a long way ahead; some improvements are not likely to be begun until the middle 1970s.

Work is nearing completion on the national highway from Eastern Switzerland to Bellinzona, capital of the Canton Ticino. From the north this has two approaches, uniting at Sargans, one from Zürich, along the south-west side of the lake, and then through Ziegelbrücke and along the south shore of the Walensee, and the other from Winterthur, St. Gallen, Rorschach and up the Rhine valley. This bypasses the important town of Chur. Tunnelling was needed on the Walensee section, and extensively through the Via Mala, beyond Thusis, while the biggest task has been the 4-mile San Bernardino tunnel.

A second north-south national highway will be the road counterpart of the Gotthard Railway. From Lucerne onwards a dual carriageway is now in use, partly tunnelled (under the Lopperberg) and carried over the reinforced concrete Acheregg bridge into Stans. From here the road will proceed on the west side of the Lake of Lucerne (instead of the east side as now) to Beckenried, and then with a tunnel $2\frac{3}{4}$ miles long under the Seelisberg peninsula and several subsequent tunnels to Flüelen. Here it will be joined by the road from Zürich. The latter has now been improved by a tunnel under a spur of the Fronalpstock, which bypasses Brunnen; and another tunnel, 2 miles long, under the Uetliberg, is to expedite the exit from Zürich. Works of some magnitude are being carried out up the Reuss valley, but the greatest enterprise of all is the new road tunnel under the Gotthard Pass, just over 10 miles long, work on this, began in 1969, and is now well under way. But the tunnelling on the west side of the Lake of Lucerne is not contemplated until 1972 or later.

Work is now in progress on an improvement of the road communication between Basle and the south, which includes a new tunnel under the easternmost ridge of the Jura, 2 miles in length, not far from the 5-mile Hauenstein tunnel on the Basle-Olten railway line. This will link up west of Aarburg with a very lengthy new highway which is now being built to improve the communication between Zürich and Berne, and also Solothurn, Biel, Neuchâtel and the south-west; the latter starts west of Lenzburg and passes to the south of Aarau and Olten to Oensingen, where the Berne and Solothurn roads separate.

Another route of importance is that from Lucerne to Interlaken, Thun and Berne by way of the Brünig Pass; out of Lucerne this shares, as far as Acheregg, the dual carriageway already mentioned. This road also will provide the means of access to a very important project which lies in the more distant future. This is to extend the present road up the Simme Valley from Spiez through Zweisimmen to Lenk, by a new road to cut through the Alps into the Rhône valley at Sierre, which will involve a $2\frac{1}{4}$-mile tunnel under the Rawyl pass. The value of this road will be to provide a much more direct route than now from Berne, Biel and all the populous surrounding area, to the central part of the Rhône valley. So the modernisation and improvement of Swiss road communications is proceeding just as vigorously as that of the railways.

FIFTEEN

Swiss Lake Steamers and Motorships

No BOOK on Swiss transport would be complete without some description of the passenger services on the different lakes, which give pleasure and recreation to such vast numbers of holiday-makers. In addition, of course, these lake craft provide many lakeside towns and villages with their only direct communication, so that the services on most of the lakes, even if in a reduced form, operate throughout the winter as well as in summer. As in most mountainous countries, the lakes are numerous, and as some of them extend into the heart of the High Alps, they afford both magnificent views and also provide access to mountain railways and suspension lines, so making possible an attractive combination of lake and mountain excursions.

A number of the best-known lakes are on the frontiers, and are therefore shared by Switzerland with other countries. In the north there is the Lake of Constance, or Bodensee, with Germany on its northern shore and Austria at its eastern end. In the south-west most of the southern shore of the Lake of Geneva is French territory, with Switzerland on its northern side and round its eastern extremity. In the extreme south, in the Canton Ticino, the Lakes of Maggiore and Lugano are both bordered in part by Italian territory; indeed, Lake Maggiore is mainly Italian. The Lake of Lugano is unique in that on its eastern side the town of Campione is in a little enclave of Italian territory completely separated from the mother country; otherwise this lake is mainly Swiss. These international complications mean that the Swiss Government must maintain passport and customs posts at all piers called at by the lake steamers and motorships which also serve piers in the other countries, and that passengers landing must carry their passports. Switzerland also must maintain a small "navy" of fast launches to keep a check on the smuggling which otherwise might be indulged in on an extensive scale.

The principal Swiss lakes on which passenger services are run are those of Lucerne, Geneva, Thun, Brienz, Zürich, Constance, Lugano and Maggiore, and, on a minor scale, those of Neuchâtel, Biel, Zug, the Greifensee and the Hallwilersee. The Lötschberg Railway owns the ships on the Lakes of Thun and Brienz, and the Swiss Federal Railways run certain of the services across the Lake of Constance between Romanshorn and the German port of Friedrichshafen and between Rorschach and Lindau; the former include ferries carrying both railway wagons and motorcars, which thus can move directly between Switzerland and Germany and avoid crossing two Austrian frontiers by having to travel round the east end of the lake through St. Margrethen, Bregenz and Lindau. The ships on all the other Swiss lakes are operated by private companies, which with the railways have vied with one another in building some extremely fine craft, particularly the later diesel-driven ships, with the most modern of equipment. We have now to deal in detail with the principal lakes.

The Lake of Lucerne

In my judgment, which I think may be shared by anyone who knows Switzerland well, there is no rival in both beauty and diversity to the Lake of Lucerne. For this pre-eminence there are several reasons. The diversity is due to the irregular shape of the lake, cruciform and with its southern extremity turning at a right-angle to reveal a view totally different from what has been seen up to that point. At the centre of the lake, where the four arms meet, the scene is well-nigh incomparable. Over the blue water in the foreground there are the densely wooded slopes of the Bürgenstock, part of the forests that gave the lake the name of Vierwaldstättersee—the "Lake of the Four Forest Cantons" of Lucerne, Unterwalden, Schwyz and Uri, which border its shores. To the right the bold shapes of Pilatus, the Stanserhorn and other mountains are backed by the distant snows of the Bernese Alps. Then by the time we turn the right-angled corner of the lake at Brunnen, we are introduced directly to the High Alps themselves—a stretch of water like a Norwegian fjord, hemmed in by mountain slopes that are in part precipitous, with the glaciers of the Uri-Rotstock to the right, and the lovely cone of the Bristenstock providing a stately background to the head of the lake at Flüelen.

The total length of the lake, from Lucerne to Flüelen, is 23 miles, but the course of the steamers covering the whole distance is anything but direct and extends for 30 miles. The town of Lucerne is situated at the extremity of the relatively short north-western arm. On reaching the central cross of the lake, we have to the left the much longer north-eastern arm, up to Küssnacht, and to the right the south-western arm, which appears to terminate at Stansstad, at the foot of the buttress of Pilatus known as the Lopperberg, but then passes through a narrow opening—now bridged by the Lucerne–Stans–Engelberg Railway and a dual carriageway—into the Alpnachersee, on which is situated the village of Alpnachstad, lower terminus of the Pilatus Railway. Ahead is the solid barrier of the Bürgenstock ridge, cutting the lake almost in half.

This the Flüelen steamer then rounds, in an easterly direction, calling at Weggis and Vitznau, on the lower slopes of the Rigi. The steamer then has to turn south, between the two "noses"—the Untere Nase, at the eastern extremity of the Bürgenstock, and the Obere Nase, just beyond Vitznau—into another stretch of the lake running from west to east and eventually to the north-east, to Brunnen. All this time we have been cruising along the base of the Rigi ridge, which is almost entirely surrounded by water, from Küssnacht round to Brunnen on this side, and with the Lakes of Zug and Lowerz bordering much of the north-east side. Finally, as already mentioned, there is the complete turn through three parts of a circle to the southern extremity of the lake, from Brunnen to Flüelen.

The piers at which direct railway connections are made are those at Lucerne and Flüelen, with the Gotthard main line of the Swiss Federal, rail and boat tickets being interchangeable; at Vitznau for the Rigi Railway and at Alpnachstad for both the Pilatus Railway and the Brünig line of the Swiss Federal. Stansstad for the former Stansstad–Engelberg Railway used to be a fifth, but since the latter has been linked with Lucerne by rail, the pier at Stansstad is about half-a-mile from the new railway station. During the summer season there are five daily steamers in each direction over the full length of the lake between Lucerne and Flüelen. Those calling at most of the piers have their times considerably increased by doubling to and fro across the lake, between Kehrsiten and Weggis; Vitznau, Buochs and Beckenried; Beckenried and Gersau; Gersau and Treib; and Treib and Brunnen.

The long established 2.55 p.m. steamer from Flüelen, which collects up most of the holiday-makers who have been making mountain trips round the lake, takes 3 hours 30 minutes on the journey, and often needs the capacious flagship of the fleet, the *Stadt Luzern* (and at times of pressure also a relief steamer from Vitznau) to provide enough accommodation. The 2.25 p.m. from Flüelen, however, which has five intermediate calls only, makes the run in 2 hours 4 minutes. In general, 2¾ to 3 hours is the time occupied. There are other services between Lucerne and Vitznau and in winter the boats ply only between Lucerne and Brunnen, with a single trip from Brunnen to Flüelen and back each day,

Then there is the service between Lucerne, Stansstad and Alpnachstad, now carried on entirely by the modern diesel motorships, which have sufficient clearance to pass under the bridge at Stansstad into the Alpnachersee. These boats almost all call at Kehrsiten pier, on the Bürgenstock, where they connect in many cases with the Flüelen steamers, so providing a service between Vitznau and Weggis and the Stansstad and Alpnachstad piers. Küssnacht has three motorships a day from Lucerne in summer, but a Sunday service only in winter; this arm of the lake is, of course, served by the Gotthard line trains to and from the stations of Meggen and Küssnacht. Which is a reminder that the only direct communication between Lucerne and some of the lakeside resorts served, such as St. Niklausen, Kastanienbaum, the two Kehrsiten piers, and one or two other points, is by water; towns such as Buochs and Beckenried are accessible by rail from Lucerne to Stans and postal motorcoach from there, but the ships provide direct transport without change. The lake service is completed by the launches which ply round the Lucerne arm of the lake, serving Seeburg, the Hermitage and Tribschen, and by the Beckenried-Gersau motorcar ferry.

The Schiffahrts-Gesellschaft des Vierwaldstättersees, or Lake of Lucerne Ship Company, can claim the distinction of building its own ships, and they are indeed a long-lived race. The first was the paddle-steamer *Rigi*, which began service in 1848 and continued to work for 104 years; she is now permanently on exhibition, and serves as a restaurant, in the grounds of the Transport Museum at Lucerne.   Nine of the older ships, six now withdrawn, have covered over a million miles on the lake; the record was held by the S.S. *Gotthard*, which between 1889 and 1965 achieved a total mileage of no less than 1,455,508 miles.

This leaves six paddle-steamers, of which the largest and finest is the oil-fired *Stadt Luzern*, 197 ft. long, 25 ft. 6 in. in the beam and of 1,300 h.p.; she took the water in 1929, and is the last of the steam-driven ships.   The first class passenger accommodation is quite luxurious.   At the maximum the *Stadt Luzern* is allowed to carry 1,200 passengers, though in such conditions she is extremely crowded!   The first experiment in screw propulsion with diesel engines was in 1912, with a launch called the *Neptun*, limited to 95 passengers; this was followed by the *Mythen*, *Rütli* and *Reuss*, used mostly for the short trips round the bay of Lucerne.

But it is with the last of the eleven diesel-driven ships, the *Schwyz*, the *Winkelried*, the *Pilatus* and the 1970 *Gotthard*, that the finest development has been reached. The *Winkelried* and the *Gotthard*, each accommodating up to 1,200 passengers, are 180 ft. long, 27 ft. 6 in. in the beam, and of 900 h.p. The *Gotthard* has a new internal arrangement; the first class upper deck has a magnificent combined saloon and restaurant seating 156, and comfortable seats partly under cover and partly in the open for 271 more; while the second class lower deck has a restaurant with 55 seats, a saloon seating 98 and 168 seats in the open. All the last three ships have been built at Lucerne by the S.G.V.

Traffic in the summer fluctuates greatly with the weather, as may be imagined.   On August 4, 1965, for example, a record total of 36,537 passengers was carried in a single day, whereas on the previous day the number was 13,645 only, and on the 22nd of the same month the figure dropped to 5,417!

The Lakes of Thun and Brienz

The town of Interlaken derives its name, fairly obviously, from being situated "between the lakes"—the two lakes of Thun and Brienz, which provide part of the scenic glory of the Bernese Oberland.   On both the service is operated most efficiently by the Bern–Lötschberg–Simplon Railway, but though the two lakes are little more than two miles apart, it is not possible for the lake steamers and motorships to pass between one and the other, because the level of Brienz is 20 ft. higher than that of Thun. One of the earliest railways in Switzerland, the Bödelibahn, was laid down from Bönigen, on the Lake of Brienz, through Interlaken to Därligen on the Lake of Thun, to provide communication between the early steamers on the two lakes.

In the matter of beauty, the Lake of Thun undoubtedly has the advantage.   From the level of the castle that dominates the town of Thun a magnificent view unfolds itself to the south-east.   Beyond the wooded slopes that border the lake, and the lower mountains, there tower the ice-clad summits of a row of great peaks—the Wetterhorn, Schreckhorn' Eiger, Mönch, Jungfrau and Blümlisalp. Then, to the right beyond the perfect cone of the Niesen, there is the serrated ridge dominated by the Stockhorn—a perfect Alpine picture. The Lake of Brienz is less spectacular; it is hemmed in by mountains of a fairly even height, and only as we reach the eastern end, at the approach to the town of Brienz, does some prospect appear of the snows of the Grimsel region, beyond Meiringen.

Some of the larger Lötschberg motorships, which ply on the Lake of Thun, are among the finest lake craft in Switzerland, and are very heavily patronised in summer; railway tickets between Thun, Spiez and Interlaken are inter-available on them. From Thun they leave the quay adjacent to the railway station, and pass through a channel leading out to the lake, into which, in the reverse direction, they proceed stern first. Most of them call at the lakeside resorts of Hünibach, Hilterfingen, Oberhofen with its picturesque castle, and Gunten, before crossing the lake to Spiez, a most attractive centre, with its little harbour, dominated by another castle, and with the conical Niesen towering in the background.

Here the pier is about a mile from the railway station, but the two are connected by a frequent motorbus service which climbs the intervening 200 ft. After Spiez the ships cross the lake again to call at Merligen and Beatenbucht, the lower terminus of the funicular railway to Beatenberg, and then, after a halt on most services at Neuhaus, with its "Lido", they turn stern first to make their way up the 1¾-mile canal to the terminus adjacent to Interlaken-West Station. There are fifteen piers in all between Thun and Interlaken; certain courses are varied in order to serve the piers of minor importance. Running the entire length of the lake takes about two hours or slightly less.

The motorships on the Lake of Brienz start from a quay adjacent to Interlaken-Ost Station, but time can usually be saved by taking one of the motorcoaches which work between this station and the pier at Bönigen. Services on the Lake of Brienz are maintained entirely by motorships, smaller than those on the Lake of Thun. The most important call is at Iseltwald, on the south side of the lake; Giessbach, with its famous waterfall, is the next stop; and the ships then cross to the piers at Brienz-Dorf and Brienz, the latter adjacent to the railway station on the Swiss Federal Brünig line.

The run between Bönigen and Brienz takes 45 to 55 minutes, and to and from Interlaken-Ost from 20 to 25 minutes longer. On the Lake of Brienz the service throughout the winter is almost as ample as in the summer; with some places served, such as Iseltwald, the only communication is by water. On the Lake of Thun, however, operation is confined mainly to a shuttle service across the lake between Spiez and Gunter.

The Lötschberg fleet now comprises sixteen ships, eleven of which sail on the Lake of Thun and the other five on the Lake of Brienz.

No paddle-steamers now remain on Lake Thun; the last of them, the *Blümlisalp*, dating back to 1906, was replaced in 1971 by a most handsome new diesel-driven *Blümlisalp*, carrying up to 1,200 passengers.

The first diesel experiment was in 1901, with a small craft named *Spiez*; five of these, with accommodation for 70 to 400 passengers, carry out the minor duties. But in addition to the new *Blümlisalp*, the pride of the fleet is in the *Jungfrau, Stadt Bern* and *Bubenberg*, three truly magnificent ships carrying from 900 to 1,100 passengers, and of from 620 to 700 h.p. The *Bubenberg* was built in 1962, and there is one later vessel of smaller capacity, the *Beatus*, which took the water in 1963. On the Lake of Brienz one paddle-steamer is still available, the *Lötschberg*, capable of carrying 1,000 passengers, but most of the work is done by the motorships *Rothorn* and *Interlaken*, accommodating up to 400 and 550 passengers respectively, with a couple of large motor launches chiefly for the reduced winter service.

The Lake of Geneva

By comparison with the lakes already described, navigation on the Lake of Geneva is like that of an open sea, and at times, indeed, with a strong westerly wind, it can become distinctly rough. The lake is 45 miles long, and at its widest point 8½ miles across; it covers an area of 224 square miles, roughly two-fifths of which is French territory. A curious phenomenon experienced on the lake, probably caused by sudden variations in atmospheric pressure, is the *seiches*, or miniature tidal waves, which have been known to rise to a height of as much as 6 ft.; some run longitudinally, and others cross the lake in about ten minutes.

The lake service is operated by the Compagnie Générale de Navigation du Lac Leman, or C.G.N., nicknamed the "Nana" by the lakeside residents. It possesses a fleet of seven paddle-steamers, eight motorships, three *vedettes* or large launches, and one hydrofoil, the *Albatross*, which has been making special trips at speeds up to nearly 40 m.p.h. With a total of 37 landing-stages at which to call, the majority of the services on the Lake of Geneva are local, rather than running the length of the lake, which can take anything from five to six hours. By far the busiest service is that across the lake between Ouchy, Lausanne's pier, and Evian, with some sailings prolonged to Thonon-les-Bains, on the French side. Of this a unique feature is the 1.0 a.m. trip from Evian, for the benefit of Lausannois who have been sampling the excitements of Evian's casino, and it is supplemented on Sunday mornings by a further run at 2.15 a.m.

In summer, for those who wish to spend most of the day on board, there is a *Translémanique*, leaving Geneva at 10.15 a.m., calling on the outward journey only at Ouchy, Vevey, Montreux and the Château de Chillon to Villeneuve, at the eastern extremity of the lake; on the return journey the calls are at Chillon and Montreux, and then on the French side at Evian and Thonon, the return to Geneva being by 5.40 p.m. Other ships at various times make a "Tour du Haut Lac" and a "Tour du Petit Lac", the former of the eastern end of the lake from and to Ouchy, and the latter from Geneva round the western end, calling at all the local piers in each case.

The C.G.N. owns some very fine lake craft, most of them of a handsome clipper design, with sharply pointed bows, and with first class restaurant facilities. The paddle-steamers are the most capacious; the *Simplon* and *Helvétie* are rated as capable of carrying a total of 1,600 passengers apiece, 1,200 of them seated; *La Suisse* accommodates 1,500; and the *Rhône*, *Savoie* and *Général Dufour* 1,100 each. Of the motorships, only the *Léman* carries as many as 1,000; the *Italie*, *Vevey* and *Genéve* are limited to 900 and the *Lausanne* to 850. All the bigger ships have appointments of which their owners may well be proud; evening trips in the summer are made with orchestras on board and dancing for those so disposed by the *Helvétie*, illuminated from stem to stern.

The Lake of Constance

There are similarities between the Lakes of Geneva and Constance that are of no small interest. Both are roughly equal in size; Constance is 40 miles long and has a maximum breadth of 8¾ miles, as against the 45 miles by 8½ miles of Geneva. In both Switzerland has no more than a part interest, the opposite shores being the territory of other nations. The two lakes are fed by two of the principal European rivers, both of which rise in Switzerland, Constance by the River Rhine and Geneva by the River Rhône. Very curiously, also, both lakes are at the extreme corners of Switzerland, Constance in the north-east and Geneva in the south-west. Scenically, Constance, or Bodensee, cannot compare with such lakes as Lucerne and Thun, and falls short even of the eastern end of Geneva; its only mountains are those bordering the eastern or Austrian end of the lake, and the *massif* of the Säntis, as seen well to the south. But in the varied interest of its lake craft Constance has no rival in Switzerland.

This interest is due to two facts. One is that all three nations bordering the lake—Switzerland on the south, Germany on the north, and Austria in the east—have their own steamers and motorcraft, owned in each case by the national railways (the Swiss Federal, German Federal and Austrian Federal) whose names each vessel bears on its stern. The other is that, as already mentioned, to avoid the necessity of running round the eastern end of the lake and the double crossing of the Austrian frontier, both motorcars and railway wagons are ferried across the lake from the Swiss port of Romanshorn to Friedrichshafen on the German side, which is probably the most important port on the lake. "Port" is a very suitable description, for Friedrichshafen has a large harbour, enclosed by long breakwaters; Romanshorn and the German Lindau are equipped similarly, and such protection is of considerable value in storms, which can be even more violent here than on the Lake of Geneva.

The Romanshorn–Friedrichshafen crossings, which take 40 minutes and in summer are made up to ten times daily in each direction (and more frequently on Sundays), are shared by Swiss and German vessels. Whether motorcar-carrying or wagon-carrying, these ships have wide decks bridged over by saloons high up above, which gives them a most curious appearance, especially the wagon-carrying Swiss *Romanshorn*, with its enormous superstructure crowned by cabins at both ends from which the manoeuvring of the vessel to its berths on both sides of the lake is carried out. But most of the wagon-carrying vessels do not accommodate passengers, though the motorcar carriers all do. Many of the motorcar crossings are made by the German ferry-boat *Schussen*, but unfortunately the German railways have not established at Friedrichshafen handling facilities for wagons equal to those constructed at considerable cost by the Swiss Federal Railways at Romanshorn.

The Swiss Federal Railways have some modern passenger ships which are used on the Rorschach–Lindau crossing, and in summer serve the coastal resorts between Rorschach and Romanshorn, also crossing to piers on the German side, such as at Meersburg and Mainau; some also run to and from Bregenz in Austria. But the Austrian end of the lake is served mainly by the Austrian ships, which work as far as Friedrichshafen, and the length of the German shore by those of the German Federal Railways. At its western end the Lake of Constance divides into three, two arms extending to the towns of Ludwigshafen and Radolfzell, and the third, the southernmost, passing through a narrow channel between the towns of Konstanz and Kreuzlingen into what is known as the Untersee. This most attractive stretch of water is served by an independent company, the Untersee und Rhein, which maintains a service between Kreuzlingen and Stein-am-Rhein and then down the river itself as far as Schaffhausen, just short of the Rhine Falls, the whole trip taking $3\frac{1}{4}$ hours. The company's latest motorship, the *Thurgau*, completed in 1964, is 154 ft. 6 in. long and 30 ft. 6 in. broad, and can accommodate 600 passengers. Other minor services are conducted with motorboats on various parts of this large sheet of water, for the most part in summer only.

The Lake of Zürich

The company responsible for the heavily patronised services on the Lake of Zürich, the Zürichsee Schiffahrts-Gesellschaft or Z.S.G., earns distinction in that its fleet of 18 ships is the biggest owned by any individual lake company in Switzerland. Navigation on the lake began early, as far back as 1835, with a British-built ship known as the *Minerva*, long before there were any railways on both shores of the lake. It is a far cry from this primitive vessel to the latest motorships, the *Linth*, completed in 1952, carrying a maximum of 1,400 passengers; the *Limmat*, 1958, with a capacity for 1,100; and the majestic *Helvetia*, introduced in 1964, accommodating no fewer than 1,500. One striking feature in each of the latest vessels is the capacious first class saloon, with its glazed semi-circular forward end affording an all-round view to the passengers comfortably seated at its many tables. There are full restaurant facilities on all the bigger ships.

The Lake of Zürich is long and narrow—25 miles in length but no more than $2\frac{1}{2}$ miles across at its widest—and covers an area of 34 square miles. Its north-western end is enclosed by the city of Zürich and its suburbs, and its shores are densely populated almost throughout. It bends gradually to due east, coming to an end at Uznach, but its eastern extremity is cut off by the Seedam, the causeway between Rapperswil and Pfäffikon which carries the South-Eastern Railway (Südostbahn) and a public road across the lake. No regular steamer or motorship services run east of Rapperswil, but it is possible to get through to the Linth Canal, which cuts through the marshy ground to the south-east of Uznach to proceed past Ziegel-brücke to link the Lake of Zürich with the Walensee. Throughout most of the length of the lake, in clear weather, the distant snowclad Alps are in view, more particularly Glärnisch, Tödi and the Windgallen, Bristenstock and Uri-Rotstock.

The most important landing-stages on the lake, apart from those at the end of the Bahnhofstrasse and near the Theatre in Zürich, are at Thalwil, Wädenswil and Rapperswil. Even in summer no more than five ships each way run the whole course of the lake between Zürich and Rapperswil, taking about two hours, but on Sundays their numbers are doubled. There are many local sailings between Zürich and Thalwil, and also a frequent cross-lake service, carrying motorcars as well as passengers, run by an independent company between Horgen and Meilen, about midway between Zürich and Rapperswil. Other short-distance runs across the lake are between Wädenswil and Männedorf, and Erlenbach and Thalwil, all of which make possible the avoidance of what otherwise would be very lengthy circuits round the ends of the lake. The long-distance ships also vary their calls, zigzagging to and from across the lake, so that every lakeside community has a very adequate service, and, though of course reduced in frequency, in winter as well as in summer.

The Lake of Lugano

Scenically the Lake of Lugano resembles that of Lucerne in that its extremely irregular shape presents the traveller by water with a consider-able variety of views, though surrounded by mountains of a good deal less height, and, except in winter, without any sight of the snows. Although the lake is partly Italian, the company operating its fleet of 13 ships, the Società Navigazione del Lago di Lugano, or S.N.L., is Swiss. Early in the 1960s the last paddle-steamers on the lake disappeared, and the present fleet is entirely diesel-driven.

The four principal vessels—the *Italia*, *Lugano*, *Ticino* and *Elvezia*—all can carry a maximum of 550 to 600 passengers; they are from 150 ft. to 155 ft. long and 30 ft. broad, and are particularly sleek in their design with all upper work kept well down in height, because of the necessity of passing under the arches carrying the railway and road across the causeway between Melide and Maroggia, at the centre of the lake. With the recent widening of the causeway to carry a double line of railway and a dual road carriageway, however, the old arches have been replaced by reinforced concrete spans, which have increased the height above water level from 19 to 22 ft. and the available width from 50 ft. to 66 ft. 6 in., greatly easing the problems of ship design and navigation. Most of the remaining motor vessels can carry from 110 to 280 passengers.

The curiously shaped Lake of Lugano has its north-eastern extremity in

Italian territory at Porlezza, separated by a narrow neck of land from Menaggio, on Lake Como. This arm of the lake then runs south-westwards into Switzerland, past Gandria, perched on the steep mountainside and beloved by artists, until it reaches Castagnola, at the foot of Monte Bré. Here the lake opens out on the north side to the wide bay which has the town of Lugano on its north side, and the suburb of Paradiso on the south. The lake now turns almost to the south, skirting the precipitous flank of Monte San Salvatore on the west, and the Italian enclave of Campione, already mentioned, on the east, and then reaching the Melide causeway.

Beyond this point one arm of the lake takes a south-easterly direction to Capolago, terminus of the rack-and-pinion railway up Monte Generoso, while the other describes a complete semi-circle, finally pointing due north. At its southern extremity is the Italian Porto Ceresio, terminus of the North Milan Railway, and at the most westerly point of the northern turn is Ponte Tresa, on the Swiss-Italian frontier, from which it is but a short run by road to Luino, on Lake Maggiore. The plan of the lake thus resembles a running man, with the head at Lugano, one arm pointing upwards to Porlezza, one foot at Capolago, and the other leg doubled upwards, with its knee at Porto Ceresio and its foot up at Agno. Monte San Salvatore separates the two main parts of the lake, and this accounts for the magnificent view to be obtained from that bold peak.

In summer there are three services each day between Lugano and Ponte Tresa, taking about $1\frac{3}{4}$ hours for the run, and a number of others between Lugano and Porto Ceresio only, while a frequent service also is maintained between Lugano and Gandria, with the proviso that in the event of *cattivo tempo*—bad weather—most of these boats will not run. Porlezza and Capolago both get four summer services each way daily from and to Lugano. In winter the service is almost entirely confined to the Lugano–Porto Ceresio run, which makes it possible to reach Milan in $2\frac{3}{4}$ to 3 hours from Lugano, or very little more than the all-rail journey *via* Chiasso.

Other Lakes

Maggiore, the biggest of all the Italian lakes, is mainly Italian, and its services are operated entirely by an Italian company located at Verbania–Intra. The only Swiss port of importance on the lake is Locarno, and local services operate from here round the northern part of the lake as far south as Brissago, summer and winter alike. It is round the southern part of the lake, entirely on Italian territory, however, that the greatest passenger patronage is obtained, particularly between Luino and Intra, Pallanza, the famous Isola Bella and Stresa.

To the east of the Jura there are three lakes—Neuchâtel, Bienne (or Biel) and Morat (or Murten)—which, being at the same level, are connected by canals. Neuchâtel, the biggest, is 24 miles long and from 4 to 5 miles broad; in 1878 its level was raised by 8 ft. to that of the Lake of Bienne by converting the Thièle stream, which connects the two, into a canal.

The latter lake is smaller, 9½ miles long and 2½ miles broad. These two, running from north-east to south-west, are in line with one another; the smallest of the three lakes, Morat, is a little further east, and is connected with the north-eastern end of the Lake of Neuchâtel by the Broye Canal. A company known as the Société de Navigation sur les lacs de Neuchâtel et Morat S.A., or L.N.M., with eight ships, operates on the Lakes of Neuchâtel and Morat, and another company, the Bielersee Schiffahrts-Gesellschaft, or B.S.G., with six ships, on the Lake of Bienne.

From Neuchâtel there is a local service throughout the year across the lake to Cudrefin and Portalban; in summer ships run the length of the lake to and from Estavayer-le-Lac and Yverdon. Using the canals there are through services between Neuchâtel and Bienne, which on the way provide the only communication with St. Petersinsel, formerly a wooded island on the Lake of Bienne with a monastery which has been converted to a hotel, but now connected by a causeway with the mainland. The Lake of Morat has its own services. In summer all three lakes are served by a motorship which on certain days starts from Bienne at 9.0 a.m. gives tourists 2¾ hours in Morat, proceeds to Neuchâtel for an hour there, and is back in Bienne by 6.40 p.m., an attractive cruise made possible by use of both the Thièle and Broye canals.

One or two minor services may be mentioned. In summer the Lake of Zug sees one daily trip along its length from Zug to Arth-am-See and back, and seven each way on Sunday; the operating company owns two small motorships. On the Hallwilersee, a small lake midway between Zürich and Olten, three motorships cruise between Beinwil and Meisterschwanden, on opposite sides of the lake, with calls at Birrwil, but in winter on Sundays only. The Greifensee, an even smaller lake east of Zürich, also has services with six small motor vessels, making the circuit of the lake from Maur back to Maur, with calls at Uster and elsewhere, operating quite intensively throughout the year. For so relatively small a country, far from any ocean, this very considerable activity on the water, with many palatial motorships of ultra-modern design, is a great credit to Switzerland.

SIXTEEN

Making the Most of Swiss Travel

OVER SHORT DISTANCES Swiss travel in general is on the expensive side, but as the length of journey increases, so the rate per kilometre decreases; indeed, over long distances, despite the fare increases in November 1971, Swiss fares are some of the cheapest in Europe. The tourist also benefits by a variety of fare concessions, which can reduce still further the cost of his travel.

Normal fares are charged in accordance with a sliding scale; over distances of 10, 20, 30, 50, 100 and 150 km (6½, 12½, 18½, 31, 62 and 93 miles) the rates are Sw.fr.1.80, 3.40, 5.00, 8.00, 15.00 and 23.00 respectively, second class. At the Anglo-Swiss exchange rate ruling at the beginning of 1972 this works out at from 2.9p down to 2.1p per mile. But at above 150 km the rate decreases so rapidly that no more than Sw.fr.3 are added for each additional 50 km (31 miles), so that when we get to 500 km (310 miles) the rate has dropped to 1.45p per mile. First class tickets are charged at roughly 50 per cent above the second class fare, and return tickets at 50 per cent over the single fare.

The most expensive journeys in Switzerland are those on the purely tourist lines, as, for example, from Kleine Scheidegg to the Jungfraujoch or Zermatt to the Gornergrat. It has to be remembered, however, that the operating costs of such lines are high, and that patronage on a large scale is only during the summer months and the winter sport season, and, furthermore, that in bad weather traffic over such lines is greatly reduced. At one time many of the smaller railways, especially those reaching high altitudes, had to charge high fares for similar reasons, but in 1958 the Federal Government passed a new law compelling all the railways which met social needs to reduce their fares to the national kilometric standard (with slight increases where specially justified), the difference between revenue at the new rate and that at the national standard being made good by Government subsidy. As an example, fares on the Furka–Oberalp Railway are now only about two-fifths of what they were formerly, though this is certainly an extreme case.

The various mountain lines, of whatever kind, have their own standards of fare charging; in general, those that reach the highest altitudes charge the most, while chair-lifts, which can be operated with the smallest staffs, are the cheapest. There follow some details of the excursions offered.

The Swiss Holiday Ticket
The most familiar type of ticket for the tourist is the Swiss Holiday

Ticket, which is a cover enclosing, in the form of paper tickets, all the journeys that he proposes to make between entry and exit. A fixed charge, Sw.fr.24 second class, and Sw.fr.36 first class (*plus* an issuing fee of Sw.fr.3) is made, and then the total length of the itinerary is calculated at a rate per kilometre considerably lower than the ordinary fares. The longer the itinerary, therefore, the less it costs per kilometre, and it is in the purchaser's interest to include in it the more lengthy trips that he may have in mind, as, for example, to Lugano and back if he is staying at Lucerne, so that he may see the length of the Gotthard line, or the famous tour of the "Three Passes"—Grimsel, Furka and Süsten—if he is in the Bernese Oberland, for postal motorcoach services as well as railways may be included in any itinerary.

On the outside back cover of the Holiday Ticket there are five coupons which the holder can use on the days of his own choice for his more expensive excursions, and which then are charged to him at half-rate. If the five get used up, three more coupons may be bought for Sw.fr.5 second class or Sw.fr.7 first class. The validity of the Swiss Holiday Ticket is one month, but can be extended for a further ten days on payment of Sw.fr.7 second class or Sw.fr.10 first class. The starting and finishing points of the itinerary must be at a frontier station or an airport.

The Half-Fare Season Ticket

Those who wish to do a maximum of travelling in the country— as, for example, railway enthusiasts who are keen on seeing as much as they can of the Swiss railways—can profitably invest in a Half-Fare Season Ticket, especially if they are able to remain in the country for a 15 days or more. This costs Sw.fr.35 for 15 days, Sw.fr.50 for one month, Sw.fr.100 for three months and Sw.fr.300 for one year, irrespective of class. It gives the holder the right to buy all his tickets at half rate, not only on the SBB, but also on many of the minor railways, on the lake steamers and on the postal motorcoaches, over a total of some 8,700 route miles.

Moreover, the holder may buy, for an additional Sw.fr.50 second class or Sw.fr.75 first class, a complementary card permitting him, on three days of his own choice, free travel anywhere in the country; for Sw.fr.70 second class or Sw.fr.105 first class this privilege may be extended to five days. and for Sw.fr.120 and 180 respectively to ten days. In addition there are, of course, season tickets over any line or group of lines chosen by the purchaser, or over the entire Swiss Railway system. The last-mentioned, available for a year, costs Sw.fr.1,200 (about £121) second class and Sw.fr.1,800 (£184) first class. These tickets can be purchased only in Switzerland.

The Swiss Holiday Pass

A new concession, introduced in 1972, is that the tourist may buy a pass with the same coverage as the Half-Fare Season Ticket which entitles him to unlimited travel during the period of its validity. This can be a period as short as eight days, or alternatively, fitfeen days or a month. For eight days the charge is Sw.fr.90 second class or Sw.fr.125 first class; for fifteen days Sw.fr.125 or 175; and for a month Sw.fr.170 or 240 respectively. The pass must show the first and last days of validity, the passenger's name and country of residence, the number of his passport or identity card, and the date stamp of the issuing office (which for a British subject must be in Great Britain). This is a travel bargain of an exceptional kind, and should enjoy extensive patronage.

Regional Season Tickets

In all the principal holiday areas the Regional Holiday Season Tickets are by far the most attractive and economical facility offered to those who wish to make the most possible of the lake, mountain railway and coach travel in their particular areas. These tickets have certain features in common. They are available for 15 days. Each region has a network of routes —lake steamer, rail and postal motorcoach—over which the holder has unlimited travel freedom on five days of his own choice; on the remaining days he may travel over any part of this network at half-fare. The Locarno and Lugano Regions differ, in that their tickets are available for 7 days only, on all of which free travel is allowed. Also within and surrounding each area there are a number of supplemental routes over which the holder is entitled at any time to reduced fares, mostly one-half but in a few cases three-quarters of the ordinary fares. The accommodation in general is first class on the lakes and second class on the railways.

In every region production of a Swiss Holiday Ticket entitles the purchaser to a 25 per cent reduction in the cost of the Regional Season Ticket, subject to three of the five excursion ticket coupons on the outside cover of the Holiday Ticket being cancelled. The Regional Season Ticket must be signed by the holder. There are in all ten regions offering this facility; space forbids the setting out in detail of the precise coverage of each, but very briefly the routes are as follows.

1   Vevey and Montreux

Region No. 1 is the eastern end of the Lake of Geneva, and its five-day free railway coverage includes the Montreux-Oberland Bernois line from Montreux to Château d'Oex and Gstaad, the G.F.M. lines from Vevey to Châtel St. Denis, Bulle, Gruyères and Montbovon and the mountain lines to the Rochers de Naye and Les Pléiades. The supplemental or half-fare lines extend from Gstaad to Interlaken, the Swiss Federal main line from Geneva to Lausanne, Montreux, and Aigle; the mountain lines from Aigle to Diablerets and the Glacier-des-Diablerets and all the lines round Gstaad; also all the services on the Lake of Geneva.

2   Bernese Oberland

Region No. 2 Season Ticket offers probably the best value of all six regions. In the general Bernese Oberland area in which the five free days operate are the Lakes of Thun and Brienz; the whole of the Bernese Oberland group of railways described in Chapter 4 (save only from Kleine Scheidegg to Jungfraujoch); the Lötschberg Railway from Thun to Interlaken, Kandersteg and Hohtenn, and to Zweisimmen; the Swiss Federal line from Interlaken to Brienz, Meiringen and Brünig-Hasliberg; and the Brienzer Rothorn Railway. The free coverage of cableways includes Grindelwald-First, Beatenberg-Niederhorn, Kandersteg-Stock-Sunnbühl; Mülenen-Niesenkulm and Zweisimmen-Rinderberg. There is an immense range of routes at half-fare, including Thun-Berne, Hohtenn-Brigue, Brigue-Visp-Zermatt, the Furka-Oberalp line from Brigue to Gletsch and Andermatt; the popular Three Passes motor-coach tour (Grimsel-Furka-Susten) and Zweisimmen to Gstaad and Montreux by the M.O.B. Lastly, at 25 per cent. reduction there are the lines from Kleine Scheidegg to Jungfraujoch, Zermatt to the Gornergrat, and Stechelberg to Mürren and the Schilthorn. *In toto*, so wide a range could hardly be exhausted in the course of a fortnight's stay.

3   Lake of Lucerne

Region No. 3 is the Lake of Lucerne area. In this case the full coverage is of the lake itself, the Lucerne–Stans–Engelberg Railway from Hergiswil onwards, the mountain lines up Pilatus and the Stanserhorn, the lines from Vitznau and Arth–Goldau up the Rigi, the short line from Treib to Seelisberg, and the mountain ascents from Engelberg to Brunni and to Gerschnialp, Trübsee and the Joch Pass. Also covered is the attractive trip by motorcoach from Brunnen to Schwyz and Schlattli, funicular to Stoos, and chair-lift from there to the summit of the Fronalpstock. In the supplemental area one may travel at half-rate over the Swiss Federal line between Lucerne, Arth-Goldau, Brunnen and Flüelen, the Brünig line as far as Lungern, and the Südostbahn from Arth-Goldau to Einsiedeln, Wädenswil and Rapperswil. The summit of Pilatus may be reached by the suspension lines from Kriens *via* Fräkmüntegg, and similar ascents are possible from Lungern to Schönbüel, Stockalp to Melchsee-Frutt, and the new line from Trübsee (Engelberg) to the Kleintitlis.

4   Region of the Grisons

In the Canton of the Grisons there were formerly three different types of season ticket, one for Chur and Arosa, a second for the Davos region, and a third for St. Moritz, Pontresina and the Engadine generally, but these have all now been merged into one, with a coverage even greater than that of the Bernese Oberland. The five free days cover the entire Rhaetian Railway system, including the main line from Chur to Thusis, Tiefencastel, St. Moritz and Pontresina, the line from Landquart through Klosters and Davos to Filisur, the line down the Lower Engadine from Bever to Schuls, the Chur–Arosa line, the Bernina line from St. Moritz to Tirano, and the line up the Vorder Rhein valley from Reichenau to Disentis. In the half-rate category are all the mountain lines in the Canton, including Piz Corvatsch, Piz Nair, Diavolezza and Piz Lagalb in the St. Moritz area, the ramified group round Davos and Klosters, the Arosa Weisshorn, the Parpaner Rothorn and many others. Finally there is a vast coverage at half-rate of motorcoach routes, including Chur–Lenzerheide–Tiefencastel–the Julier Pass–St. Moritz; St. Moritz–the Maloja Pass–Soglio; Thusis–Splügen–San Bernardino–Bellinzona; Chur–Flims–Ilanz and Ilanz to both Vals and Vrin; Disentis–the Lukmanier Pass–Olivone–Acquarossa; and Zernez to the Fuorn, Umbrail and Stelvio Passes as well as to Munster. This season ticket may well claim to be one of the finest travel bargains that Switzerland has to offer.

5, 6 *Locarno and Lugano*

The Regional Holiday Season Tickets for the Locarno and Lugano areas are in a sense interchangeable, in that the five-day free routes for one are half-rate routes for the other, and *vice versa*. The Locarno free routes are the Centovalli Railway as far as Santa Maria Maggiore, the cableway up to Orselina, the steamers on Lake Maggiore as far south as Brissago and Ranzo, and a number of local motorcoach routes. Those at Lugano include the local railway to Ponte Tresa, the mountain railways to Monte Bre, Monte San Salvatore and Monte Generoso, the cableway from Miglieglia to Monte Lema, and also one or two local motorcoach services. Half-rate tickets are available on the Swiss Federal Railway from both Locarno and Lugano to the junction at Giubiasco, and from there northwards to Bellinzona. The Swiss Federal also may be used between Bellinzona and Locarno. The Locarno and Lugano Season Tickets are available in first class on both trains and ships. It may be added that in addition to these Regional Holiday Tickets it is possible to obtain a General Season Ticket, at a moderate cost of Sw.fr.35, for the whole of the postal motorcoach services, some 75 in number, in the Canton Ticino, including such long-distance routes as from Lugano to St. Moritz and Bellinzona to Chur in Switzerland—a bargain indeed.

The table following gives the price, in Swiss Francs, of all ten Regional

No	Region	Full Rate	With Holiday Ticket	Period of issue	No of Days
1	Vevey and Montreux	42	32	May-October	15
2	Bernese Oberland	64(a)	48(a)	May-October	15
3	Lake of Lucerne	62(b)	47(c)	April-October	15
4	Region of the Grisons	60(d)	45(d)	May-October	15
		90(e)	67(e)	May-October	15
5	Locarno	29(f)	22(f)	May-October	7
6	Lugano	32(f)	24(f)	May-October	7

(a) Sw.fr.6 extra for first class on ships. (b) Sw.fr.7 extra for first class on ships. (c) Sw.fr.5 extra for first class on ships. (d) Second class on trains. (e) first class on trains. (f) First class on trains and ships.

Season Tickets. It should be emphasised, of course, that these are the quotations in force at the time of writing. Pamphlets showing the precise facilities offered by each Regional Season Ticket, illustrated by small maps, are obtainable from the Swiss National Tourist Office in London, or from travel agents.

It should be added that most of the Swiss lakes issue their own season tickets, for use on the ships only, except that in certain cases they include limited land facilities also.

Party Rates

One final note is that in Switzerland there are the customary concessions for parties. These are a 20 per cent. reduction on ordinary fares for 10 to 24 persons, 30 per cent. for groups of between 25 and 399, and a 35 per cent. reduction for 400 persons and over.

Timetables

A number of different timetables are published in Switzerland, but by far the most valuable is the *Amtliches Kursbuch* or *Indicateur Officiel*, a compact and beautifully printed compilation of over 800 pages which sells at Sw.fr.3.50. It opens with a mass of general information, a station index (which shows the precise altitude of every station, mountain railways and *téléphériques* included, and fare tables); then follow all the through services to neighbouring countries, including a list of "T.E.E." trains; the major part of the book is occupied with the country's passenger train services, which include the precise composition of every main line train, and at the end a list of all the funicular railways, chair-lifts, *Gondelbahn* and *Luftseilbahn* lines (including the length of and height through which the passenger is lifted by each); following are the times of all the lake steamers and motorships; and the book concludes with a lengthy section giving the times of all the ramified postal motorcoach services all over the country. The whole is a *vade mecum* indeed of Swiss travel and a mine of information. In many holiday areas, such as Lucerne, the Bernese Oberland and Montreux, a few *centimes* will buy small local timetables that can be slipped into the pocket and are very handy when making excursions, but the *Kursbuch*, issued twice annually, is indispensable to any student of Swiss transport.

Sightseeing from Trains in Switzerland

To obtain the best views on the principal scenic routes, travellers should if possible sit on the sides of the trains indicated in the table following (looking in the direction in which the train travels).

Railway	Route	Side of Train
Swiss Federal	Berne–Lausanne–Geneva	Left
„ „	Vallorbe–Lausanne–Brigue	Right
„ „	Lausanne–Neuchâtel–Bienne	Right
„ „	Lucerne–Flüelen–Erstfeld	Right
„ „	Erstfeld–Göschenen	Left
„ „	Airolo–Bellinzona–Lugano	*Right
„ „	Lugano–Chiasso	Left
„ „	Zürich–Sargans–Chur	Left
„ „	Lucerne–Alpnachstad	Left
„ „	Alpnachstad–Meiringen	†Right
„ „	Meiringen–Interlaken	†Left
Bern–Lötschberg–Simplon	Thun–Spiez–Interlaken	Left
„ „ „	Spiez–Kandersteg–Brigue	*Right
Berner Oberland	Interlaken–Lauterbrunnen	Right
„ „	Interlaken–Grindelwald	Right
Wengeralp	Lauterbrunnen–Kleine Scheidegg	*Right
„	Grindelwald–Kleine Scheidegg	Right
Jungfrau	Kleine Scheidegg–Eigergletscher	Right
Montreux–Oberland Bernois	Zweisimmen–Gstaad	Right
„ „ „	Gstaad–Montreux	Left
Rhaetian	Chur–Thusis–St. Moritz	*Right
„	Landquart–Klosters–Davos	*Right
„	Samedan–Schuls–Scuol	Right
„	St. Moritz–Pontresina–Tirano	*Left
„	Chur–Ilanz	Right
„	Ilanz–Disentis	Left
„	Chur–Arosa	Right
Furka–Oberalp	Brigue–Oberwald	Right
„ „	Oberwald–Gletsch–Andermatt	Left
„ „	Andermatt–Oberalp–Disentis	*Right
Bodensee–Toggenburg	Romanshorn–St. Gallen–Rapperswil	Right
Südostbahn	Rapperswil–Arth–Goldau	*Left
Lucerene-Stans–Engelberg	Lucerne–Engelberg	*Left
Vitznau-Rigi–	Vitznau–Rigikulm	Left
Arth-Rigi	Arth-Goldau–Staffel	Right
„	Staffel–Rigikulm	Left
Pilatus	Alpnachstad–Aemsigenalp	Right
„	Aemsigenalp–Pilatuskulm	Left
Brigue–Visp–Zermatt	Visp–Zermatt	Left
Gornergrat	Zermatt–Gornergrat	Right
Martigny–Châtelard	Martigny–Vallorcine	Left
French National	Vallorcine–Chamonix	Right
Bex–Villars–Bretaye	Bex–Villars-sur-Ollon	*Right
Aigle–Sépey–Diablerets	Aigle–Le Sépey	‡*Left
„ „ „	Le Sépey–Diablerets	‡Right
Rochers-de-Naye	Montreux–Rochers-de-Naye	Left

*Views mainly on this side. †No need to change seats at Meiringen, as the train reverses direction here. ‡No need to change seats at Le Sépey, as the train reverses direction here. When travelling in the opposite direction to that indicated, change the seating from right to left, or vice versa.

APPENDIX 2

Maximum Altitudes Attained on Swiss Adhesion Railways

SUMMIT	RAILWAY	SECTION	ALTITUDE		STEEPEST APPROACH GRADIENT		GAUGE
			metres	feet	per cent	1 in.	
Bernina Hospice	Rhaetian (Bernina)	St Moritz-Tirano	2,257	7,403	7·0	14	Metre
Albula Tunnel	Rhaetian (Main line)	Chur-St Moritz	1,823	5,982	3·5	29	Metre
Arosa	Rhaetian	Chur-Arosa	1,742	5,715	6·0	16½	Metre
Wolfgang	Rhaetian (Davos loop)	Landquart-Davos	1,633	5,359	4·5	22	Metre
Saanenmöser	Montreux-Oberland-Bernois	Montreux-Zweisimmen	1,269	4,163	7·3	13¾	Metre
Lötschberg Tunnel	Berne-Lötschberg-Simplon	Spiez-Brigue	1,240	4,067	2·7	37	Standard
La Givrine	Nyon-St Cergue-Morez	Nyon-St Cergue	1,230	4,035	6·0	16½	Metre
Gotthard Tunnel	Swiss Federal	Arth-Goldau-Chiasso	1,154	3,786	2·7	37	Standard
Les Diablerets	Aigle-Sépey-Diablerets	Aigle-Diablerets	1,154	3,786	6·0	16½	Metre
La Corbatière	C. de F. Neuchâtelois	La Chaud-de-F.-Les Ponts	1,112	3,648	4·0	25	Metre
Breuleux-Eglise	C. de F. du Jura	Tavannes-Le Noirmont	1,073	3,520	5·0	20	Metre
Ste Croix	Yverdon-Ste Croix	Yverdon-Ste Croix	1,069	3,507	4·4	22½	Metre
Le Lieu	Le Pont-Brassus	Le Pont-Brassus	1,050	3,445	2·3	43½	Standard

APPENDIX 3

Swiss Rack-and-pinion Railways (Zahnradbahn type)

LOWER AND UPPER TERMINALS OF LINE	LENGTH OF LINE		ALTITUDE				TOTAL ASCENT		MAXIMUM GRADIENT	
			LOWER TERMINUS		UPPER TERMINUS					
	km	miles	metres	feet	metres	feet	metres	feet	per cent	1 in.
Brienz-Rothornkulm*	7·60	4·72	568	1,863	2,249	7,378	1,681	5,515	25	4
Alpnachstad-Pilatuskulm	4·27	2·66	437	1,434	2,066	6,778	1,629	5,344	48	2
Montreux-Rochers-de-Naye	10·32	6·41	395	1,296	1,969	6,460	1,574	5,164	22	4½
Zermatt-Gornergrat	9·34	5·80	1,604	5,262	3,089	10,134	1,485	4,872	20	5
Kleine Scheidegg-Jungfraujoch	9·23	5·73	2,061	6,762	3,454	11,333	1,393	4,571	25	4
Wilderswil-Schynige Platte	7·26	4·51	584	1,916	1,967	6,453	1,383	4,537	25	4
Capolago-Generoso Vetta§	8·99	5·50	273	896	1,592	5,223	1,319	4,327	22	4½
Vitznau-Rigikulm	6·85	4·26	439	1,440	1,750	5,741	1,311	4,301	25	4
Lauterbrunnen-Kleine Scheidegg†	10·47	6·51	797	2,615	2,061	6,762	1,264	4,147	19	5¼
Arth-Goldau-Rigikulm	8·55	5·31	518	1,699	1,750	5,741	1,232	4,042	20	5
Grindelwald‡-Kleine Scheidegg†	8·64	5·37	944‡	3,097‡	2,061	6,762	1,117	3,665	25	4
Blonay-Les Pléiades	4·90	3·04	620	2,034	1,348	4,422	728	2,388	20	5
Villars-Col-de Bretaye	4·66	2·90	1,253	4,111	1,808	5,932	555	1,821	17	6
Rorschach-Heiden	5·69	3·54	399	1,309	794	2,605	395	1,296	9	11
Rheineck-Walzenhausen	1·90	1·18	405	1,332	672	2,205	267	873	26	4
Ouchy-Lausanne	1·48	0·92	374	1,227	479	1,571	105	344	13	7¾

*Steam-operated   †Wengernalp Railway   ‡Grindelwald Grund   §Diesel operated
All lines electrically operated with the two exceptions shown

APPENDIX 4

Swiss Rack-and-adhesion Railways

(On which the steepest sections only are operated with rack-and-pinion)

SECTION OF LINE	LENGTH OF LINE		ALTITUDE				TOTAL ASCENT		MAXIMUM GRADIENT	
			LOWEST ON LINE		HIGHEST ON LINE					
	km	miles	metres	feet	metres	feet	metres	feet	per cent	1 in.
Brigue-Furka*	52·05	32·34	671	2,201	2,160	7,088	1,489	4,887	11	9
Aigle-Leysin	6·21	3·85	404	1,325	1,398	4,587	994	3,252	23	4½
Brigue-Visp-Zermatt	43·98	27·33	671	2,201	1,605	5,266	934	3,065	12½	8
Disentis-Oberalppasshöhe*	19·01	11·81	1,130	3,706	2,033	6,670	903	2,964	11	9
Bex-Villars-Chesières	13·84	8·60	411	1,348	1,253	4,110	842	2,762	20	5
Martigny-Châtelard§	18·36	11·41	458	1,503	1,228	4,029	770	2,526	20	5
Andermatt-Furka*	15·89	9·87	1,436	4,710	2,160	7,088	724	2,378	11	9
Aigle-Ollon-Monthey-Champéry	23·18	14·40	393	1,289	1,046	3,432	653	2,143	13½	7½
Andermatt-Oberalppasshöhe*	9·72	6·04	1,436	4,710	2,033	6,670	597	1,960	11	9
Lucerne-Brünig-Interlaken†	73·54	45·70	436	1,430	1,002	3,287	566	1,857	12	8½
Lucerne-Stans-Engelberg	¶24·56	¶15·26	435	1,427	999	3,278	564	1,851	25	4
Alstätten-Gais	14·26	8·86	430	1,411	971	3,186	541	1,775	16	6¼
Zweilütschinen-Grindelwald‡	11·15	6·93	652	2,139	1,034	3,392	382	1,253	12	8½
Göschenen-Andermatt*	3·52	2·19	1,106	3,629	1,436	4,710	330	1,081	18	5½
St. Gallen-Gais-Appenzell	19·43	12·07	670	2,198	919	3,015	249	817	16	6¼
Interlaken-Lauterbrunnen‡	12·30	7·64	567	1,860	797	2,615	230	755	9	11

*Furka-Oberalp Railway.   †Swiss Federal Railways.   ‡Berner Oberland Railway.
§Trains work through to Vallorcine, 18·36 km (13·45 miles), altitude 1,263 m (4,143 ft).
¶From Hergiswil to Engelberg.

APPENDIX 5

Swiss Funicular Railways (Drahtseilbahn type)

(500 metres long or over)

LOWER AND UPPER TERMINALS OF LINE	LENGTH OF LINE		ALTITUDE ABOVE SEA LEVEL				TOTAL ASCENT		GRADIENT		CAPACITY OF EACH CAR
			LOWER TERMINUS		UPPER TERMINUS				AVGE	MAX	
	metres	yards	metres	feet	metres	feet	metres	feet	%	%	persons
Sierre–St. Maurice–Montana*	4,207	4,601	540	1,772	1,471	4,826	931	3,054	22	48	65
Davos–Höhenweg–Weissfluhjoch*	4,048	4,427	1,557	5,106	2,663	8,737	1,106	3,631	29	48	156/168
Stans–Stanserhornkulm†	3,913	4,280	450	1,476	1,850	6,069	1,400	4,593	42	63	40
Mülenen–Schwandegg–Niesenkulm*	3,495	3,842	693	2,274	2,336	7,664	1,643	5,390	54	68	60
Punt Muragl–Muottas Muragl	2,185	2,390	1,742	5,715	2,448	8,031	706	2,316	34	54	80
Neuchâtel (La Coudre)–Chaumont	2,091	2,287	514	1,686	1,084	3,557	570	1,871	29	46	70
St. Moritz–Chanterella–Corviglia*	2,080	2,277	1,846	6,056	2,486	8,156	640	2,100	34	46	110/140
Beatenbucht–Beatenberg	1,695	1,854	568	1,837	1,121	3,651	553	1,814	35	40	100
Biel–Magglingen	1,681	1,839	435	1,427	873	2,864	438	1,437	27	32	140
Lugano (Paradiso)–San Salvatore*¶	1,629	1,781	282	925	873	2,864	591	1,939	47	60	71
Cassarate–Suvigliana–Monte Bré*	1,599	1,749	287	942	916	3,005	629	2,063	48	61	43/70
Vevey–Mont Pèlerin	1,578	1,726	389	1,277	806	2,644	417	1,367	27	54	90
Interlaken–Harderkulm	1,435	1,569	567	1,860	1,304	4,278	737	2,418	59	64	65
Lauterbrunnen–Grütschalp	1,421	1,554	796	2,612	1,481	4,859	685	2,247	55	61	62
Schwyz (Schlattli)–Stoos	1,361	1,488	587	1,926	1,290	4,232	703	2,306	61	78	70
Piotta–Piora (Ritom) ||	1,358	1,485	1,011	3,317	1,793	5,883	782	2,566	71	88	35
Châtelard–Barberine	1,310	1,432	1,128	3,701	1,821	6,001	693	2,300	63	87	42
Linthal–Braunwald	1,294	1,415	666	2,185	1,254	4,114	588	1,929	51	64	100
Zug (Schönegg)–Zugerberg	1,261	1,379	561	1,841	927	3,042	366	1,201	30	47	80
Lucerne (Halde)–Dietschiberg	1,243	1,360	442	1,450	628	2,060	186	619	15	25	44
Cossonay Station–Cossonay‡	1,219	1,333	430	1,412	563	1,847	133	435	11	13	50
Unterwasser–Iltios	1,195	1,307	911	2,989	1,339	4,393	428	1,404	38	46	75
Ligerz–Tessenberg	1,183	1,293	439	1,440	818	2,683	379	1,243	34	40	60
Treib–Seelisberg	1,134	1,241	440	1,443	770	2,526	330	1,083	30	38	90
Bern (Wabern)–Gurtenkulm	1,045	1,143	575	1,886	833	2,733	258	847	27	33	100
Kehrsiten–Bürgenstock	934	1,021	434	1,424	874	2,867	440	1,443	53	58	80
Biel–Evilard	920	1,006	452	1,483	694	2,277	242	794	27	36	100

LOWER AND UPPER TERMINALS OF LINE	LENGTH OF LINE		ALTITUDE ABOVE SEA LEVEL				TOTAL ASCENT		GRADIENT		CAPACITY OF EACH CAR
			LOWER TERMINUS		UPPER TERMINUS				AVGE	MAX	
	metres	yards	metres	feet	metres	feet	metres	feet	%	%	persons
Lucerne (Kriens)-Sonnenberg	830	908	496	1,627	706	2,316	210	689	26	43	30
Locarno-Madonna del Sasso	811	887	207	679	380	1,247	173	568	22	30	80
Zürich-Waldhaus Dolder	805	880	447	1,467	547	1,795	100	328	13	18	70
St. Imier-Mont Soleil	728	796	832	2,730	1,173	3,849	341	1,119	53	61	54
Reichenbach-Reichenbachfall	707	773	600	1,968	844	2,769	244	801	37	62	24
Davos Platz-Schatzalp	702	768	1,557	5,108	1,861	6,106	304	998	47	47	80
Territét-Glion‡	630	689	391	1,283	689	2,261	298	978	54	57	50
Mürren-Allmendhubel	536	586	1,649	5,410	1,907	6,257	258	847	55	61	65
Les Avants-Sonloup	515	563	976	3,202	1,156	3,793	180	591	38	55	50
Engelberg-Gerschnialp	512	560	1,000	3,281	1,266	4,154	266	873	61	68	75

* Two independent sections. † Three independent sections. ‡ Operation by water balance . ‖ Operated by single car, raised and lowered from upper terminus. ¶ Operated by two single cars, meeting at middle station.
Note: There are 13 additional funicular railways in Switzerland of less than 500 yd. in length. All lines electrically operated, except where otherwise shown.

APPENDIX 6

Swiss Chair-lifts with Open Chairs (Sesselbahn type)

(Lines completed to 1971)

LOWER AND UPPER TERMINALS OF LINE	NEAREST TOWN	LENGTH OF LINE		ALTITUDE ABOVE SEA LEVEL				TOTAL ASCENT		CAPACITY OF EACH UNIT
				LOWER TERMINUS		UPPER TERMINUS				
		metres	yards	metres	feet	metres	feet	metres	feet	persons
Grindelwald-First†‡§	Grindelwald	4,354	4,762	1,066	3,492	2,171	7,122	1,105	3,625	2
Lenk-Betelberg*‡	Lenk	3,632	3,972	1,100	3,609	1,947	6,388	847	2,779	2
Flims-Foppa-Alp Naraus*‡§	Flims	3,444	3,745	1,091	3,579	1,843	6,046	752	2,467	2
Savognin-Somtgant*	Tiefencastel	3,315	3,647	1,174	3,852	2,107	6,912	933	3,060	2
Lenk-Mülkerblatten*	Lenk	3,293	3,601	1,590	5,211	1,937	6,349	347	1,138	2
Tannenheim-Prodkamm*	Unterterzen	3,252	3,556	1,224	4,016	1,949	6,394	725	2,378	1
Nods-Chasseral	Neuchâtel	2,950	3,226	882	2,894	1,549	5,082	667	2,188	2
Val Sporz-Piz Scalottas*	Lenzerheide	2,940	3,215	1,521	4,990	2,324	7,625	803	2,635	2
Furt-Pizolhütte*	Sargans	2,823	3,087	1,523	4,996	2,221	7,287	698	2,291	1/2
Wildhaus-Oberdorf-Gamsalp*‡	Wildhaus	2,781	3,041	1,018	3,346	1,761	5,778	743	2,432	2
Miglieglia-Monte Lema‡	Lugano	2,690	2,942	708	2,323	1,553	5,095	845	2,772	2
Gstaad-Wassemgrat*‡	Gstaad	2,585	2,827	1,117	3,665	1,943	6,375	826	2,710	2
Beatenberg-Niederhorn*‡§	Interlaken	2,583	2,825	1,161	3,809	1,949	6,394	788	2,585	2
Miraniga-Alp Stein*	Flims	2,539	2,771	1,437	4,715	1,800	5,078	363	1,191	2
Pardiel-Laufböden*‡	Bad Ragaz	2,443	2,671	1,631	5,351	2,224	7,295	593	1,944	1/2
Oberdorf-Weissenstein*‡§	Solothurn	2,369	2,581	661	2,169	1,280	4,199	619	2,030	2
Krümmenschwil-Rietbach	Nesslau	2,108	2,305	732	2,402	1,121	3,678	389	1,276	2
Braunwald-Kleine-Gumen*‡	Linthal	2,084	2,279	1,314	4,311	1,904	6,247	590	1,936	2
Schönried-Horneggli	Gstaad	2,036	2,227	1,236	4,055	1,773	5,817	537	1,762	2
Melchsee Frutt-Balmaregghorn	Sarnen	1,900	2,078	1,896	6,220	2,291	7,516	395	2,316	1/2
Alpboden-Haldigrat	Stans	1,853	2,026	1,236	4,055	1,942	6,371	706	2,316	2
Leontica-Cancori	Acquarossa	1,853	2,026	929	3,048	1,464	4,803	535	1,755	2
Glaris-Jetzmeder	Davos	1,814	1,984	1,460	4,790	2,060	6,758	600	1,968	2
Churwalden-Pargitsch	Chur	1,783	1,950	1,248	4,094	1,725	4,571	477	1,565	2
Morgins-Le Corbeau*	Morgins	1,768	1,934	1,341	4,399	1,988	6,522	647	2,123	1/2
Sattel-Mostelberg‡	Arth-Goldau	1,730	1,892	777	2,549	1,185	3,888	408	1,339	2
Bettmeralp-Schönboden	Mörel	1,724	1,885	1,955	6,414	2,285	7,497	330	1,083	2

L

LOWER AND UPPER TERMINALS OF LINE	NEAREST TOWN	LENGTH OF LINE		ALTITUDE ABOVE SEA LEVEL				TOTAL ASCENT		CAPACITY OF EACH UNIT
				LOWER TERMINUS		UPPER TERMINUS				
		metres	yards	metres	feet	metres	feet	metres	feet	persons
Möser-Tschentenegg	Adelboden	1,687	1,845	1,435	4,708	1,935	6,348	500	1,640	2
Startgels-Nagens	Flims	1,682	1,838	1,590	5,216	2,172	7,125	582	1,909	2
Filzbach-Haberschwänd	Weesen	1,624	1,776	739	2,455	1,282	4,206	543	1,751	2
Visperterminen-Giw	Brigue	1,602	1,752	1,381	4,531	1,962	6,437	581	1,906	2
Zermatt-Sunnegga‡	Zermatt	1,590	1,739	1,614	5,295	2,291	7,516	677	2,221	2
Wengernalp-Lauberhorn	Wengen	1,578	1,726	1,830	6,004	2,326	7,631	496	1,627	2
Stoos-Karrenstöckli	Schwyz	1,565	1,712	1,296	4,252	1,742	5,715	446	1,463	1/2
Churwalden-Alp Statz	Chur	1,524	1,667	1,248	4,094	1,929	6,329	681	2,235	2
Les Collons-La Trabanta	Sion	1,492	1,632	1,802	5,912	2,195	7,201	393	1,289	1
Käserstatt-Hohsträss	Brünig	1,490	1,629	1,827	5,994	2,178	7,145	351	1,151	2
Alt St. Johann-Alp Sellamatt	Wildhaus	1,485	1,624	897	2,943	1,395	4,577	498	1,634	1/2
Geilsmäder-Hahnenmoos	Adelboden	1,479	1,617	1,714	5,623	1,957	6,421	243	798	2
Seebli-Spirstock	Einsiedeln	1,468	1,605	1,446	4,750	1,771	5,816	325	1,066	2
Trübsee-Jochpass	Engelberg	1,448	1,437	1,774	5,820	2,213	7,260	439	1,440	1/2
Brämbrüesch-Hühnerköpfe	Chur	1,438	1,573	1,611	5,285	1,950	6,397	339	1,112	1/2
Grimentz-Bendolla	Vissoie	1,430	1,564	1,605	5,266	2,136	7,008	531	1,742	2
Morgins-La Failleuse	Morgins	1,420	1,553	1,305	4,281	1,814	5,951	509	1,670	1
Kiental-Gehrihorn	Spiez	1,413	1,545	932	3,058	1,415	4,642	483	1,584	1
Kandersteg-Oeschinen‡	Kandersteg	1,405	1,536	1,200	3,937	1,685	5,528	485	1,591	2
Amden-Niederschlag	Weesen	1,394	1,525	934	3,064	1,294	4,245	360	1,181	1/2
Ste. Croix-Les Avattes‡	Ste. Croix	1,390	1,520	1,160	3,806	1,460	4,790	300	984	2
Schönengrund-Hochhamm	Herisau	1,346	1,472	883	2,897	1,210	3,970	327	1,073	2
Schwarzsee-Riggisalp	Fribourg	1,337	1,462	1,052	3,451	1,494	4,901	442	1,450	1/2
Moléson Village-La Vudalla‖	Gruyères	1,320	1,444	1,110	3,642	1,664	5,460	554	1,818	2
Bruson-La Côt	Le Châble	1,318	1,441	1,090	3,576	1,530	5,019	440	1,443	2
Seebli-Sternen	Einsiedeln	1,314	1,437	1,465	4,806	1,856	6,089	391	1,283	2
Geils-Luegli	Adelboden	1,303	1,425	1,724	5,655	2,066	6,776	342	1,121	2
Adelboden-Tschentenalp‡	Adelboden	1,268	1,387	1,370	4,495	1,938	6,358	568	1,863	2
Greicheralp-Blausee	Mörel	1,256	1,374	1,894	6,214	2,219	7,280	325	1,066	2
Wildhaus-Gamplüt	Wildhaus	1,250	1,367	1,098	3,600	1,370	4,494	272	894	2
Champex-La Breya	Champex	1,240	1,356	1,506	4,941	2,184	7,165	678	2,224	1
Pontresina-Alp Languard*	Pontresina	1,232	1,347	1,841	6,041	2,275	7,465	434	1,424	1/2
Buttes-La Robella	Fleurier	1,230	1,345	769	2,523	1,212	3,976	443	1,453	2

LOWER AND UPPER TERMINALS OF LINE	NEAREST TOWN	LENGTH OF LINE		ALTITUDE ABOVE SEA LEVEL				TOTAL ASCENT		CAPACITY OF EACH UNIT
				LOWER TERMINUS		UPPER TERMINUS				
		metres	yards	metres	feet	metres	feet	metres	feet	persons
Gummi-Honegg	Interlaken	1,228	1,343	1,798	5,899	2,165	7,103	367	1,204	2
Archette-La Barillette	Nyon	1,208	1,321	1,166	3,825	1,459	4,786	293	961	1
Leysin-Solacyre	Leysin	1,182	1,293	1,373	4,505	1,831	6,008	458	1,503	2
Grötzenbüel-Seblengrat	Linthal	1,177	1,287	1,558	5,112	1,895	6,218	337	1,106	2
Bächital-Seblengrat	Linthal	1,174	1,284	1,461	4,793	1,895	6,218	434	1,424	2
Rublo-La Videmanette	Château d'Oex	1,163	1,272	1,751	5,745	2,012	6,601	261	856	1
La Forclaz-Mont d'Arpille	Martigny	1,150	1,258	1,527	5,010	2,042	6,699	515	1,689	1
Stock-Sunnbüil	Kandersteg	1,141	1,248	1,834	6,017	1,936	6,352	102	335	1
Unterbach-Brand	Visp	1,130	1,236	1,232	4,042	1,595	5,233	363	1,191	1
Sedrun-Cungieri	Disentis	1,102	1,205	1,454	4,769	1,840	6,035	386	1,266	1/2
Col de Bretaye-Chamossaire	Villars	1,070	1,170	1,812	5,945	2,103	6,900	291	955	2
Kalberhöni-Vordereggli	Gstaad	1,066	1,166	1,331	4,367	1,667	5,469	336	1,102	2
Bretaye-Chavonnes	Villars	1,035	1,132	1,708	5,607	1,817	5,964	109	357	1
Kippel-Haispiel	Kippel	1,030	1,126	1,394	4,574	1,870	6,136	476	1,562	1
Croce-Brusada	Faido	1,026	1,122	1,650	5,413	1,948	6,391	298	678	2
Hühnerköpfe-Furggabüel	Chur	1,021	1,116	1,951	6,400	2,175	7,135	224	735	2
Ovronnaz-Jorasse	Sion	1,015	1,110	1,389	4,557	1,748	5,735	359	1,178	2
Lac Noir-Chaux Ronde	Villars	1,003	1,097	1,723	5,653	1,987	5,917	264	866	2
Herrenboden-Hochstuckli	Arth-Goldau	1,002	1,096	1,187	3,894	1,493	4,895	306	1,001	2
Cardada-Cimetta‡	Locarno	931	1,018	1,336	4,383	1,650	5,413	314	1,030	1/2
Gd. St. Bernard-La Chenalette	Gd. St. Bernard	731	799	2,475	8,120	2,772	9,095	297	975	1

* Two independent sections. †Four independent sections. ‡ Automatic attachment and detachment of chairs at terminals; on all other lines chairs permanently attached to haulage cable. § Through running of chairs between sections by transfer at junctions. || Passengers travel standing in bucket-shaped cabins.

Note: The figures 1/2 in the last column indicate that the line concerned can be operated at will as a single or double chair-lift according to traffic demand.

There are a number of chair-lifts also of less than 1,000 yd. in length.

APPENDIX 7

Swiss Chair-lifts with Enclosed Cabins (Gondelbahn type)

(Lines completed to 1971)

LOWER AND UPPER TERMINALS OF LINE	NEAREST TOWN	LENGTH OF LINE		ALTITUDE ABOVE SEA LEVEL				TOTAL ASCENT		CAPACITY OF EACH CABIN
				LOWER TERMINUS		UPPER TERMINUS				
		metres	yards	metres	feet	metres	feet	metres	feet	persons
Zweisimmen-Rinderberg*	Zweisimmen	5,056	5,529	950	3,117	2,011	6,598	1,061	3,481	2
Kriens-Fräkmüntegg*†	Lucerne	4,968	5,433	516	1,693	1,415	4,643	899	2,950	4
Col des Mosses-Pic Chaussy*	Château d'Oex	4,038	4,416	1,454	4,770	2,311	7,582	857	2,812	4
Flims-Startgels	Flims	3,729	4,078	1,099	3,606	1,591	5,220	492	1,614	4
Bad Ragaz-Pardiel*	Bad Ragaz	3,495	3,822	508	1,667	1,629	5,344	1,121	3,677	4
Tannenboden-Maschgenkamm	Unterterzen	3,310	3,619	1,398	4,587	2,010	6,595	612	2,008	4
Wangs-Furt*	Sargans	3,239	3,542	541	1,775	1,526	5,007	985	3,232	4
Crans-Cry d'Err*‡	Montana	3,165	3,461	1,507	4,944	2,260	7,416	753	2,472	4
Charmey-Vounetse	Bulle	3,151	3,446	876	2,874	1,617	5,305	741	2,431	4
Rougemont-La Videmanette*	Château d'Oex	3,112	3,403	971	3,186	2,158	7,080	1,187	3,894	4
Arosa-Hörnli	Arosa	3,087	3,376	1,835	6,020	2,500	8,202	665	2,182	4
Gstaad-Hohi Wispile*†	Gstaad	3,030	3,314	1,051	3,775	1,911	6,270	860	2,495	4
Mörel-Greicheralp	Mörel	2,825	3,089	770	2,526	1,913	6,276	1,143	3,750	4
Veysonnaz-Thyon	Sion	2,760	3,018	1,370	4,495	2,142	7,028	772	2,533	4
Zaumiau-Cabane des Violettes*	Montana	2,598	2,841	1,509	4,950	2,224	7,296	715	2,346	4
Barboleusaz-Les Chaux	Villars	2,572	2,813	1,218	3,996	1,774	5,820	556	1,824	4
Gd. St. Bernard-Col de Menouve	Gd. St. Bernard	2,555	2,794	1,933	6,342	2,764	9,068	831	2,726	4
Montana-Cry d'Err	Montana	2,499	2,733	1,534	5,033	2,259	7,412	725	2,379	4
Saas Fee-Spielboden†	Saas Fee	2,455	2,685	1,803	5,915	2,456	8,057	653	2,142	4
Savognin-Radons	Tiefencastel	2,454	2,684	1,192	3,911	1,703	5,587	511	1,676	4
L'Aminona-Petit Mont Bonvin	Montana	2,440	2,668	1,526	5,007	2,390	7,842	864	2,835	4
Les Diablerets-Isenau	Diablerets	2,392	2,616	1,192	3,911	1,767	5,797	575	1,886	4
Twing-Käserstatt	Brünig	2,380	2,603	1,171	3,840	1,835	6,018	664	2,178	2
Scuol-Motta Naluns	Scuol-Tarasp	2,333	2,551	1,295	4,248	2,150	7,054	855	2,806	4
Turren-Schönbüel	Lungern	2,310	2,526	1,519	4,984	2,012	6,601	493	1,617	4
Celerina-Saluver	Celerina	2,302	2,518	1,752	5,748	2,280	7,480	528	1,732	4
Tortin-Col de Chassoure	Verbier	2,302	2,518	2,064	6,772	2,761	9,059	697	2,282	4

LOWER AND UPPER TERMINALS OF LINE	NEAREST TOWN	LENGTH OF LINE		ALTITUDE ABOVE SEA LEVEL				TOTAL ASCENT		CAPACITY OF EACH CABIN
				LOWER TERMINUS		UPPER TERMINUS				
		metres	yards	metres	feet	metres	feet	metres	feet	persons
Klosters-Albeina	Klosters	2,296	2,510	1,140	3,740	1,887	6,191	747	2,451	4
Villars-Roc d'Orsay	Villars	2,278	2,491	1,272	4,173	1,952	6,404	680	2,231	4
Haute Nendaz-Tracouét	Sion	2,270	2,483	1,388	4,554	2,200	7,218	812	2,664	4
Saas Fee-Plattjen	Saas Fee	2,220	2,428	1,805	5,922	2,572	8,438	767	2,516	2
Champéry-Planachaux	Champéry	2,216	2,423	1,097	3,599	1,787	5,862	690	2,263	2
Les Creux-Savoleyres	Verbier	2,210	2,417	1,592	5,223	2,336	7,664	774	2,441	4
Crans-Chetseron	Montana	2,185	2,390	1,481	4,859	2,113	6,933	632	2,074	4
Anzère-Pas de Maimbré	Sion	2,133	2,333	1,552	5,091	2,362	7,748	810	2,657	4
Marbach-Lochsitenberg	Langnau	1,958	2,141	888	2,913	1,476	4,842	588	1,929	4
Reigoldswil-Wasserfalle	Liestal	1,933	2,114	544	1,785	928	3,045	384	1,260	4
Leysin-Berneuse	Leysin	1,888	2,065	1,333	4,373	2,040	6,693	707	2,320	4
Les Crosets-Pointe des Mossettes	Champéry	1,877	2,053	1,676	5,499	2,252	7,389	576	1,890	4
Croix des Ruinettes-Téte des Vaux	Verbier	1,858	2,032	2,199	7,215	2,729	8,957	530	1,742	4
Schatzalp-Strelapass	Davos	1,727	1,889	1,887	6,189	2,362	7,747	475	1,558	2
Ried bei Brig-Rosswald	Brigue	1,721	1,882	1,037	3,402	1,820	5,971	783	2,569	4
Verbier-Croix des Ruinettes I	Verbier	1,657	1,812	1,534	5,033	2,200	7,218	666	2,185	4
Verbier-Croix des Ruinettes II	Verbier	1,637	1,790	1,531	5,023	2,195	7,201	664	2,178	2
Pra Perron-La Montagnette	Château d'Oex	1,635	1,788	1,218	3,996	1,630	5,348	412	1,352	2
Col du Pillon-Pierres Pointes	Diablerets	1,579	1,727	1,552	5,092	2,200	7,218	648	2,126	4
Vercorin-Crêt du Midi	Sierre	1,570	1,717	1,301	4,268	1,836	6,023	535	1,755	4
Emmetten-Stockhütte	Beckenried	1,520	1,662	761	2,497	1,283	4,210	522	1,713	4
Gstaad-Eggli	Gstaad	1,470	1,608	1,046	3,432	1,561	5,122	515	1,690	4
Hauts Geneveys-Tête de Ran	Chaux-de-Fonds	1,470	1,608	1,030	3,379	1,399	4,590	369	1,211	2
Les Marcottes-La Creusaz	Finhaut	1,393	1,523	1,125	3,690	1,780	5,839	655	2,149	4
Känzeli-Brämbrüesch	Chur	1,387	1,517	1,190	3,904	1,597	5,240	407	1,336	2
Moléson Village-Plan Francey	Gruyères	1,310	1,433	1,114	3,655	1,523	4,997	409	1,342	4
Sunnegga-Unterrothorn (1st Sec)	Zermatt	1,233	1,348	2,293	7,522	2,579	8,460	286	938	4
Saas Fee-Hannig	Saas Fee	1,126	1,231	1,825	5,987	2,340	7,677	515	1,690	4
Melide-Carona	Lugano	619	677	325	1,066	582	1,909	257	843	4
Montana-Grand Signal	Montana	560	612	1,534	5,033	1,715	5,627	181	594	2

* Two independent sections. † Cabins permanently attached to haulage cable (non-stop running). ‡ Through running of cabins between first and second sections.

Note: On all *Gondelbahn* lines the cabins detach from the haulage cables at the terminals and come to rest.

APPENDIX 8

Swiss Cableways or Téléphériques (Luftseilbahn type)

(Lines completed to 1971)

LOWER AND UPPER TERMINALS OF LINE	NEAREST TOWN	LENGTH OF LINE		ALTITUDE ABOVE SEA LEVEL				TOTAL ASCENT		CAPACITY OF EACH CABIN
				LOWER TERMINUS		UPPER TERMINUS				
		metres	yards	metres	feet	metres	feet	metres	feet	persons
Stechelberg-Mürren-Schilthorn‡	Mürren	6,931	7,580	875	2,871	2,967	9,740	2,092	6,869	‡100/80
Zermatt-Furgg-Trockener Steg†	Zermatt	5,810	6,354	1,646	5,400	2,927	9,603	1,281	4,203	80/100
Reusch-Glacier des Diablerets†	Gstaad	5,591	6,114	1,358	4,455	2,946	9,665	1,588	5,210	40/60
Fiesch-Eggishorn*	Fiesch	4,776	5,223	1,070	3,510	2,878	9,442	1,808	5,932	30/21
Surlej (Silvaplana)-Piz Corvatsch*	St. Moritz	4,435	4,850	1,877	6,158	3,305	10,843	1,428	4,685	80/80
Mulania-Crap Sogn Gion	Flims	4,156	4,545	1,099	3,606	2,230	7,317	1,131	3,711	125
Andermatt-Gemsstock*	Andermatt	4,020	4,396	1,445	4,741	2,955	9,695	1,510	4,954	40/40
Erlenbach-Stockhorn*	Spiez	4,008	4,383	735	2,411	2,145	7,037	1,410	4,626	60/23
Zermatt-Schwarzsee*	Zermatt	3,885	4,249	1,642	5,387	2,590	8,498	948	3,111	40/40
Saas Fee-Felskinn	Saas Fee	3,622	3,969	1,851	6,073	2,997	9,833	1,146	3,760	100
Bernina-Diavolezza	Pontresina	3,609	3,947	2,101	6,893	2,984	9,790	883	2,897	62
Trübsee-Kleintitlis*	Engelberg	3,498	3,825	1,810	5,938	3,033	9,950	1,223	4,012	80/80
Lenzerheide-Parpaner Rothorn*	Lenzerheide	3,385	3,702	1,509	4,950	2,864	9,405	1,358	4,455	35/35
Unterterzen-Tannenbodenalp*	Unterterzen	3,370	3,685	436	1,430	1,390	4,560	954	3,130	30/45
Stockalp-Melchsee	Sarnen	3,321	3,632	1,089	3,573	1,916	6,286	827	2,713	33
Cabane des Violettes-Plaine Morte	Montana	3,234	3,537	2,231	7,319	2,894	9,494	663	2,175	80
Jakobsbad-Kronberg	Appenzell	3,223	3,525	883	2,895	1,655	5,428	772	2,533	40
Arosa-Weisshorn*	Arosa	3,217	3,518	1,758	5,768	2,646	8,687	888	2,919	60/75
Gornergrat-Stockhorn*	Zermatt	3,180	3,478	3,113	10,212	3,413	11,196	300	984	40/40
Davos-Ischalp-Jakobshorn*	Davos	3,138	3,432	1,543	5,082	2,571	8,455	1,028	3,373	40/40
Beckenried-Klewenalp	Beckenried	3,103	3,393	457	1,499	1,599	5,246	1,142	3,747	40
Mörel-Riederalp	Mörel	3,061	3,348	773	2,536	1,929	6,329	1,156	3,793	15
Klosters-Gotschnagrat*	Klosters	2,935	3,210	1,196	3,924	2,293	7,523	1,097	3,599	55/38
Mörel-Greicheralp	Mörel	2,810	3,073	770	2,526	1,913	6,276	1,143	3,750	12
Stalden-Staldenried-Gspon*	Visp	2,762	3,031	804	2,638	1,899	6,230	1,095	3,592	12/12
Schönenboden-Brienzer Rothorn	Brienz	2,740	2,996	1,248	4,094	2,288	7,504	1,040	3,410	80
Brülisau-Hoher Kasten	Appenzell	2,716	2,970	934	3,064	1,791	5,877	857	2,813	60

LOWER AND UPPER TERMINALS OF LINE	NEAREST TOWN	LENGTH OF LINE		ALTITUDE ABOVE SEA LEVEL				TOTAL ASCENT		CAPACITY OF EACH CABIN
				LOWER TERMINUS		UPPER TERMINUS				
		metres	yards	metres	feet	metres	feet	metres	feet	persons
Rickenbach-Rotenfluh*	Schwyz	2,583	2,825	614	2,014	1,529	5,016	915	3,002	10/15
Betten-Bettmeralp*	Mörel	2,482	2,714	838	2,749	1,931	6,335	1,093	3,586	50/50
Corviglia-Piz Nair	St. Moritz	2,424	2,651	2,496	8,189	3,030	9,941	534	1,752	40
Parsennhütte-Weissfluhjoch	Davos	2,390	2,614	2,211	7,254	2,676	8,780	465	1,526	50
Curtinatsch-Piz Lagalb	Pontresina	2,380	2,603	2,117	6,945	2,902	9,520	785	2,575	60
Grächen-Hannigalp	St. Niklaus	2,359	2,580	1,613	5,292	2,116	6,942	503	1,650	50
Dallenwil-Niederrickenbach	Stans	2,349	2,568	513	1,683	1,163	3,816	650	2,133	25
Weggis-Rigi Kaltbad	Weggis	2,320	2,537	507	1,663	1,436	4,695	924	3,032	51
Rhäzüns-Feldis	Chur	2,302	2,518	671	2,201	1,472	4,839	801	2,628	10
Pierres Pointes-Cabane Diablerets	Diablerets	2,250	2,460	2,203	7,227	2,948	9,672	745	2,445	30/60
Gerschnialp-Trübsee I	Engelberg	2,227	2,435	1,271	4,170	1,802	5,912	531	1,742	33
Alp Naraus-Fil de Cassons	Flims	2,193	2,398	1,846	6,056	2,644	8,674	798	2,618	23
Gerschnialp-Trübsee II	Engelberg	2,188	2,393	1,273	4,176	1,803	5,915	530	1,739	80
Küssnacht-Seebodenalp	Küssnacht	2,180	2,384	463	1,519	1,029	3,376	566	1,857	10
Raron-Unterbach	Visp	2,160	2,362	640	2,100	1,228	4,029	588	1,929	16
Schwägalp-Säntis	Appenzell	2,157	2,359	1,362	4,469	2,483	8,146	1,121	3,677	45
Airolo-Sasso della Boggia	Airolo	2,068	2,261	1,185	3,888	2,071	6,795	886	2,907	32
Dallenwil-Wirzweli	Stans	2,060	2,253	577	1,893	1,228	4,029	651	2,136	25
Orselina-Cardada	Locarno	2,040	2,231	395	1,296	1,340	4,396	945	2,100	23
Dörfji-Mitteltalli	Davos	2,017	2,206	1,808	5,932	2,491	8,173	683	2,241	100
Riddes-Isérables	Martigny	1,988	2,174	500	1,640	1,117	3,664	617	2,024	20
Leukerbad-Gemmipass	Leukerbad	1,971	2,156	1,430	4,692	2,346	7,697	916	3,005	20
Gampel-Jeizinen	Visp	1,957	2,140	640	2,100	1,525	5,003	885	2,903	10
Turtmann-Oberems	Sierre	1,940	2,122	640	2,100	1,335	4,380	895	2,280	10
Zinal-Sorebois	Zinal	1,892	2,069	1,663	5,456	2,438	7,999	775	2,543	80
Flüelen-Eggbergen	Flüelen	1,878	2,054	440	1,443	1,452	4,763	1,012	3,320	15
Chalais-Vercorin	Sierre	1,820	1,990	519	1,703	1,301	4,268	782	2,565	10
Blatten-Belalp	Brigue	1,780	1,947	1,333	4,373	2,100	6,890	767	2,517	10
Lungern Obsee-Turren	Lungern	1,761	1,926	709	2,326	1,537	5,043	828	2,717	25
Raron-Eischoll	Visp	1,757	1,921	645	2,116	1,217	3,993	572	1,877	10
Kräbel-Rigi Scheidegg	Arth-Goldau	1,745	1,908	770	2,526	1,648	5,407	878	2,552	10
Weglosen-Seebli	Einsiedeln	1,718	1,870	1,050	3,445	1,465	4,806	415	1,361	125
Champéry-Planachaux	Champéry	1,660	1,815	1,084	3,556	1,789	5,869	705	2,313	18

LOWER AND UPPER TERMINALS OF LINE	NEAREST TOWN	LENGTH OF LINE		ALTITUDE ABOVE SEA LEVEL				TOTAL ASCENT		CAPACITY OF EACH CABIN
				LOWER TERMINUS		UPPER TERMINUS				
		metres	yards	metres	feet	metres	feet	metres	feet	persons
Wengen-Männlichen	Wengen	1,620	1,772	1,308	4,291	2,239	7,346	931	3,055	50
Château d'Oex-Pra Perron	Château d'Oex	1,592	1,741	965	3,166	1,223	4,012	258	846	33
Kandersteg-Stock	Kandersteg	1,580	1,728	1,200	3,937	1,825	5,988	625	2,051	16
Croix des Ruinettes-Les Attelas	Verbier	1,540	1,684	2,200	7,218	2,734	8,970	534	1,752	30
Wasserauen-Ebenalp	Appenzell	1,498	1,638	873	2,684	1,596	5,236	723	2,552	34
Elsigbach-Elsigenalp	Frutigen	1,492	1,632	1,329	4,360	1,802	5,912	473	1,552	15
Fellboden-Bannalpsee	Stans	1,490	1,629	898	2,946	1,577	5,174	679	2,228	8
Fräkmüntegg-Pilatuskulm	Lucerne	1,373	1,501	1,421	4,662	2,066	6,778	645	2,116	40
Dorenaz-Champex d'Alesse	Martigny	1,342	1,468	454	1,490	1,127	3,698	673	2,208	10
Cry d'Err-Bellalui	Montana	1,300	1,422	2,264	7,428	2,527	8,291	263	863	61
Schattdorf-Haldi	Altdorf	1,257	1,375	486	1,594	1,086	2,562	600	1,968	10
Kies-Mettmen	Schwanden	1,250	1,367	1,040	3,412	1,617	5,305	577	1,893	10
Gamsen-Mund	Brigue	1,249	1,366	668	2,192	1,199	3,933	531	1,741	10
Unter dem Birg-Engstligenalp	Adelboden	1,199	1,311	1,407	4,616	1,966	6,450	559	1,834	12
Engelberg-Brunni	Engelberg	1,193	1,305	1,023	3,356	1,605	5,266	582	1,910	40
Plan Francey-Le Moléson	Gruyéres	1,101	1,204	1,527	5,010	1,986	6,516	459	1,506	35
Sunnegga-Unterrothorn (2nd Sec.)	Zermatt	1,101	1,204	2,584	8,478	3,100	10,171	516	1,693	81
Chur-Känzeli	Chur	1,099	1,202	600	1,969	1,194	3,937	594	1,969	23
Turtmann-Ergisch	Sierre	1,085	1,187	640	2,100	1,079	3,543	439	1,443	10
Adliswil-Felsenegg	Zürich	1,048	1,146	503	1,650	810	2,657	307	1,007	30
Grindelwald-Pfingstegg	Grindelwald	1,037	1,134	1,027	3,369	1,387	4,551	360	1,182	36
Spielboden-Längfluh	Saas Fee	934	1,021	2,461	8,074	2,872	9,442	411	1,348	24
Brusino Arsizio-Serpiano	Lugano	920	1,006	290	951	655	2,149	365	1,198	10
Les Attelas-Mont Gelé §	Verbier	872	954	2,741	8,993	3,009	9,872	268	879	40§
Matt-Wissenbergen	Elm	810	886	852	2,795	1,261	4,137	409	1,342	10
Weissfluhjoch-Weissfluhgipfel	Davos	685	749	2,669	8,756	2,823	9,262	154	1,405	50
Le Chargeur-Lac des Dix	Sion	640	700	2,142	7,027	2,376	7,795	234	768	12
Furgg-Schwarzsee	Zermatt	399	436	2,436	7,982	2,589	8,484	153	502	75§

* Line with two independent sections. † Line with three independent sections. ‡ Line with four sections: on two lower sections single cabins raised or lowered from Gimmelwald, but interconnected: single cabin only, upper section. § Single cabin raised or lowered from upper terminus.
Note: Above lines have all been built under Federal concessions; there are also a number of minor lines built under Cantonal concessions, with cabins holding 4 to 8 passengers only.

APPENDIX 9

Some Swiss Railway and Cableway Records

HIGHEST ALTITUDE ATTAINED

	Location	Railway or Cableway	Metres	Feet
Main line	Lötschberg Tunnel	Bern-Lötschberg-Simplon	1,240	4,067
Metre gauge through line	Bernina Hospice	Rhaetian	2,257	7,403
Mountain Line	Jungfraujoch	Jungfrau	3,454	11,333
Funicular	Weissfluhjoch	Davos-Parsenn	2,663	8,737
Luftseilbahn	Stockhorn	Gornergat-Stockhorn	3,413	11,196
Gondelbahn	Col de Menouve	Gd. St. Bernard-Col de Menouve	2,764	9,668
Chair-lift	La Chenalette	Gd. St. Bernard-La Chenalette	2,772	9,095

GREATEST LENGTH OF MOUNTAIN LINE

	Location	Railway or Cableway	Metres	Yards
Funicular	2 sections	Sierre-Montana	4,207	4,601
,,	1 section	Punt Muragl-Muottas Muragl	2,185	2,390
Luftseilbahn	4 sections	Stechelberg-Mürren-Schilthorn	6,931	7,580
,,	3 sections	Zermatt-Furgg-Trockener Steg	5,810	6,354
,,	1 section	Fiesch-Eggishorn	4,776	5,223
Gondelbahn	2 sections	Mulania-Crap Sogn-Gion	4,156	4,545
,,	2 sections	Zweisimmen-Rinderberg	5,056	5,529
Chair-lift	1 section	Flims-Startgels	3,729	4,078
,,	4 sections	Grindelwald-First	4,354	4,762
,,	2 sections	Lenk-Betelberg	3,632	3,972
,,	1 section	Nods-Chasseral	2,950	3,226

MAXIMUM ASCENT BETWEEN TERMINALS

	Location	Railway or Cableway	Metres	Feet
Luftseilbahn	4 sections	Stechelberg-Mürren-Schilthorn	2,092	6,869
Gondelbahn	3 sections	Reusch-Glacier des Diablerets	1,588	5,210
,,	4 sections	Bad Ragaz-Pardiel	1,121	3,677
Chair-lift	4 sections	Grindelwald-First	1,105	3,625
Funicular	2 sections	Mülenen-Niesenkulm	1,643	5,390
Rack-and pinion railway	1 section	Brienz-Rothornkulm	1,681	5,515

STEEPEST GRADIENT

	Railway or Cableway	per cent	I in.
Adhesion railway	Montreux-Oberland Bernois	7¼	13¾
Rack-and-pinion railway	Alpnachstad-Pilatus	48	2
Funicular railway	Piotta-Piora	88	1⅛
Luftseilbahn	Pierres Pointes-Cabane des Diablerets	125	1¾
Gondelbahn	Emmetten-Stockhütte	86	1⅛
Chair-lift	Champex-La Breya	89	1⅛

LONGEST SPAN BETWEEN PYLONS

	Railway	Metres	Feet
Luftseilbahn	Jakobsbad-Kronberg	2,220	7,283

FASTEST START-TO-STOP SPEEDS OF SWISS TRAINS

In Switzerland: Train No. 293 Sion-Montreux: 42.3 miles in 37 min., 68.6 m.p.h.

Outside Switzerland: TEE "Cisalpin" Paris-Dijon: 195.3 miles in 140 min., 83.7 m.p.h.

INDEX